TORVILL & DEAN

John Man is the author of *The Survival of Jan Little* and co-author of *Stay Alive, My Son* (with Pin Ya-Thay) and *Going Back* (with Simon Weston). Other non-fiction books include *The Waorani: Jungle Nomads of Ecuador* and Penguin's *Atlas of D-Day*. He devised and wrote BBC Radio 4's *Survivors* series.

TORVILL & DEAN

The Autobiography of Ice
Dancing's Greatest Stars

With John Man

A Birch Lane Press Book
Published by Carol Publishing Group

Carol Publishing Group Edition, 1996

A Birch Lane Press Book
Published by Carol Publishing Group
Birch Lane Press is a registered trademark of Carol Communications, Inc.

Editorial, sales and distribution, rights and permissions inquiries
should be addressed to Carol Publishing Group, 120 Enterprise Avenue,
Secaucus, N.J. 07094

In Canada: Canadian Manda Group, One Atlantic Avenue, Suite 105,
Toronto, Ontario M6K 3E7

Carol Publishing Group books may be purchased in bulk at special
discounts for sales promotions, fund-raising, or educational purposes.
Special editions can be created to specifications. For details, contact
Special Sales Department, Carol Publishing Group, 120 Enterprise Avenue,
Secaucus, N.J. 07094

Published with permission from Simon & Schuster Ltd, London

Manufactured in the United States of America
10 9 8 7 6 5 4 3 2 1

Library of Congress Cataloging-in-Publication Data
Torvill, Jayne, 1957–
    [Facing the music]
    Torvill and Dean : the autobiography of ice dancing's greatest
stars / Jayne Torvill and Christopher Dean with John Man.
        p. cm.
    Originally published : Facing the music. London : Simon & Schuster
1995.
    "A Birch Lane Press book" —T.p. verso.
    ISBN 1-55972-390-4
    1. Torvill, Jayne, 1957– . 2. Dean, Christopher, 1958– .
3. Skaters—Great Britain—Biography. 4. Ice dancing. I. Dean,
Christopher, 1958– . II. Man, John. III. Title.
GV850.T63A27 1996
796.91'2'092—dc20
[B]   96-32900
                                               CIP

To Jill and Phil for their love and understanding.

Acknowledgement

We would like to thank our families, whose love and support we receive and continue to receive, our close friends and associates, who have shared and enriched our lives with their friendship. And to everyone who has watched and supported our careers over the last two decades, we take this opportunity to applaud you.

Prologue

Sheffield Arena, May 24, 1994

W e are in a tiny space, surrounded by gossamer-thin fabric, made to seem like a wall by the darkness beyond, creating a private universe, all our own. We are on the ice, on our knees, mere shadows, feeling the tension, but also the strength we give each other.

The moment lasts only a few seconds. It ends with the quiet, insistent beat of a side-drum. The fabric rises, spotlights glare, and suddenly we are in a different universe. Out there, in the darkness beneath the spotlights, there are 8,000 people. There is a reassuring murmur of apprehension, and a ripple of applause. For about the 1,500th time, we are starting *Bolero*.

We have been dancing it for 10 years, and each time it has to be real, tense, concentrated. We have always owed that to the audience, and to ourselves. Even now, as soon as we hear the opening beats, we become those doomed lovers, locked together, with eyes only for each other. The tension is there — *has* to be there — every time.

Yet this *Bolero* is different. Our still moment together was preceded by four other spotlit couples out there on the ice, each swaying in turn to music that foreshadows the main theme. After we have finished, with our death-fall on to the ice, 20 skaters will sweep in to the gorgeous fanfare that opens Janacek's *Sinfonietta*. All these other dancers are international stars in their own right, a panoply of talent moulded into a company that is, as far as we know, unique.

And it is ours, our show, the first night of the Torvill and Dean 1994–5 World Tour.

It's not just *our* show, of course. The skating talent, the managerial and financial back-up, the lighting, the music, the costumes — all of that has to be done by others. But still it amazes us to have a multi-million pound show depending on us, and to have so many people who are willing to come and see it.

All our lives, we have done what we love doing as well as we can. That apart, we're ordinary people. How did Jayne and Chris, the working-class kids from Nottingham, get to be 'Torvill and Dean'? How did an insurance clerk and a policeman become a 'fairytale couple' for so many people?

The fairytale long ago acquired a life of its own, trailing us in its wake. As a result, we seem to have spent most of our amateur and professional lives surprised by our success and popularity. By hindsight, an understanding of how and why it all happened often vanished in a fog of fast-unfolding events. We lived for the present, and the immediate future, while the past receded into uncertain memory.

Yet the past is there, a hidden part of the present, waiting to be explored. This book is an attempt to explain ourselves to ourselves, and to anyone who wants to know the realities, as opposed to the myths.

1

In my life

Chris

I was 10 when I first saw an ice-rink. It was probably Betty, my stepmother — 'Tee' as I called her — who started it, because she had skated as a child, and suggested to my dad that I should have some skates for Christmas. It was only sensible to see if I had any interest, so off we drove from the little town of Calverton, into Nottingham, eight miles away. That was an adventure in itself because I had hardly ever been into the big city.

The ice-rink was a wonder. Nottingham ice-rink, near the middle of town, looks as if it had once been a cinema — patterned brick with swinging glass doors and a huge lobby leading up steps to the stadium itself, with its rectangle of ice, arched roof, dirty yellow walls, banks of splintery wooden seats, and an organ at the far end. I had never seen anything like it. All those people swishing round on the white expanse; the cavernous, echoing hall; the screams of the children; the wail of the piped organ music — it was as strange and thrilling as seeing a Christmas card come to life.

The look on my face told Tee and Dad it was worth getting the skates. Not that it would have been much of a risk: I would have responded to almost any new sporting challenge. And on Christmas Day, when I felt the hard leather and the glistening blades, I wanted to get back down there right away.

So, the first Saturday after Christmas, off we went again. Once in the rink, I was in a world of my own. Most kids, when they start, work their way round the rink holding on to the barrier at the side. I suppose there was something driving me from the first, because I didn't work myself in by pulling myself round the outside. I tried to skate straight away. Of course, I fell over at once, got up, staggered and slid into the middle, fell over, and went on falling over and staggering around for the full two hours.

Sometimes Jayne and I wonder if she was part of the crowd on that day, and maybe saw me as I slipped and waved my arms. Probably not, because she was already on to higher and better things. If she *was* there, she was one of those kids drifting effortlessly past me as I crashed down for the hundredth time. I remember that the sides of the boots were scuffed by all the falling over. But it didn't seem to bother me. No one was looking at me, except Tee and Dad watching from the seats. It was total, self-absorbed happiness.

Every Saturday they brought me in. I loved the place, the

noise, the music, the crowds that gave me the right combination of togetherness and privacy. It was all very basic.

Nowadays, to resurface the ice, a specially designed
machine, a Zamboni, slices off the top layer and spreads a
regular layer of water which refreezes in a few minutes. In
Nottingham in the 1960s, when the ice had been cut up by
several hundred kids for an hour or two, it was resurfaced
by a wartime tractor towing a blade that ploughed off the
top layer of ice, with its pulverised 'snow'.

The blade was guided by a man on skates dragging along
behind. When the blade had a good pile of 'snow', the
tractor drove near a wooden box, the man behind hit a
lever, and the blade rose, leaving a pile of 'snow' behind,
which was scooped into the 'snow'-pit later. The blade
clunked down, and the man was pulled on straight through
the pile of 'snow', ready to tackle the next section of the
rink. Then a man with a hose sprayed on fresh water.

The whole operation took about half an hour. I loved
watching it. I always wanted to be the man at the back
being pulled by the tractor.

Soon I could get myself along forwards pretty well. Then
I wanted to go backwards. Then do turns. And at each
stage I would start a new round of falling over, so I must
always have looked pretty useless. One thing that gave me
particular pleasure was when I first did a skid-stop, jumping
sideways and stopping short with a shower of ice exploding
from the blades. I thought that was really cool.

Tee and Dad took to the rink as much as I did, because it
was a useful base to drop me off when they went shopping
on Saturdays. Often I was left to make my own way in the
crowd, but when they were there I used to like seeing them

standing at the edge, or up in the seats. When I knew they were watching, I didn't skate just for myself, but for them as well.

For weeks, every Saturday morning, I experimented happily on my own, never saying hello to anyone. My only friend was Fred, the man who ran the skate-hire booth in the lobby. He would keep an eye on me for Tee and Dad when they went off shopping.

I wasn't much interested in having lessons, probably because I was shy. But after a while, when I began to go in on Thursday evenings as well as Saturdays, Tee and Dad told me to give the Ice Cubs a try. For a while, I was part of a group, one of several groups on the ice, all of different standards. I felt I was doing OK, certainly I was never bothered by all the falling over, so Tee eventually said, 'How about having a lesson?'

'Yes. OK. Why not?'

But what did I want to learn? Free-skating? Or dancing? I had no idea, of course. Tee settled it. She and Dad used to go ballroom dancing socially. 'I think you should do dancing,' she said firmly.

After the freedom I'd had, I found lessons a bit galling. But it was good for me. There was a discipline in learning my first dance steps and getting the feel of moving to music. I'd never listened to music properly. We'd had music at school – mainly making plaintive little noises on a flute recorder – but, to me at that time, it was so boring I never took anything in. Now, I *had* to listen, especially when I started proper dance sessions.

On Thursday evenings, the public sessions stopped for

three 15–minute dance intervals. The only available partner, at least for beginners, was the teacher, in my case
Pat Beet. It cost a shilling (five pence) to dance with her.
The music was by courtesy of Dougie Walker, playing in
rigid tempo on the Hammond organ, with the metronome
ticking away beside him, and his wife – all prim make-up
and bleached-blonde hair – turning the pages. That was
how I got my introduction to the Prelim Foxtrot and the
Prelim Waltz.

All the while, I was gaining more control on the ice,
and always pushing myself to do more, not because I had
any idea of doing anything special, but just for the joy of
achievement and the excitement of moving fast over the ice.
I was taking it more seriously too. At first I had worn jeans
to skate. Then, when I was 12, I got an ill-fitting catsuit, a
cheap one made of navy-blue jersey, with wrinkly leggings.
That was the gear you had to have. I felt terrific.

One Saturday afternoon, I had just had my skates
sharpened and joined in with the other kids and grown-ups
in the mêlée of the public session. I was tearing round as
fast as I could, zoomed up to the wooden barrier at the
edge of the ice where skaters got on and off, turned to
do my famous skid-stop, and hit the edge. I fell, and felt
a sharp pain in the leg. Next I knew, Fred, the skate-hire
man, was feeling my leg.

'You've broken it, Chris,' he said, and took me off to
hospital.

By the time my parents came to pick me up, my leg was
encased in a plaster cast. I quite enjoyed learning to use
crutches. The first time going down stairs, I tried leading
with my plastered leg, toppled forwards on my crutches

9

and tumbled to the bottom. It didn't bother me. I treated the experience as a challenge.

Six weeks later, just after I was out of the cast, there was a try-out at school for the football team. More than anything, I loved sport – football, swimming, gymnastics and running. I had been captain of football at junior school, and I wanted to be in the team here as well. Tee had told me I couldn't play, because I was still recovering from a broken leg, and a further injury would stop me getting back on the ice. I couldn't see why being a skater should stop me playing football. So I just stayed on after school and joined in the trial.

Tee guessed what I was up to, of course. I was horrified to see her walking across to the touchline, and calling out right in the middle of the game, 'Chris! Come on! You're not doing that!'

I was appalled – embarrassed at the humiliation, angry at being denied my chance to realise an ambition.

But she wouldn't stand any nonsense, and I didn't dare defy her outright.

'But Tee!' I protested, as she led me away, 'I want to play football!'

'Football!' she said. 'What about your skating?'

I hadn't seen myself as a skater in particular up until then. But after that I did.

While doing this book, I looked further back still, trying to find out exactly how and why the commitment to skating emerged.

One of my very first memories is playing in the Co-op in Calverton, because my mother – my biological mother,

Mavis — worked there at the meat counter, and before I started school she used to take me along from our council flat with its flight of three ducks on the wall and its lino floor. We didn't go out much into the rolling countryside, let alone to Nottingham, which was just a name of a faraway place.

The Co-op was my own private world. I went back there recently, and was surprised to see that it's only an ordinary suburban store, mainly one big room with windows along the front. But to me, a four-year-old with hair so blond it was almost white, the Co-op was magic.

Behind the counter where my mum worked was a big storeroom, with boxes piled up on the wooden floor: a universe of building blocks and secret hiding places — and reassuring smells. Back then, remember, packaging wasn't what it is today, and there were piles of orange-crates, apple-boxes, bacon, tea.

My mum was just outside, and I felt secure in the feeling that I was special. I remember being dressed in red and blue woollens that my mum had knitted, and no other mum brought her kids in, so there was no one else to share the Co-op with. In this safe world I built cardboard-box palaces, planes and cars, sometimes venturing out to explore the shop itself, always within easy reach of Mum's open arms.

So school, when it came, was a bit of shock. It was only a stone's throw from the Co-op, on the opposite corner of the street, but I can still feel how I felt then, abandoned with children I didn't know behind the wire-mesh fence that surrounded the playground. I remember staring through the mesh at the Co-op, knowing my mum was in there, and also knowing, as if I was in some huge empty void, that this would last a long, long time.

In a way, it did, because my mum left when I was six. I had no idea what was happening, or why. She was going to stay with friends, and she took me along, and the friends brought me home again. I just remember her going, and me crying, crying, and the same terrible, empty feeling: *this is for ever.*

I have seldom spoken to my biological mum, and never discussed the details of what happened. So even now, in the child that still lives in my memory, there is a void. I can't remember if it affected my behaviour, but I do have one vivid memory of sitting inside a cardboard box with a square hole cut in it, surrounded by drawings of switches and dials, pretending I was locked away in something like a cockpit or a racing driver's seat. I seem to have spent my skating life re-creating some version of that exclusive, exciting place.

In one very important way, I was lucky. Into my life came Tee, who in a completely different way became a second mother to me. She had been a friend of the family for a while, so when both marriages collapsed and she moved in with my dad it gave me the feeling that things might be OK, if I could make Tee pleased with me.

Tee had had a family of her own, twins, who were already grown up. It must have been a tough time for Dad and Tee. My father had been down the mines as an electrician all his life, and was content with his role, with the mine – the towers were just out of sight over the hill from the Co-op – and with his workmates. He was one of the most stable and contented of men.

12

He and Tee must have had some difficult times, because this was a small, tight-knit mining community, and divorce was quite rare in the 1960s. For her to move in with my dad — she didn't finally divorce until quite a while afterwards — must have been a tough decision. It worked out well, though. The twins and I, despite the difference in our ages, became close, as close as if they had always been my older brother and sister.

Tee was a very different sort of person from my biological mother — practical, clear-headed, strong, authoritative. She had to be: she worked in a variety of book-keeping jobs, and she had the flat to run as well. She was the sort of person who would not only make you do as she said, but make you *want* to do as she said. I liked to meet her off the bus after school and carry her bags for her. She made me feel I had to do well for her, in school, in schoolwork — it was thanks to her that I did OK academically — and in sport.

Sports in particular, mainly running, football and swimming, all of which I was keen on and had been good at from the age of seven or eight. I looked forward to the 100 yards on school sports day, and sometimes won. It made me stand out a little, which was certainly not something I would get from my classroom work. Skating was similar. No one else at school skated, so it made me feel different.

And there was always the support of Tee and Dad. Dad especially took increasing pride in what I was doing, though he never said so right out. To me, he was a man of few words, but even in the simplest of practical remarks — 'Eh-up, Buster. You ready? Time to go!' — I felt the strength of his commitment. I don't think he was ambitious for me to achieve for the sake of achievement. He just took pleasure in my joy and my growing skill.

Tee saw that my progress gave us all satisfaction, and was equally supportive. Without that support – the evenings in Nottingham, the bussing and driving back and forth, the hours it took every week, the money spent on lessons – I would never have continued.

So there I was, learning the Prelim Foxtrot from Pat Beet. I suppose I felt I made progress, because I kept at it for a couple of years, three times a week, and more as time went by. I never felt I was anything special among the others, because there were many good skaters there, figure-skaters and dancers – a whole clique, friends and rivals at the same time.

Jayne and her partner were up there with the best of them, way beyond anything I could contemplate. I remember their trainer, Thelma, charging round the rink to clear a way for them when they were running through their programmes.

My first partner was Sandra Elson, who became one of Jayne's best friends. We were both 13 when we teamed up, or rather when she teamed up with me, which was what it felt like, because right from the start she was the dominant one. We always seemed to be arguing over little things. In the end I learned to give as good as I got – almost – but often that just led to an argument. 'I'm off!' she'd say, and that was it for the day.

Still, in the four years we were together, we progressed well, working our way up to win the British primary and junior dance championships. The primary was the first championship we had entered, and winning it, in my navy-blue catsuit and frilly fluorescent pink samba sleeves, was the greatest thrill of my life so far. I was just 14.

I remember the feeling of pride and achievement as I performed the ritual I had so often seen others perform – coming out on to the rink for the first practice after we had won, with a silver trophy filled with champagne, making sure all the other skaters had a sip.

There were other competitions, one abroad in Czecho-slovakia, where I first met the Russian skater Andrei Bukin, soon to be a major rival. I remember him well, because of a muddle over the medals. At that time, Andrei was dancing with his wife, not his future partner Natalya Bestemianova. Sandra and I won the bronze, the Bukins the silver. When we came off the ice, Andrei, who didn't speak much English, pointed to my medal and then his, back and forth.

'Yes,' I said, puzzled and uncertain. ''Er thank you very much . . . Congratulations to you too.'

'No, no. Look. Is wrong.'

Then it dawned on me. The judges had given us the wrong medals, the silver to me, the bronze to him. We swopped, and parted with a handshake and laughter.

In 1974, Sandra and I came sixth in the British senior championships, the peak of our career together.

By then schooldays were over. Long before, I had decided that I wanted to be a policeman, because at school, when I was doing the Duke of Edinburgh Bronze Medal Award Scheme, we had to learn about one of the services, and a policeman came to talk to us. That was the first time anyone had made me think about what I was going to do

15

after school. It sounded exciting, and I never wanted to do anything else.

Also, I couldn't wait to learn to drive, to be in control of a machine behind a lot of switches and dials. I always dreamed of driving a nice car, because Dad could never afford one that worked well.

'She's not going to make it, Buster!' he'd say with a slow shake of his head before some long journey. 'What wouldn't I give for a Mercedes!'

He was for ever messing around under a bonnet, encouraging me to clean a carburettor or the plugs. So I knew a little about about cars, and shared Dad's dream. Driving and the police: those were my two ambitions.

So even before I left school, I had been accepted as a police cadet, and now I was going to cadet training every day on a moped.

Sandra was now an extremely attractive 16-year-old, and restless. She was fed up with living at home, just about to leave school, didn't know what she was going to do, and was as much interested in her social life as skating. And I had gained in self-confidence.

Perhaps it was the change in me that led to the final break, or perhaps our disagreements after our teacher moved to Grimsby. Sandra was all for going there. I would be able to go only at weekends, and wanted to train during the week as well. Besides, the 60-mile journey would be time-consuming, expensive and a terrible imposition on my parents, who would probably have volunteered to drive me there.

It might have worked out, because we began work in Nottingham with a new teacher, Janet Sawbridge, a

five-foot-nothing bundle of nervous energy, with a beehive
pile of curly hair. Janet, a former national ice-dancing
champion, had spent most of her adult life training and
competing, living in London, but had recently moved to
Birmingham to teach, and had then been invited to
Nottingham by one of the other Nottingham trainers,
Mick Wilde. She was looking for dancers, and Sandra
and I needed a teacher. It seemed a good idea to me. She
had a real passion for skating.

We'd hardly started with her, though, when Sandra and
I had our final row — what actually caused it I've no idea —
and decided we weren't going to dance together again.

'What a waste!' Tee said. 'Four years! Now it's all
gone!'

But it had all gone anyway, because we couldn't handle
the rows.

Soon afterwards, when word of the break got round,
Sandra had an offer from a boy in London who wanted
her as a partner. So off she went, all high hopes, to a
new life.

That left me on my own, with a good teacher, but
without a partner.

2

Roots

Jayne

At that time, I was without a partner, too.

I had been skating two years longer than Chris — I started when I was almost nine, and I'm almost a year older than he is — so skating was already a way of life.

Dad, Mum and I lived in Clifton, an estate of new council houses on the edge of Nottingham. Dad worked most of his life for Raleigh Cycles, which was good for me because I got a new bike every couple of years. I didn't have any brothers or sisters, but I was surrounded by family. Two of Mum's sisters and a brother of Dad's lived on the same estate. We were always in and out of each other's house for birthday parties and Christmases. Good strong roots.

Home was a safe place to be. I used to like walking back for lunch at my aunt's house with one of my cousins, who went to the same infants' school. I remember once during my last year there — I must have been five or six — being confronted by a tough little boy in the playground.

'I'm going to *get* you,' he said. I was terrified, because he had a gang. Next time I saw him and his gang together, I ran into the schoolhouse, banged on the staffroom door and burst sobbing into the middle of the coffee break.

'They're going to hit me!' I said tearfully. They didn't take me seriously, and sent me back out to what I was sure was going to be a terrible fate.

Nothing happened right then, but a few days later, the gang followed my cousin and me back to my aunt's. By the time we noticed them, we were almost at the house.

'Come on!' I yelled to my cousin. 'They won't follow us into the house!' And they didn't. They prowled around the outside, peering through windows — but inside we were safe.

I think that feeling of safety has stayed with me. It takes a lot to make me really upset and angry. It's as if there was always a home of some kind to protect me, so when emotions run high I can just withdraw until the storm blows over.

When I was eight, in junior school, my teacher decided to organise a trip to the Nottingham ice-rink. It was a Friday. We all went there in a little bus, and got fitted up with some hired skates. Mine were brown, which I didn't like because the white ones some of the other skaters had looked nicer. Then we tottered on to the ice, corralled at one end by a rope across the rink.

I took to it right away. For some reason, I had a good sense of balance, and managed to stay upright. Then the

20

rope came down, and we were allowed to skate all around the rink.

I was hooked. Suddenly, for a few seconds, I was doing something that seemed impossible, sailing fast and effortlessly over solid ground with the wind brushing my cheeks. I wanted more of the speed and the freedom. The skating teacher told me I could come back — that the next day, Saturday, there was a something called 'ice cubs' where everyone was put into a class according to standard.

As soon as I got home, I pestered Mum and Dad to take me, and they did. I could see from all the other skaters that I could have more of that glorious feeling — with practice. So soon, after my parents bought me some second-hand skates (white ones), I started having private lessons on Friday evenings.

Thelma Perry was my first teacher. She taught me to foxtrot and waltz, to jump, spin, do my first figures. She was tall, attractive, inspiring, and terrific with kids, always willing to keep an eye on me for my parents. I liked her a lot, which is the main thing. As a result, I made good progress. Thelma probably confirmed this to Mum and Dad.

So onwards and upwards. Soon I was having two lessons a week, then three — one on Friday, two on Saturday, one of which was for ice-dancing, with a male teacher, because Thelma told me, 'If you ever want to take tests, you'll have to dance with a man.'

I took to dancing as readily as any other discipline, though the music you danced to then wasn't very inspiring. Thelma had a stock of gramophone records. I can remember her leading me upstairs to her dressingroom and pulling out a record from her dusty collection, saying, 'Yes, I think this will do for you.' She would make a tape of it, scratches and all, and play it over the loudspeaker system.

Basically, if there was a crash or a drumbeat, that was when you had to do a jump. The same music had served for other children the previous year, and would serve yet others the year after. There was no flicker of originality in this. But at that age, who cared? No one had any idea of choreography, any more than children taking musical grades know anything of composition.

I just enjoyed it all — my developing skills, the music, the movement. At home, I had a flute recorder, on which I practised, driving my parents crazy, and the radio was on a good deal. I was always dancing around to whatever music came from the radio. Sunday mornings I remember in particular, when we had classical music on. Some people find it hard to move in time to music, but it seemed to come quite naturally to me.

After a while, I started to take the National Skating Association tests in figure-skating and ice-dancing. The certificates began to mount up, which gave me a satisfying sense of progress. Some of my friends got really nervous before tests, but I enjoyed them, responding to the challenge and the small audience of proud mums.

Besides, in these tests, it didn't matter if you weren't quite up to standard first time around, because they allowed you to reskate one of the elements. I was quite proud that I got through to my Silver Dance Test without a reskate. No problems, just fun, pure and simple.

Then, at the age of 12, I teamed up with my first partner, Michael Hutchinson, not as ice-dancers but as pair-skaters, a couple working together to incorporate all the elements of free-skating. That was a new excitement. Skating in a pair is harder in some ways, easier in another, because you have support.

But the main difference is psychological. You feel a sense of responsibility to yourself and your partner. Besides, Michael was terribly good-looking, and four years older than I, so there were always other girls around trying to catch his eye. He always seemed to have a girlfriend. I was too young to be jealous; in fact I rather enjoyed it. It was as if he was a big brother, who was the focus of admiration from other people, yet here he was skating with me! Whenever he got talking to older girls, I just used to roll my eyes.

We did well. There were never many other competitors, perhaps three or four, because pair-skating was not as popular as some of the other categories, so we won almost anything we went in for, becoming British junior champions in 1970. Then we were second in the senior championships. That was enough to get us into our first international as intermediate pair-skaters in a little Alpine town, Oberstdorf, in southern Germany.

We were shepherded there, and stayed only a few days, so I hardly had time to take in anything but the competition. I certainly had no inkling what the place would mean to me later.

There were only two couples in the competition. We came second, or last, whichever way you care to look at it. But simply competing was good for us.

The next year, 1971, we were selected for the European championships in Gothenburg. We came last again, not surprising really, and no great disappointment, because I

23

was still only 14. In fact, I had a great time, seeing skating stars famous from TV in the flesh.

But it wasn't all fun. I shared a room with the then number-three ice-dancer, Rosalind Druce. As an only child, I wasn't used to sharing a room, and once, when I came in late after watching a late-night competition with Michael, I woke her up. She gave me a terrible ticking off next morning.

I met her recently when we were on the 1994–5 World Tour in Chicago, where she was teaching at a rink. She saw the show, came round the back afterwards and said, 'Remember how I had a go at you for coming in late?' Remember! It had been one of the most memorable things about my stay in Gothenburg.

Soon after that the partnership began to run out of steam for Michael. We had done a fair bit of travelling around in our short career, and he had blossomed, meeting people everywhere we went. He was now 18, had an office job in Nottingham and had acquired a steady girlfriend – Janet – with whom he wanted to spend more time.

Not that he was ever anything but kind to me personally. For my birthday, he gave me some little skate-shaped golden earrings made by his father, a dental technician who used gold in his work. It was the first time anyone other than family had ever given me a present, and I treasured them. Still do, in fact – I wear them in every performance.

But that didn't mean he was committing himself to me as a partner for ever. Not surprising, really, because I had no particular ambition, at least not consciously. I just did what I enjoyed doing, living for the present, or the immediate future, the next competition, the next rung of a ladder that led upwards. To what? I had no idea, and didn't worry about it.

It was quite a blow when he told me he was planning to give up skating with me. I blamed it on poor Janet, and disliked her, although I hardly knew her. The break wasn't immediate, but things were not the same after that. We stopped training so hard. In the next Senior Pairs, we didn't skate very well – I fell over, actually, and ended up in tears – and we dropped to second place. It was a sign that the partnership was as good as over.

Then he had an offer of a new skating partner in London, and he left. I couldn't understand how he was going to manage, with Janet in Nottingham – who turned out to be really nice when I got to know her – and a skating partnership in London, but it seems to have worked out OK, because he married Janet later. Eventually, he moved to Canada, to teach at an ice-rink there.

That left me without a partner. It never occurred to me to give up, just because my partner had left. Skating was almost the only thing I really wanted to do. It was already a way of life, a home from home, as solid as that.

So I started skating on my own again, with my new teacher, Norma Bowmar. Having been pair-skating with Michael, I had fallen a bit behind in solo work. I was now too old to compete in the junior championships – you had to be 14 or under – and I hadn't got the test qualifications to compete in the seniors. So I concentrated on getting the next figure test, the silver. I wanted the silver because it would qualify me for senior competition, but I was never very strong in figures because I found them boring. So I failed, twice. But I still did a few local competitions, winning one

25

in Sheffield, which was enough of an inspiration to keep me going.

To improve my skating, Norma suggested I should go to ballet class. So, along with another skater, I went to a local ballet-teacher named Sissy Smith.

She was a wonderful character. She must have been in her sixties then, and had been famous briefly as a partner for Robert Helpmann, one of the greatest dancers and choreographers of the century. Her husband had just died, and the shock, together with her vivid memories, made her easily distracted.

'Now. First position,' she would say, then stare out of the window, leaving us standing at the bar, suppressing giggles and rolling our eyes, while she launched into a recollection of her time with Robert Helpmann. The classes tended to go on a bit, and lacked focus, so I never derived much benefit from them. But I loved Sissy Smith.

Later, Chris and I went there a few times and always made a point of being in touch when we were performing in Nottingham. Sissy died in a car crash a few years ago. I always regret not having been able to take in more with her when I was young.

At 16, I left school, and started work at the Norwich Union Insurance Company, still living at home, but feeling grown up because I was earning my own money, even if it was only a small wage. I was in the motor insurance department, talking to people on the phone and filling in forms with the details of their lives.

It was at this time, when I had been skating solo for a year or so, that I first became aware of Chris. He was always there, very much in Sandra's shadow, the quiet one who was sometimes part of our group if we went bowling, or something.

It was Sandra herself I got to know. She became a good friend. We were the same age, and began to go out together at weekends, just the two of us. We were too young for pubs, but there were discos. If you were a teenager in Nottingham then, you'll remember drinking Cokes and dancing to 45s played by a DJ at the Palais, though the Palais was cool only on certain nights. Other nights, when the Palais was not cool, we would go to The Boat, a club on the River Trent.

Sandra was great to be with because she was so outgoing. She made up for my mousy shyness. I would probably never have gone out if it hadn't been for her, certainly not talked to anyone. But with her, you couldn't help it. Tall and good-looking, she had presence enough to make herself a focus of attention, introducing herself to people, making friends for both of us.

Anyway, when Chris and Sandra broke up, I knew soon enough, as everyone else did. But it never occurred to me to give up solo work and team up with Chris.

3

Partners

Jayne and Chris

So we were around at the same place, at the same time, and both ready for another partner. We had even danced together once or twice, at a dance club event called Drawn Partners.

We had dance clubs every Thursday evening, from 6:50 to 7:30, just before the public session. It was a whole mass of older people, in their twenties, who all seemed middle aged to us. We were the babies. Three judges would come into the rink, and all the names would go into a hat, and you would find yourself skating with anyone, just by the luck of the draw. We were partners twice, and even won once. But it never occurred to either of us that we might really become partners.

We never knew exactly how we were put together. Tee

apparently overheard Jayne in the 'buffet,' as the arena's tacky old café styled itself, saying something about going back to ice-dancing. That sparked an idea.

'You know,' she said to Chris's dad, Colin, later, 'Chris would be all right with Jayne Torvill.'

Colin was doubtful, because Jayne seemed such a retiring little thing, certainly up against Sandra, Chris's first partner. But Tee stuck to her guns. 'I bet she'd be fine. Let's go and see what her parents think.' So they went over to see them, and Jayne's parents thought it would be worth a try. Then, after a few phone calls, Chris's teacher, Janet, took to the idea.

Jayne

It made quite good sense actually, because we were at about the same standard, as measured by the tests we had passed. The only thing that might have mattered was that I hadn't done much dancing in the last couple of years. On the other hand, I had done a bit of everything, and Janet must have seen that I would be adaptable.

The first I knew of it, Janet, and Mick Wilde, who always seemed to be with her at the time, beckoned me off the ice. I think it was Mick who put the suggestion into words: 'How would you like to skate with Christopher Dean?'

I never react much, so I just sort of shrugged, 'Yes, why

not? I'll give it a try.' Inside, though, I was quite excited by the idea, because it would be good to have a partner again. Once again, I would have a reason to continue skating, which was what I really enjoyed.

Chris

Same thing with me: a quick suggestion on the ice-rink. It would never have occurred to me to skate with Jayne, because I knew Jayne only as a pair-skater and free-skater, not a dancer. For her, this would be a real career move, almost like starting anew. But I knew she was talented and willing, so I said I'd give it a try.

Jayne and Chris

Choosing a partner for Chris was a big deal for Janet as well. As a former champion, she felt that her self-esteem was at stake. Besides, to make her mark as a trainer, it would be important for her that we succeed.

First, though, we all had to be happy with the new arrangement. In case it all went wrong, and because Janet knew we'd feel uncomfortable, that first session needed to be as private as possible. So Janet said we had better come when there was no one else around and we would be sure to have 'private ice' — at 6:00 a.m! It was a Thursday morning — Thursday was the only day we had early-morning skating, and Chris was used to coming in at that time, before work, because that was when Sandra and he had practised.

Janet and Mick picked Jayne up on the way to the rink, because Janet was driving in from that direction. Chris arrived on his moped, ready to go on to police college afterwards.

Janet made us stand and hold each other in a dance position, really close, bodies pressed together, probably to find out if we were inhibited about touching each other. We'd both had partners before, of course, so that didn't bother either of us, but we were still painfully shy about everything else.

We hardly even dared look at each other. Janet put some of Dougie Walker's organ music on a cassette-player, and told us to do some basic steps. We went off and did as we were told, then came back and looked at her, waiting for more orders, just like a couple of obedient schoolkids. Then back and forth we went for an hour and a half, doing basic dance steps, waltz three-turns and foxtrot chassés.

The main thing she told us before we left for work was how Jayne should compensate for the difference in our height — Chris is 10 inches taller — by raising her free leg higher. That was something Janet knew all about, because she was Jayne's size, and her partner had been much taller, too.

It must have gone OK, because we danced together in

the dance interval that evening, which was like a public statement. All the other skating kids and their proud parents saw us, and everyone knew we were the new couple. We were very conscious of being on display. At one point, Jayne fell and banged her head, and had to pretend it wasn't anything.

A few days later, Janet asked, 'Do you think you'll stay together?' And we looked at each other, and um'd and ah'd and said we'd give it another week.

That's how it remained. We never really said we would skate together, and eventually it seemed as if it would bring bad luck if we did. So it was always, 'Well, we'll give it a bit longer. Another month, then we'll see.'

Of course, the time stretches out when you have high-level competitions to prepare for. But still, we always had this feeling that if we said we would stick together, we wouldn't. It's odd to think it's now been 20 years of just another month, just another year.

Chris

I remember my next day off going for an illicit drink with Paul Dale, who was going on 17, more than a year older than I was, and a more advanced skater, too, so he was someone to be looked up to.

'Are you really going to skate with Jayne?' he asked.

'Yes, I think I'll give it a go,' I said. There wasn't much

I could do about it now, anyway, without offending Janet, and my parents, and Jayne's parents, and Jayne herself probably, though I didn't know how she felt about it since we then hardly dared talk to each other.

'Well,' Paul said with a dismissive shrug, 'it's up to you. Good luck.'

Jayne

I had a bit more encouragement than that, from Sandra Elson of all people – Chris's first partner. She was still coming back home at weekends, and we were still going out on Saturday nights. I would go back home with her sometimes, and spend the night there. I remember fixing up a date with her over the phone, and telling her I'd been asked to skate with Chris. For her Chris was obviously history, because she just said, 'Oh, go for it, then!' So we were fine together, though I think her parents were a bit surprised.

Before long, Chris was definitely my partner, because I gave him a platinum Parker fountain pen for his 16th birthday. The only person I'd ever given anything to before was Michael, so I was a bit shy about doing it. My mum pushed me into it: 'Of course you must give him a present – it's his birthday!'

Jayne and Chris

So we started skating with Janet. And she was a genuine inspiration, because she was so driven. It was as if skating was all there was to life, and right then skating meant *us*. Off the ice, she was small, even nondescript, but on the ice she came alive, and grew, and became this larger-than-life person, whom we were eager to do well for.

Soon we had a tough schedule: a lesson several evenings a week for half an hour, followed by an hour and a half in the public session on our own, dodging through the mêlée of 200 or so other skaters; two hours early on Thursdays and Mondays; and all of Sunday mornings.

At the same time, Janet was coaching Jayne for her silver singles figure test, the one she had failed twice. Later we were skating every evening except Tuesdays, because there was only a half-hour gap in the schedules on that day.

'Why don't you skate Tuesday?' said Janet.

'It's only half an hour.'

'So what? Half an hour is half an hour! You come in and skate!' She could be really tough when she wanted to be.

We did as we were told, almost without thinking, and enjoyed ourselves. Later, when Jayne got a Mini, we became more independent, but in the early days it was our poor uncomplaining parents who suffered, because they often had to run us back and forth to the rink, and make most of the travel arrangements for competitions. It would all have been impossible without them.

Within a few months we were placed in a couple of club competitions, and began to look ahead. First we would take the inter-gold-medal test (the 'inter-gold', as it was known), which was the exam requirement for national competition set by the National Skating Association. We had to have it to enter the 1976 British championships.

Along the way, Janet said she was putting us forward for selection for two competitions in Europe, in Oberstdorf in southern Germany, and St Gervais, in France, near Grenoble. The two competitions were long-established stepping-stones for would-be senior competitors on the route to major international championships – not that we were looking very far ahead.

Now we could start work on the elements needed both for national and international competitions. These elements, as defined by the International Skating Union, were to govern our skating lives for the next nine years, and are still at the heart of amateur ice-dancing.

They are:

The 'compulsories' – with rigidly set steps. The demands are highly technical, the skating equivalent of piano scales. There were nine of them at that time, three being selected for performance just before competition. Nowadays, four are prescribed, and two selected for the competition.

An *Original Set Pattern (OSP)* – now known as the Original Set Dance, in which you dance your own steps to a set tempo, like a rumba or a paso doble. The tempo is set a year in advance.

A *Free Dance* — four minutes of music and dance-steps of your own choice. Here you are limited only by the time, and other rules governing holds, lifts, numbers of separations and the amount of time spent apart during the separations.

Although we hardly knew it yet, we were on the roundabout that would, if everything went well, take us from national to international and Olympic competitions. First in the skating season came the British National Ice-Dance Championships in November, traditionally held in Nottingham. The European championships, held in a different city every year, followed in January, with the World championships in March.

In addition, every four years, the Olympics slotted into the schedule in February. It's a gruelling round, for which you have the summer to prepare. You skate the same programme in each competition, because you have time to make only minor changes.

And many of the judges make the same circuit, building up their opinions of performers and performances. This fact, and the tightness of the timing, mean that you have to look at the three competitions (or four, if you include the Olympics) as a unit: the international skating year. In ice-dancing there are no overnight sensations. It's a long, arduous haul.

And it's all designed to win the judges' approval. In a sport that is so dependent on opinion, the judges constantly search for something firm as a basis for judgement. Supposedly, the rules provide that. But the rules are complicated and ever-changing.

All too often, behaviour and attitudes, on and off the ice, play a role. Nothing is ever certain. As time went on, we would also slowly see the inadequacies of the rules, conventions and traditions, and begin to get a feel for the disagreements, prejudices, ambitions, loyalties and animosities that the rules could not iron out.

All of this can be learned only by experience. You have to live it to understand it. Some come along faster than others of course — and now kids seem to adapt with astonishing speed — but it took us a good two to three years before we felt comfortable in competitions. At the time, of course, we had hardly an inkling of any of this, no idea how the world of amateur skating would become for us a life within our lives.

But we weren't even at the stage of devising a Free Dance yet. The inter-gold tests would be an OSP and compulsories. Janet, though, decided it was time to prepare for the future. 'Well,' she said, 'you'd better go off and find some music.'

We stared at her.

'You know, go to a music shop.'

That shocked us. We had been used to teachers turning up with music, and making up steps for us. We had never been on our own together outside the rink, and never thought about choosing our own music. But we did as we were told, telling each other, 'We'd better bring back something, or she won't let us skate again.'

So we met up, explored a couple of record shops, and spotted something that looked nice with a bright red cover. It was a Ted Heath Big Band album. We bought it on spec. It included a version of *Fever*, which we liked.

That was what we used as the main part of our first Free Dance. By now we knew that the Free Dance was not free at all. It was bound by rules, and tradition. Besides the rules on holds, lifts and separation, you had to display your skill with no more than four pieces of music, all within about four minutes. So the tradition had arisen that you always had four pieces of music — it didn't matter what, it didn't matter how they were cut, you'd just slap a tango next to a piece of jazz next to a minute of slushy strings, Gypsy music, Latin or Spanish, all cut at random to fit into the time available.

For a while we tried buying LPs for our music, but it was expensive and risky. We couldn't listen to everything in the shops, and ended up buying things just because they had nice covers, and were often disappointed. Then, after doing a local interview for BBC Radio Nottingham, we wandered past the music library, a room with shelves of records, thousands of them, a treasure-house of music. We stared, murmuring how wonderful it would be if we could have access to all that. We plucked up courage, and asked, and were given permission. At once, we began to haunt the place. Although we used to huddle in a corner like intruders, we could listen to anything, to our hearts' content.

Soon, a friend of Janet's, a former skater named Brian Saunders who had become a BBC sound engineer in London, started to help us, taping records and editing extracts together using a razor-blade and sticky tape. With his help, we built up a whole collection. Because the speed of players varied from rink to rink — either 7.5 or 15 inches per second — we had two versions of our programmes done,

39

turning up to competitions bearing a pile of eight reels and handing them to officials on arrival.

Looking back, we realise that the choreography, if you can call it that, was as basic as the music. In our four pieces, we developed little tricky steps or sequences, 'highlights' as we called them, which look difficult, and then we strung them together as well as we could, fitting them into the rhythm we were dancing to. It was all very ballroom, since that was the tradition, firmly established because the British had dominated ice-dancing and derived their moves from ballroom dancing. It didn't make the best use of ice-dancing as a form of expression, let alone try to do anything that carried through the full four minutes.

As teenagers, we didn't criticise, just responded to the demands of the sport, and enjoyed ourselves, inspired by every small success. Quite quickly, we began to emerge from the crowd. In our practice sessions, people would stop and watch as we ran through our free dance, and clap at the end. It was as if we were in the middle of a race being lifted by the crowd, onwards and upwards towards something we couldn't even glimpse yet.

The trip to Oberstdorf and St Gervais was our baptism of fire. The National Skating Association gave us our tickets and we took days off that were owing to us. We drew out our pocket money, hoping it would be enough for the two weeks we were to be away. The rest was up to us, which was going to be a big adventure, because it was the first time we had been abroad unsupervised. We couldn't afford to pay for Janet to come with us.

So off we went, with matching zip-up cardigans knitted

by Tee with red and white flashes on the arms, and our blue tops with the British team badges on, and our pile of tapes. We were both nervous. Chris had been to Czechoslovakia with Sandra for a competition, but we'd never been away from Nottingham by ourselves.

It was a summer Sunday when we left, with hardly any traffic on the motorway. Jayne's parents drove us down to Heathrow for the flight, because Chris's dad's car was on the point of breaking down, as usual.

Oberstdorf is down near the Austrian border, not far from Munich, but for some reason we were flying to Zurich and had tickets on a train the next morning to get us to Oberstdorf. It never occurred to anyone, apparently, that we were arriving in Zurich in the evening, and getting a train the next morning. So where were we to sleep? To adults, these things are simply routine, but we were hardly more than kids.

We arrived at Zurich airport quite late at night, and the whole airport seemed shut up. We didn't know where to go or what to do, didn't want to spend any money on a restaurant — well, we'd never been in a foreign restaurant — so we just sat in the airport lounge and dozed.

Then, first thing in the morning, we found a bus outside the airport that went to the station. 'Change at Immenstadt,' we were told. We found the train, and piled in our cases. Then Chris became nervous, almost hyperactive, wondering if we were really on the right train. He ran out again to check, running back in panic just in time before departure.

Still not satisfied, he asked other passengers, 'Are we OK for Immenstadt?' Then we discovered the train was going to divide, and we were in the wrong section, so off we went as fast as we could back along the train, our baggage banging along the banks of seats.

When we got over the border, we scanned each station anxiously wondering if this was Immenstadt. Then the change, wrestling with the bags, and the same frantic concern about whether it was the right train, and what to do if it wasn't, because we didn't know a word of German.

Well, it was all right, and one of the German organisers was there to meet us. We hardly had time to admire the setting — Oberstdorf is right on the edge of the Alps, in a valley hemmed in by peaks — when we were taken to our accommodation. These were simple, bare rooms in a modern, functional rather grim boarding school, an *Internat*, as it's called in German, which was empty for the summer holidays, though it was now gradually filling with other skaters there for the competition.

We didn't know anyone — the other team members were all older — we had no idea what was expected of us, and we had hardly any money. So from that first evening we just stayed together, like babes in the wood. We wandered about the village and had some fishcakes and chips at a fish shop, the Nordsee, which was an odd thing to find in an Alpine village. But once we'd found it, we stuck to it, and ate there every evening.

It was the cheapest place we could find, but we were still afraid of running out of money the next week. It was a relief the following morning to discover that breakfast at the *Internat* was free, and there was lots of it, even if they had things that struck us as really odd — warm ham instead of bacon, and cheese and paté. Anyway, we ate as much breakfast as we could, until we felt sick, hoping we could get through the rest of the day until our Nordsee supper.

Being hungry and broke: those are the dominant memories of our first visit to Oberstdorf. Close behind comes the rink itself. It was a 15-minute walk from the *Internat*, a *wet* walk because it seemed to rain all the time. It's different now, but then the rink, although roofed, was open on three sides. At night, the bright lights brought out the moths. We skated with our mouths tight closed in case we swallowed one. It was damp, and it was humid.

We felt like outsiders, but we made the best of it because we didn't know enough — didn't have enough money — to do anything but skate. There was no one to guide us, no one to tell us how to behave. We had our practice times over the first three days, and we just went to the rink, ran through our numbers, and sat down on the seats afterwards to watch without talking to anyone.

So it was a real surprise, and an exhilaration, when we came second, behind a Russian pair, but ahead of a British couple who had finished in the top five in the British championships the previous year.

It was all surprisingly low-key. Just a few congratulations, but no sense of where it might be leading. That became apparent only after the six-hour bus journey to the next competition in St Gervais. Chris found himself sharing a room with a man who was to us already a living legend of skating, Robin Cousins. With all the authority of his international experience, he said that Oberstdorf was like a dress rehearsal for St Gervais so 'you're going to do really well here.'

As it happened, we did better than anyone could have predicted, because the Russians were not competing.

After the compulsories and the OSP we were in the lead, on course to win. But it was a close call, because the food at the hotel was so awful Chris got food poisoning. He was throwing up the day of the Free Dance, and just as we were going on to the ice, he said, 'Jayne, I don't feel good.' Somehow – perhaps it was the adrenalin – he kept his stomach under control for the dance.

And we won. Our first international win. We should have felt nothing but unalloyed joy. But the edge was taken off it by what was happening to Chris's insides.

Chris

I remember after the Free Dance sitting uselessly in the dressingroom, flaked out, too weak to stand. Someone helped me up, but it was no good.

Jayne

The officials sent for an ambulance, and off he went to

hospital. Changing quickly into ordinary clothes, I tried to go with him, but one of the officials said, 'No, please, you have to go to the podium. The photographers— There will be no one standing in first place!' So I went and stood there by myself, flanked by the couples placed second and third, feeling not so much proud as embarrassed in my skirt and blouse.

Chris

Meanwhile, I arrived in hospital, still wearing my navy-blue catsuit with its silver lamé collar and carrying my skates. It was a pretty miserable night. The doctor spoke no English, I was sick, I was cold, I had no friends to talk to, other than Jayne who came by briefly after the ceremony.

And next day, when she came to fetch me, she forgot my clothes. I had to leave in my catsuit.

Jayne and Chris

Still it was a good experience as far as skating went. Not only did we win, but the whole adventure, which really seemed an epic to us at the time, had cemented us as a

45

team. We had been thrown together to work things out the best we could, and we had done it together. There hadn't been much to do but travel and work and eat — almost everything but sleep together — and everything was a joint decision.

Winning was a tremendous boost. Not that you would have guessed it from the reactions at home. When we got back, Jayne's dad picked us up again. We hadn't called to tell anyone the news, and we can't remember what he said when we told him we'd won. 'Oh, that's nice,' probably.

It was the same with Jayne's mum and Chris's parents, and Janet. None of them were ones to make a display of the pride they felt.

But in terms of our career it laid a foundation. We had taken a leap away from junior into senior status. Now we could concentrate on the inter-gold and, with luck, go on to the national championships.

Our career almost ended there and then, with the inter-gold. The skaters perform as a couple twice but are assessed individually by the three judges. We were dancing a rumba, in which there is a change of emphasis that is hard to achieve. Chris failed. The second time was Jayne's turn to be assessed and, because we got the timing right Jayne passed. Through Janet, we reapplied immediately for another attempt a month later, practised hard, danced a perfect rumba, giving Chris his medal, and leaving us ready for the British championships.

It's hard now to remember any particular high points of the next two years — there were so many. The important thing was that we were steadily moving up. Fourth in our first British championships, then third the next year. That lifted us to another level, making us one of the three couples entered for the European championships in Strasbourg in 1978.

When we were chosen, we were ecstatic. If we never did anything else in our lives, we felt we would die happy. It was one of those marvellous moments you usually get only in childhood, when there is no burden of expectation, no future of imagined failure, to mar the purity of happiness.

There was also the awareness, though, that we were at some sort of turning point, because Janet told us so. 'Enjoy yourselves, because it's your last chance to do so,' she said.

Whatever happened, we would never feel the same elation and freedom from responsibility again. 'It's your first time, you've got nothing to lose.'

Then she gave us good advice: 'I want you to watch as many practices as possible. Watch everything. _Everything._ Free-skating, pair-skating, ice-dancing, the lot. You can learn from watching something bad as much as something good. Just watch, and take it all in.'

In Strasbourg, we did our best to live up to what we imagined to be the expectations placed upon us. We were ice-dancers, we were athletes, so we walked round in the hotel in our track-suits, because that's what real athletes did. We'd never included much running in our training, and we knew we were going to be allowed only an hour or so on the ice every day, so we thought we had better keep fit. The first evening we went running. The next morning, our calves were in agony.

It was another baptism of fire, that competition. In those days no one ran through their whole number in practice. We'd just do bits and pieces, a few steps here, a tricky bit there, then drift over to Janet for comments. So, compared with later performances, we really weren't fully prepared.

Then in our first dance, the compulsories, we were drawn almost last in our group. We thought that was fine. But we hadn't reckoned with the effect of 18 pairs of skaters, all doing the same thing one after the other.

By the time we came to skate, the ice was cut into tramlines. That, combined with the fact that we hadn't skated the sequences through for quite a while, made the experience utterly exhausting. Overall, we came ninth, which we were more than happy with.

In the end, it was not so much the competition that mattered as what and whom we saw. The people who really impressed us at Strasbourg were the winners, a couple we had admired for a while as a result of seeing them on TV.

They were Russians called Irina Moiseyeva and Andrei Minenkov. The Russians always made a particular impact. They had dominated skating for 10 years, they were serious athletes, with all the advantages of government backing, and they carried this aura of excellence and nobility and distance, partly because you couldn't talk to them easily.

Even among Russians, Moiseyeva and Minenkov were impressive. They were tall, balletic, as remote and glorious as creatures from another planet. We stared at them as young children look upon TV stars, unable to believe we were in the same rink with them.

It wasn't as if we were able to analyse what they did. We just watched open-mouthed. Now, of course, it's obvious why they were so impressive. They came from a tradition totally different from the false, staid, uptight ballroom background that was familiar to us, the postures and steps that had dominated ice-dancing for a decade, since before we started. Their background was the Bolshoi and Russian folk dancing.

But it was more than that. Here were two people who were obviously a man and woman in a relationship, with a story to tell. And they were dancing to bits of _West Side Story_ — still extracts, cut together with the usual variety of rhythm, but at least the extracts all came from the same source.

We found it breathtaking. But it would take quite a while yet to absorb what we had seen, and incorporate it into our work.

That was also where we first saw another couple who were to become important for us, the Hungarians Krisztina Regoeczy and Andras Sallay — Christina and Andrew, as we would call them later.

We noticed them because of the way he would give her a little kiss just before they went on the ice. It set a mood, a link between them that carried through their performance. It had never occurred to us that the dance starts before the music, that it starts when the audience — and the judges — first see you.

Although we were impressed by them, we felt honour-bound not to support them. We were rooting for the British champions, Janet Thompson and Warren Maxwell, who seemed like gods to us. It was thrilling when they actually

49

talked to us, and like a personal catastrophe when they were defeated by the Hungarians.

Jayne

The Hungarians' teacher was an English woman called Betty Callaway. She was going to play a great part in our lives, but you would never have guessed it from our first meeting. When she spoke to me and said something perfectly nice like 'I think you did a nice programme', I stared at my feet and managed no more than a little 'Mm.' It must have seemed a little rude.

The next thing was the World Championships in Ottawa, six weeks after Strasbourg. We almost didn't make it, because I got tendonitis from training. It became so bad that I had to go to hospital, where they gave me a half-cast and told me not to skate for a week. A week! And in two weeks we had the World Championships!

Chris was horrible. He came to see me at home. I had a friend from work round when he came. He took one look at the cast, one look at me, said, 'Tell me when you can skate again!' and walked out.

My friend was open-mouthed, but I knew Chris. If *he* had been in plaster, he would have been back on the ice, no matter what. But I prefer to let my body recover at its own speed, because I don't have a very high tolerance of pain.

'Oh, take no notice,' I said. 'He'll be all right. He was a bit shocked, that was all.'

Still there was no denying the danger. If the National Skating Association had heard I had a leg in plaster, they might have dropped us from the team. So I just kept my head down for a week, and it healed OK.

Jayne and Chris

Then came another blow — from Janet.

At this time, Janet was more than just a teacher, she was the rock that underlay our skating career. For a while, the three of us supplied a mutual need. We needed her, she wanted an anchor in her life. At the time the anchor was skating, and us. She was astonishingly generous with her time. Good for us, except that, with hindsight, it appears that her commitment was more than generous: it verged on the obsessive.

But recently she had acquired a different obsession. A few months previously, Janet had fallen in love with a man she had met at a sort of singles group. His name was Trevor.

Our first thought when we met Trevor was that nothing but good could come of it. But it soon became clear that things weren't going to work out quite so well, at least for us. For one thing, Trevor had nothing to do with skating, and seemed to resent the time Janet spent with us. When they got married, we weren't invited.

Naturally enough, we didn't take to him, because we believed he put pressure on her to limit her involvement with us. She began to be late for teaching, which she never had been before. Trevor used to come with her, and tell her when to leave, or come alone with a message like 'Sorry, she can't come, she's sick this morning.' Actually, there was some truth in this — she did have health problems, but they had never affected us so directly before.

Then, by the time we went to Strasbourg, she was pregnant. Now, with Ottawa looming, she said she didn't want to risk the journey.

Understandable, of course, but still devastating for us.

So we went on our own. The first trip across the Atlantic. Gawping at a big, new city. A fancy hotel — the Holiday Inn, Ottawa. We were so excited, it was hard to remember we were there to skate.

Chris

I was rooming with Warren Maxwell. Talk about sophistication. He was a fund of funny stories, and so cool that the women seemed to be all over him. At the dinners for the competitors, he had a *dinner jacket*! I was just in a Burton's off-the-peg suit, and was totally awed.

Jayne and Chris

As for the competition itself, we came 11th, but only because we were overtaken right at the end by the Austrians, Susi and Peter Handschmann. Later, when we became more cynical about judges and their motives, we wondered about that result. Placing the Handschmanns in the top 10 allowed Austria to enter two couples for the following year's World Championships, which just happened to be in Vienna. On the other hand, perhaps we just dropped a place, fair and square. Certainly, that's what we thought then, and came back reasonably pleased with our first 'Worlds'.

When we got home, Janet was in hospital, about to have her baby. Naturally, she had other things on her mind than our performance in Ottawa. We don't think she even knew how we'd done. So there we were, all enthusiastic, full of our new experiences, and all she managed was a brief, distant 'Well done.'

Then, when we started talking about getting on with training, she said, 'Well, actually, after the baby Trevor doesn't want me to teach any more.'

Of course, we should have seen it coming. But we didn't. We were so young and inexperienced that we were blind to the change in her circumstances, totally unable to see why marriage or a new baby should change things. So it was a terrible shock, like a slap in the face from a best friend. Jayne couldn't help crying.

'Don't worry,' Janet said, 'It'll work out.'

Unable to believe it, with Jayne still red-eyed, we drove

round to Janet's house to talk to Trevor. No joy. He said something that must have sounded brutally final, because Jayne just walked out and waited in the car for Chris to finish his coffee and join her.

4

Champions

Chris

So there we were, together, but without a teacher. I began to ring people who might help. One of them was an ice-skating judge, Pam Davies, who suggested Betty Callaway. That could work. We had seen her in Strasbourg, where she had been with her couple, Regoeczy and Sallay. Now, according to Pam, the Hungarians were retiring and she would have time to take on another couple.

Jayne

I wasn't so certain, but remembered that in Ottawa she had recognised a costume left at the rink as mine, and brought it back to the hotel for me. That was a thoughtful gesture, especially after my lack of response to her in Strasbourg. So I said, 'OK, let's call her.'

Jayne and Chris

She was happy to give it a try — 'Oh, yes,' she said, 'I'd like to teach an English couple again' — because she thought she was without a pair.

So she came up to see us, mainly to see whether we were all compatible. We talked in the Nottingham ice-rink buffet. She seemed to like us, and we liked her — she was quiet-spoken, calm, assured.

At the time, we were very much in awe of her — we called her 'Mrs Callaway' for quite a while — because she had almost 20 years' experience as a teacher at Richmond, as a one-time German national ice-dancing coach, and as a coach of stars like Christina and Andrew. We knew at once we were lucky to have her, though there was no way of knowing just how lucky.

It *was* luck too, because, as it turned out, Christina and

56

Andrew decided not to retire, as the result of pressure from their national skating federation to continue until the 1980 Olympics. Because she normally chose to teach one dance team at a time, that put Betty in a dilemma. She might simply have dropped us. Instead, she kept us both, with immeasurable benefit to us. Christina and Andrew turned out to be wonderful role models. And Betty's connections with Hungary and Germany were to open up new horizons for us, personally and professionally.

That year, 1978, our first with Betty, we came on fast. Christina and Andrew came up to Nottingham with Betty every weekend, and we all became good friends. That summer, Christina and Andrew moved to Nottingham, to a flat we found for them at Trent Bridge. It seemed OK to us, but it must have been a bit grim for them – they were used to international travel, and Andrew was a painter as well as a skater. Christina, a flamboyant person with great hooded eyes, said that the first thing she did was clean it from top to bottom.

Betty was meticulous, an expert in the compulsories, and her quiet authority was just right for us. She never shouted at us, always explained. She allowed us to develop our own method of practice. She also forced us to explore more on our own. Christina and Andrew had a ballet teacher in Hungary, and she thought it might be good for us as well to find someone to work with in England.

So through Nottingham County Council we contacted a teacher, Gideon Avrahami, a contemporary dance specialist from Israel who worked with the East Midlands Dance Group.

Jayne

I remember he turned up at the ice-rink draped in an enormous fur coat, as if he was going to be teaching in the Antarctic. That first time, he didn't do much but make a comment or two about a few movements, but added, 'Come and do a dance class.'

We did, but the only thing I remember was being in the changing room, ready for the class, when he came in. We had arrived in training clothes, but he came in to change, chatting to us as he did so. He took off all his clothes, until he was stark naked, still chatting away. I had never seen a naked man in the flesh before. That soon changed of course, because dancers and skaters are not exactly inhibited. But at the time I was so embarrassed that I didn't know what to do or where to look.

As for the dancing, I just wished I'd listened to Sissy Smith a bit more when I was younger.

Jayne and Chris

Then, in 1978, another opportunity opened up, the possibility that we might have a chance of winning the British Nationals. We had been third the previous year. Now the number-two pair had dropped out, and the previous winners, Warren Maxwell and Janet Thompson, had been injured. That of course meant we had a good chance, and should have felt a buzz of expectation and elation.

But we didn't. Perhaps we suppressed the emotion, to avoid the tension.

We won, ending with a Free Dance based on _Slaughter on Fifth Avenue_, with a bit of something Spanish tacked on the end. If this sounds less than ecstatic, it was probably because we felt we had won more by default than by performing to our limits. Nor were we aware of being new arrivals on a national stage.

Strangely, the immediate impact seemed to be purely local. We began to receive a lot of local press interest, and found our status at the rink enhanced, now that we had direct access to the rink's tape-machine and could put on our own music, taking our turn with the teachers.

Only gradually did we realise what we had achieved — a chance to go onwards and upwards — and began to feel a responsibility to make ourselves worthy of the role of British champions.

Onwards and upwards. But how?

Betty made a suggestion. What about coming out to Hungary for two weeks, where we could be guaranteed many more hours of ice time than the Nottingham rink could ever give us?

Chris

It was a great idea. But there was a problem. We were both working. Jayne had to take unpaid leave, and I had to negotiate time off. It turned out to be more complicated than that, however. Hungary was a Communist country, and I was a policeman. Apparently, I would be venturing into enemy territory.

I was called in for a meeting with Special Branch, and was told in all seriousness to beware of people offering me presents, and especially to beware of women wanting to go to bed with me. They would obviously be after the priceless information I had concerning the workings of the Nottingham police force. I promised to be careful.

Jayne and Chris

Then, following Betty's advice, we bought half a suitcase of Country Store cereal, biscuits and instant coffee, and off we went to Budapest, where Betty booked into a hotel, which we certainly couldn't afford, so we stayed with a family Christina and Andrew found for us.

That was a strange experience. We shared a room,

which was divided down the middle by a curtain, and had hardly any contact with the family because none of them spoke a single word of English.

Most of the time when we weren't training we were bored out of our minds. Andrew took us to a restaurant he usually ate in, a huge high-ceilinged room lined with wood panelling and full of fat ladies in fur hats. He ordered veal and pancakes.

So for the next two weeks, that's where we went, and that's what we had, every time, filling up on cereal, biscuits and coffee back in our room.

We had a beautiful city at our feet, with galleries, ballets and concerts to go to, but we didn't know what there was to experience, didn't have the confidence to explore, and anyway we didn't have any money. It was a very long two weeks.

That didn't matter, though, because our skating received a tremendous boost. Even though our hours were odd — from 10:00 a.m. to midday and from 8:00 to 10:00 in the evening — we had those four hours on the ice with only two other couples sharing it with us. We had never done so much skating before.

And, besides having Betty there to coach us, it was a real bonus working with Christina and Andrew. It's no good just having ice time when you're growing: you need to be around people you can learn from.

Jayne

And we also met their ballet teacher, Zoltan Nagy, or 'Zolli' as he seemed to be known everywhere. His background was classical ballet, and he loved women. He charmed me, in the best possible way, because he gave me a new feeling of self-confidence, both as a woman and as a skater, which is absolutely essential if you are going to project yourself with any force during a performance. He was an inspiration.

Chris

To me as well. The messages I got from his powerful combination of passion, teaching talent and masculinity were that there was nothing to be embarrassed about in ballet dancing, that it was worth striving to acquire the grace of a ballet dancer, that it was OK to express emotion in dancing. What worked in ballet, I realised, could find its parallels on ice.

Jayne and Chris

During 1979 and early 1980 we stepped further up the ladder. In the 1979 British championships, we received our first score of six. True, the mark came from Molly Phillips, a tiny, slightly eccentric octogenarian who ran a Welsh hill farm.

People used to joke that Molly gave sixes just to get her face on TV. But it was a sign that we could reach perfection in someone's eyes for one year at least, even if we knew the standards would be raised in the future.

In those years too we were sixth then fourth in the Europeans; eighth then fourth in the Worlds. (We had been lying third when we twice lost our balance during the original set pattern. The result reduced Chris to tears of anger and frustration, though Jayne's disappointment was lifted by a charming gesture: as she left the ice, the local police chief presented her with a bouquet by special request of the Nottingham Chief Constable).

And we were fifth at the Winter Olympics in Lake Placid in February 1980. Those Olympics, our first, had a lot of dramas. In an astounding sporting and political upset, the US ice-hockey team beat the Russians. There was hardly any snow – it had to be imported. And all the staff at the athletes' residences were students who became so angry at the way they were exploited that they simply quit their jobs, leaving the canteens and transport without staff. For us, the dramas were all part of a happy experience, because we weren't expected to win a place and no one took much notice of us.

Robin Cousins was the media star, winning the men's gold, so we could not have been exactly headline news. We just made sure we bought as many of the Olympic-logo T-shirts as we could, because it could easily be our one and only Olympics, and concentrated on doing as well as we could. We left content, feeling we had come on well, with Betty's influence.

That summer, Betty, as the former German national coach, was invited to teach at Oberstdorf for two weeks. They were just opening another large rink there, in addition to the established large rink and studio rink, and the invitation was part of a plan to build up Oberstdorf as a national and international skating centre. She asked us to go along, and we planned to stay for six weeks.

Oberstdorf, where we could skate at almost any hour of the day on uncrowded ice, was a revelation. Once only partially roofed, it was now all enclosed. It would have taken us months to prepare ourselves for the next season in Nottingham. In Oberstdorf, we did it in those six weeks, skating for up to six hours a day. It showed us what we might be able to accomplish, given the time and the facilities.

And with Betty behind us, it was there for the asking whenever we wanted, if only we could take advantage.

Even before we arrived home, in August, we knew we were at a turning point. Back in Nottingham, we would be facing the old routine: working during the day, skating late at night and early in the morning, fitting in as well as we could with the hundreds of other skaters.

We knew we would be getting only a few hours' sleep a night, and still wouldn't be able to have the time we needed, because we had to work. We must have been the only skaters at that level still to hold full-time jobs. We had no sponsors, so it was the only way we could afford to skate.

But if we kept the jobs on, we wouldn't be able to keep up our present levels, let alone practise harder, because every competition (like the Lake Placid Olympics) meant borrowing time against holidays, which had to be paid back with overtime, or being given time, or taking unpaid leave. And practising harder was just what it would take to become British champions again in November 1980 and give ourselves a chance to improve our position at the World championships the following March.

How we could ever find a way to continue to the Olympics, three and a half years off, we had no idea.

So we took what was perhaps the biggest risk of our lives.

Chris

I knew it was a crazy thing to do. I faced the prospect of leaving a job I loved, a job I thought was going to be a career for life, at a time when unemployment was rising fast. I remember the headlines: unemployment had just topped two million. And between us we had just about enough in the bank to get us through the Worlds the following March.

Then that would be it. If I resigned, I thought they would never have me back.

But I also knew it was crazy *not* to take the risk. There could one day be other work, though I had no idea what. But skating was here and now. It had to be. We had just three months to prepare for the next round of competitions. Whatever the pain and confusion resigning would bring, there was a part of me that knew the truth.

It was an agonising choice. I had always lived to a rigid schedule, my life mapped out in front of me, always secure. First, school, with its regular round of classroom work, sport and home. Then, with only two weeks off for a summer holiday, straight into Police Cadets. Then into the force, where I had been for almost six years. Every day, waking up, going to work, and knowing I could count on the next pay-cheque.

There was never a time when I wasn't supposed to be somewhere, never having to worry about travel arrangements, always provided with a uniform. Now, I felt as if I was on the edge of a void.

I went to the Chief Constable, Charles McClaughlin, and explained the dilemma. 'I don't know what to do,' I finished, sadly. 'I don't think I can be a policeman, and skate.'

Part of my distress was that they had been so good to me. They'd encouraged me, followed my career, given me time off, allowed me to take unpaid leave, stacked up holidays — anything to give me a chance to skate.

Chief Constable McClaughlin was a young-looking, progressive, cheerful man — he was the one who had flowers sent to Jayne after the 1980 worlds — and I'll always be grateful for his reaction.

'Well, Dean,' he said with a smile, 'what you should do now, while you have the chance, is skate. You can always come back and be a policeman later.'

His words were a huge relief. But there was more. Normally, I would have put my name down to resign, and worked out a month's notice. That's what I expected.

'If your paperwork's up to date,' he finished, 'you can be out of here in forty-eight hours.'

It solved one problem, and it was a generous response. But it was also very upsetting. I never even had a chance to say goodbye to my mates. They'd been supportive, coming to see us in the rink, even covering for me if I wanted to leave early to skate.

Suddenly, I was gone, stripped not just of my friends but of everything else that told me who I was — my shirts, epaulettes, badge, uniform, stationery. I turned them all in, back to the quarter-master's stores. At home, my cupboard was practically empty.

Jayne

It was easier for me, because I wasn't working full-time. Still, I couldn't put in enough hours to fulfil requirements.

I was always borrowing hours, which theoretically had to be repaid by working more later.

When I resigned, they said I had to make it all up in the next month. So for a month, I was sitting there, in an agony of frustration, thinking, 'I just don't want to be here.' And I was still taking time to skate, of course. So in the end, with 20 hours still owing, I said, 'Forget it. Take it off my wages.' I didn't get much for my last month's work!

Chris and Jayne

Our friends at the rink told us how to survive. Most of them were unemployed, and had been since leaving school, but they were on the dole. That was how they managed to keep up their skating. Up until then, the dole had been a vague thing that other people did. We really didn't know what the requirements were to qualify.

'That's great!' we said to each other. 'They give you money for not doing anything! How do you get it?'

'Just go and sign on.'

So off we went to the DHSS office, sat down together, and said we'd come to register.

We gave our names and addresses and then it was, 'Right, what sort of jobs are you seeking?'

'Huh?'

We stared at each other, then at the lady. 'Oh, no. We're not looking for jobs.'

'But you have to be looking for jobs.'

'But we can't. We want to be skaters.'

She stared, as if she couldn't believe her ears. All we had to say was that we would be ready to take on something. That's what everyone else did. But we couldn't.

'You're not looking for a job at the moment?'

'No. We just want to skate.'

'Well, we can't give you any money, then.'

We left with mixed feelings, glum that we hadn't got the money we'd been hoping for, glad we hadn't lied to get it.

That focused our minds on how else to get support. We started to apply to anyone we could think of for help — companies, local businesses, city corporations. But since we were bound by our amateur status and couldn't offer anything in return for the money we needed, like endorsements or advertising, they all refused.

Eventually — at Betty Torvill's suggestion — we approached Nottingham City Council.

'Dear Mr Carroll,' Jayne wrote. 'I don't know whether you have seen my partner and I recently on television . . . but if you did, you will also have heard that we have now given up our jobs to concentrate entirely on our skating . . . Our aim is to "go for gold" at the next Olympics . . . I am writing to you to see if there is any way the Nottingham City Council could help us financially as I'm sure you can imagine that we are now finding it difficult with all the outlay we have.'

They asked us for figures. We added up our living and

travelling costs, and said we could get by on about £7,000 a year each. That would eventually include renting a small flat for Chris – Jayne would be staying on at home as before. We had no idea if they would take the request seriously, and certainly had no hopes of getting help for more than a year or so.

It was a complete surprise when Radio Nottingham called to ask for our comments on the grant we had been given: £42,000, almost exactly what we had asked for on a yearly basis – but for three whole years! Enough to take us through to the Olympics, if we were good enough!

As we began to move up in the international world, Betty saw to it that we improved in presentation as well as performance. In the early days, we used to wear the most terrible fluorescent red and blue Lycra, which we changed to an equally awful green. We did it originally to be noticed. Unfortunately, we were. Once, one of the judges, who was a friend of ours, Vera Pilsworth, whispered to us, '*You have to change your costumes*!'

It was Betty who finally put us on the right road, by introducing us to Courtney Jones, both a former world champion and also a former couturier, now a long-established ice-dancing judge and secretary of the National Skating Association.

Courtney lived with his long-term companion, Bobby Thompson, a former skater and now a coach. The two of them were well-respected and influential members of the international skating establishment. To have their advice was a privilege.

We drove down to see the two of them in their

Bayswater flat. That was another revelation — to see proper interior design, glass shelves, original paintings, colour-coordinated furniture. Very awe-inspiring for two youngsters from the Midlands. Courtney himself was awe-inspiring, too: urbane, sophisticated, very upper-crust, a million miles from anything in our experience. Bobby was the one who put us at our ease, with charm and flattery.

We were there to talk about costumes. But very quickly one thing led to another, not surprisingly with two people who had been in the business so long.

To talk costumes, you have to talk about your ideas, and what music you are dancing to, and how you respond to it. It was exhilarating — the first time we had ever talked to people with an all-round vision, a total view of performance.

And as we talked, we began to relax. Courtney began to show a different side to his personality — nothing he liked more than fish and chips and apple pie, he used to say. 'Common as muck,' he'd say, putting on a northern accent.

We didn't know about that, but he was undeniably passionate about skating, as Bobby was, and both were prepared to share their views and experience with extraordinary generosity. That first session led to many others, when we would bring down records and tapes trawled from the BBC record library in Radio Nottingham.

It was Courtney who found us the two people who were to assume responsibility for the way we looked. One lived in Marlow, the other in Twickenham. As a result, when we were not in Oberstdorf, we developed a new way of life, permanently on the move.

It involved a 6:00 a.m. start from Nottingham in Jayne's Mini, a battered old thing that overheated fearfully on the motorway. On hot days, to help cool the engine, we would leave the fan-heater on. But that meant we had to have all the windows open.

Wind-blown, but still bleary with heat and fumes, we would arrive in London in the rush hour, drive to Bobby and Courtney's to discuss progress and maybe pick up some designs, go into our Berwick Street suppliers, Borovick's, to buy some material, and then head on with our cloth 30 miles to Marlow to see Chris's tailor, Mr Bishop.

Mr Bishop made costumes for numerous male skaters, so he knew all about the problems — elastic under the soles of the feet to stop trousers riding up, fixings for shirts, jackets, waistcoats and trousers so that everything held together in the middle, with just the right amount of give.

It took a lot of buttons, hooks, eyes and press-studs to make a good skating costume in those days, and considerable skill to make sure it still looked smart, however violent the movements, and whatever the speed across the ice. The crotch is the danger area. A good gusset is half the battle. There's nothing so horrible as a baggy gusset — short legs, voluminous ball-room — except a tight one that splits.

The trouble is, once you've had the one, chances are you overcorrect and get the other. We've seen some wicked outfits. But not from Mr Bishop.

Mr Bishop lived in a huge house littered with odds and ends of material. His name was appropriate, because he looked as if he should have been a vicar. He had a long neck, protruding top teeth that made his every *s*-sound whistle, and glasses. He seemed like some storybook character working mainly from a top room that was a treasure-chest of clothes, tailor's dummies and rolls of cloth.

Then back to Twickenham, to Jayne's dressmaker, Mrs Parrish, who lived in a large flat in a rambling block. She had several virtues, one of which was an ability to interpret Courtney's designs. Another was a way with skirts, which have to be sewn on to leotards and look ungainly if they are put on level, as they would be in everyday life.

The thing about Mrs Parrish was that she liked to chat. By this time it was probably early evening, and we were exhausted, slumping in our chairs, gritting our teeth and thinking, 'Mrs Parrish, please! Hurry up!'

But she wouldn't. It would be getting dark, and she had bad eyes, so there was no sewing at night. Eventually we'd leave, driving back up the motorway in our boiling car, with Chris nodding off at the wheel, getting back to Nottingham about midnight.

The dresses got later and later. It always seemed that, right in the last week before some competition or other, she would call up and say, 'Jayne, dear, do you think you can come in for another fitting?' That would mean a whole day's journey, for both of us, because Jayne wouldn't make the journey on her own. Then a final visit, and at last it was ready. Always meticulous, exquisite work.

That was how it was, right up until the 1984 Olympics.

First, though, we faced the long pre-Olympic build up. In part this was served at Oberstdorf, where Betty would help us work on the routines chosen with Courtney and Bobby. For those three years, we were out there for all the summer months, with several other shorter stays as well, staying at a new *Internat* that was part of the new training centre.

It was almost all work. Almost.

Luckily, there was someone with whom we could relax. One evening, another skater, the German champion Norbert Schramm, took us out to a club, where he introduced us to a friend of his, Clarissa von Lerchenfeld, a forceful young lady with flowing hair, a wide smile and impeccable English. We became friends, and she said, 'You ought to come out to the house one day.' When we shyly agreed, she fixed a date, and made the arrangements.

Suddenly we were in *Sound of Music* country. The house outside Immenstadt turned out to be a small castle that had been in the family for 500 years, give or take a few. It was a fairytale place crammed with paintings and antiques, the treasures of generations of von Lerchenfelds.

The father, Eckhardt, greeted us in even better English than Clarissa's — he had been to Gordonstoun. In some ways he was thoroughly traditional, often wearing lederhosen, or that thick grey and green Bavarian wool. Yet he was always surprising, funny and charming, with a flair for practical things.

He was never happier than when working with his vintage cars. He had a small collection of classic vehicles, including a fire-engine. His glasses would be perched on the end of his nose as he regaled us with intriguing anecdotes about the house.

'Do you know what this is?' he would ask, pointing to a glass-cabinet inlaid into a wall. 'The recess used to go all the way down. In medieval times, it was the toilet.'

Clarissa's mother was Austrian, equally charming, equally generous, a dirndl-clad Julie Andrews to his Christopher Plummer. That first visit, no sooner were we inside, wide-eyed, than there was a meal on a table that could seat 20, and Eckhardt was wandering up from the cellar with a bottle of wine.

'Mm, no this is too good to drink this year,' and off he went again to find another bottle. We had no idea what good wine tasted like until then.

For some reason, they made their house into a sort of refuge for us. 'Oh, Chris, Jayne,' Baroness von Lerchenfeld would say when she got to know us better. 'You can't stay at that dreadful _Internat_! Stay with us!'

It wouldn't have worked, of course. We had to be totally focused on skating. Besides, we were simply not part of their world. Once we went to a ball there, with a whole army of young-blood barons and _Grafen_, all of whom seemed equally fluent in German and English.

Clarissa took charge of us, and scanned the list of guests. 'Right,' she said. 'Let's see who's with who.' Jayne was whisked off one way, and Clarissa took Chris. Neither of us said a word through supper, feeling totally out of place. As soon as we saw the chance, we were together again in a flash.

The first real test of what we had done in Oberstdorf came not so much in the British championships in late 1980 — we retained the title — but in the Europeans in February 1981. We wanted to do well there, not just because we _always_ wanted to do well, but also to position ourselves for the Worlds less than two months later.

'Doing well' at this point meant coming no more than third. To do that we had to beat at least one pair of Russian skaters. There were three Russian couples, among them our inspiration only three years before, Moiseyeva and Minenkov. On the other hand, we didn't really expect to win, so again, and for the last time, we felt no great pressure of expectation.

To our astonishment, we took a slight lead in the compulsories. Then, with a day before the original set pattern, we began to feel the nerves, the tightness in the stomach, the effort to turn your mind away from what faces you, the sudden return of the knowledge that the events that will decide your fate are almost upon you. After the original set pattern — the cha-cha — we still led by a whisker.

It was all down to the Free Dance.

And after hours of renewed tension we kept our lead, beating not only Moiseyeva and Minenkov — 'Min and Mo' as the press called them — but also the 1980 Olympic champions Linachuk and Karponosov. It hardly seemed possible, in a way not *right*. We could not get away from the feeling that we weren't *really* better than these giants, that we were still too junior to take over the mantle from them.

Our victory left us numbed, almost apprehensive that the judges would announce there had been a terrible mistake, and the rightful order would be restored with the Russians once more in their proper place untouchably beyond us.

Nor was there much time to absorb our new position before we had to move on up, or fall.

The Worlds, six weeks later, were in Hartford, Connecticut, providing in effect a very similar line-up of opponents. In came the Americans and the Canadians, but they did not represent a challenge to the European couples. Again we would face a formidable array of Russians. Linachuk and Karponosov had retired after their defeat in Innsbruck, being replaced by another Russian couple, so there were still three Russian pairs, including Moiseyeva-Minenkov – and the Russians had won every Worlds through the 1970s.

Clearly, we were in with a chance, and felt under pressure, the more so because, the week before we left, Chris developed a stress fracture in his lower leg. There was nothing to be done about it, except try unsuccessfully to quell the rising fear. Maybe on the day he wouldn't be fit. Maybe if and when we went on the ice the leg would be too painful to continue. We had no idea what was going to happen.

After the compulsories and the original set pattern, we were leading, as we should have been, but not by enough to be sure of winning. We skated first in the Free, making good marks, but again not good enough to be certain of victory.

It would have been agony to hang on, to watch everyone else skate, and a double agony – probably impossible – to keep a tally of the scores as the competition went along.

We couldn't stand the strain, and decided to get out for a while to make the time pass more quickly. So we went for a walk in the shopping mall that is part of the Civic Centre, wandering around separately, each locked away in a separate world, not even wanting to discuss the possibilities.

It was as if we were facing execution, with this weight hanging over us by a thread, and if we so much as squeaked the thread would break and crush us.

We returned just as the last of the marks were being announced, and passed Betty. We exchanged glances, but it was impossible to read her expression. We didn't dare ask what had happened in case the news was bad. We just walked straight on, to our dressingrooms.

Jayne was sitting on her own, staring blankly at the mirror, when Betty came in, and sat down beside her. There was a moment's silence.

'Well, that's that, then,' Betty said, with her usual light tone.

That's that, thought Jayne. Oh, well.

Jayne got up, without a word, and went out into the passage, and there was Chris.

'What happened?' he asked.

'Betty said, "That's that".'

'Does that mean we lost?'

Jayne shrugged.

At that moment Betty came out to join us.

'So,' said Chris, 'where did we come?'

'Well, first,' said Betty, looking at him in surprise. She had assumed we had known all along.

We should have been elated. But no. It was so long since we skated that the high of the performance had long since dissipated. Other than feeling a sense of relief, we remained strangely blank, all elation dampened. Neither of us can remember the ceremony.

Afterwards, there was excitement, except that everyone else was more excited than we were. We were no longer in possession of our bodies or our emotions. We were drained by everything — by the six weeks of pressure, by the agonising wait, and now by the assault of cameras and questions, until we felt like empty husks.

Only hours later, back in the isolation of our hotel rooms, did we find peace, each of us on our own.

Both of us were relieved — 'Well, we've done it!' — but there immediately followed feelings that fulfilled Janet's prediction three years before. The unsullied exhilaration of childhood had gone, leaving a vague and frightening foreboding, which hung on for weeks, right through the tour always organised by the International Skating Union after the Worlds.

For all that time, we felt the responsibility of our new-found success, and saw what lay ahead. The greatest challenge, the Olympics, was three years off. Three more Europeans, two more Worlds to go before then. All the trips, costume fittings, rehearsals, anxieties over music and choreography.

How on earth could we retain motivation, sustain confidence in our ability, and remain a success? Each year, we had to be bigger and better, or fall. Our age of innocence was over.

Luckily, that mood lifted when we got home. It would have been impossible to remain down in the face of the welcome we received — a civic reception, sackfuls of mail, people everywhere congratulating us.

In every other way, too, we could not have asked for a better foundation for facing the future. We had the facilities, the teaching, recognition as world champions, everything we needed to renew our motivation. We were determined to stay on top, and to do so by doing more for ourselves.

It was good to discover that winning, which had at first seemed nothing more than a responsibility, became a stimulus. We were different now, and felt different, because winning the Worlds gave us confidence not only in our technical ability, but also in our choice of music and our choreography.

We were desperate for something new — but what? For a month in Nottingham, we dedicated ourselves to the search for music.

Chris

First, we focused on the OSP. The rhythm that year was the Blues, defined by the ISU with a range of possible tempos. The actual choice of music was up to us. I wanted to go back to basics, get away from big band sounds, to the melancholy from which the blues originated.

'In that case,' Courtney said, 'you should also skate it to the slowest tempo possible.'

When I said I thought maybe a single instrument would work, Courtney put me on the right track. 'Have you ever listened to the harmonica in an ice-rink? It has a very haunting sound.' That reminded me that I'd recently heard Larry Adler's soulful, languid version of *Summertime*.

When we heard it again, it was exactly right, except that it was so languid it took too long. Not by much, though. Working with our friend Brian Saunders, we re-recorded it fractionally faster to bring the tempo up and the time down, and that was it.

Next, the Free Dance.

This was more of a problem. It occurred to me that, in the Free Dance, all this cutting and pasting of musical bits and pieces, all this mixing and mismatching of composers, was wrong. When composers write, they have something they want to say, over a period of time, and it's definitely not a one-minute skating sequence they're thinking about. I imagined the composers turning in their graves and groaning, 'How _could_ you put my music up against _that_?'

So the thought came to me that it would be better to have a single piece of music, one composer, a unity of sound and style.

Something came to mind. Burrowing around in the Radio Nottingham library a year or so earlier, Jayne had come across this record with a scarlet cover and bold black print – a recording of a Broadway musical called _Mack and Mabel_, telling the story of the stormy affair between the silent-movie mogul Mack Sennett and his leading lady Mabel Normand.

We put it on the turntable, and liked it. The thing about this musical, as with most, was that it had an overture. Overtures have a little bit of everything from the show: the tunes, the rhythms, the emotions, all hinting at the story to come, all quite briefly stated.

Why not use the overture to _Mack and Mabel_?

Jayne and Chris

So we went back to the library and pulled it out again. And liked it. And played it to Courtney and Bobby and Betty. They weren't sure. Maybe the last bit would be all right . . . But how about putting in a rumba, or something?

No. We had done something bitty at the Worlds — some jazz from *Fame*; something Egyptian from the musical *Caravan*; *Red Sails in the Sunset* as a rumba; and a swing finale. And it now seemed embarrassing.

The more we listened and talked, the more certain we became. There was variety enough right there, in Jerry Herman's music. But in addition, if we had a full four minutes to play with, we could develop a series of related sequences, tell a story.

We began to read about the life and times of Mack and Mabel themselves. The melodrama of silent movies, man chasing girl, girl tied to railway tracks, nick-of-time rescue, tinkling piano accompaniment. Sennett's brutality, his drug habits, his girls. Mabel Normand, the on-screen idol, the off-screen victim.

Somehow, there had to be a place for some of this in what we did, not literally, but flavours, put together so that the whole four minutes had unity and purpose, other than showing off pretty steps. Up until then, we, like other skaters, had created movements, pure and simple. Now that seemed random, purposeless. Music and movement had to become one, linked by a loose storyline.

And that had another implication. If there was a story,

82

we were characters, with roles to play. We would have to act more, with all that that implied in terms of motivation, gesture and expression. As fundamentally shy and not very social people, we had always had trouble projecting. Betty, Courtney and Bobby were always having a go at Jayne for looking too serious. Well, we had learned to smile. Now we had to act.

It was Courtney who gave us our next tip about how to win an audience. Eye-contact. Typically, ice-dancers didn't engage with their partners, because they were so busy skating. Courtney explained that we had to get over that, because as soon as you look deep into your partner's eyes, it changes the whole emotional mood. At once the audience sees in you a reality that is something above and beyond the technique of skating. It is itself a technique, but it is also real. For those few minutes you become the couple you are acting, you feel the emotion, and the audience feels it too.

Through it all, we were doing our jaunts down to London for costumes from Mr Bishop and Mrs Parrish. Every detail we had to arrange ourselves. 'Gold!' Courtney declared, when suggesting costumes for Mack and Mabel. Gold, and a gold feather skirt for Jayne. Easier said than done. How do you find gold material?

We had used a stretchy ski-trouser material from Germany called _helenka_, but it came only in black, white and blue. So we bought some in white, and took it to a dyer's in Nottingham. That was a problem, because they worked only with hundreds of metres at a time. But the owner had a daughter who skated, who agreed to do the job.

83

And gold feathers for the skirt? That was another minor epic. We had to get a white boa made of ostrich feathers, have it dyed, and take it down to Mrs Parrish, who plucked them and sewed them into a skirt in clumps of half a dozen.

Finally, armed with our music, leaving Mr Bishop and Mrs Parish to finish the costumes, off we went to Oberstdorf to prepare for the coming season.

There, living in the functional *Internat*, doing nothing but skate and choreograph, checking ourselves hour by hour in the mirror that stretched the length of the little rink, we lived an almost monastic existence. We each had a double room, with bunk beds, and a communal bathroom down the corridor. The rooms were under the eaves, with sloping roofs. We called it the 'cuckoo house,' because we felt like cuckoos popping in and out.

It was not uncomfortable, just basic. And there was hardly any entertainment in the town. We ate every evening together in the *Internat*'s diningroom. Betty came and went, fitting us into her other commitments. There were perhaps 20 or so other international skaters there, most of them German. We kept ourselves to ourselves.

Chris

So I was surprised when one night there was a knock on

the door of my apartment – I was in bed reading – and this young man in his early twenties came in. He stared at me in amazement, then muttered uncertainly, 'Oh, oh . . . um . . . I think . . . I think I'm sharing with you.' He put his bags down, gave me another look, and fled.

It turned out he was half of an up-and-coming French-Canadian couple, brother-and-sister ice-dancers called Paul and Isabelle Duchesnay. Paul recognised me, of course, and had run off to find his sister overawed to find himself rooming with the world champion – just the way we'd felt about the champions in our first competitions.

The next morning, when we awoke, he didn't stir. Later he told me, 'I just didn't dare move until you'd gone!'

Jayne and Chris

Naturally, we soon got to know each other, and the two of them took to joining us for meals. It would have been odd if they hadn't, because there were no other English-speakers. Paul was easygoing, bright and jokey, but he didn't seem at ease socially, partly because his first language was French, partly because he didn't get much of a look-in against Isabelle, a pretty, chatty 18-year-old.

Chris liked Isabelle's looks, and she admired him – 'the Blond Prince' as Jayne called him, not entirely in jest – but the constant chatter at mealtimes grated on Jayne, who took to making her excuses towards the end of their meals together. If Chris accused her of being rude, she would say, 'Well, she never stops talking! She just drives me nuts!'

To cut a long season short, *Mack and Mabel*, backed by Larry Adler's *Summertime*, both worked well for us. *Mack and Mabel* in particular was a milestone for us, because it remains the oldest of the routines we still perform, and people seem to look back on it as an old favourite.

Through the end of 1981 and the start of 1982, we won the St Ivel championship in Richmond, the British, the Europeans in Lyon, and the Worlds in Copenhagen. During this run, we began to gather a string of sixes.

In the eyes of the judges we couldn't do much better — *that* year. But we knew perfectly well that the following year those sixes would mean nothing and we would be starting all over again. We knew there were heights yet to be discovered and conquered — there had to be, otherwise we might just as well give up.

That season ended with the traditional ISU tour for leading competitors in the Worlds, which took us to the Soviet Union. *Mack and Mabel* was now an old routine. We wanted a new one for next year, and started to look around for something even more demanding.

Chris

During the ISU tour in Moscow, some of the skaters were offered free tickets, a few for the Bolshoi, others for the circus. Tickets to the Bolshoi were like gold-dust, so Jayne jumped at the chance. But when I heard the word 'circus' something clicked inside my head.

'I'll go to the circus,' I said.

Jayne looked at me in astonishment. 'You don't want to go to the Bolshoi? Funny boy.'

I didn't tell Jayne then, but the word 'circus' had sparked a flow of images and characters, and the thought: maybe there's something there we can adapt.

So I trooped off, to a totally new experience. At that time, they took circus seriously there. It was a profession, with schools and a career structure, and circus buildings in big towns. Moscow State Circus was performing in this old stone building, which seemed a shadowy mess permeated with the smell of sawdust and dung.

But when the lights came on, and the little band above the entrance started, it was magic, a captivating flow of talent: ringmaster, pretty girl on a trapeze, jugglers, clowns, a strong man, high-wire act, bears, tigers.

I thought, Yes, we could use this.

Jayne and Chris

Jayne agreed, if we could find music to match.

When we got back, we found that by chance the musical _Barnum_, the story of the American circus owner, was on at the Palladium, with Michael Crawford. So we went.

Michael spotted us through the curtains, and sent a message inviting us backstage.

Michael Crawford is a circus all on his own, with a huge smile, broad expressions, and exuberant gestures, all magnified right then by the high he was feeling after the show.

'Well, what are you going to do now?' he asked after a couple of minutes.

'Well, um, that's funny, because we're looking for ideas for next year, and we had this idea about the circus.'

He asked what we needed. We explained about the four minutes of music. We already knew that there was no easy solution, because *Barnum* had no overture, and everything else was vocal, which was no good for us because the ISU rules didn't allow songs.

'Let me see what I can do,' he said, with one of his enormous grins. 'Leave it to me, and I'll get back to you.'

Not long afterwards, he did call, inviting us down to London again. There, he introduced us to the musical director Mike Reed, and the two put a suggestion to us. The music of *Barnum* could be rearranged in an overture style, and recorded especially for us.

It was a wonderful thought. The first thing that struck us was the expense. But the two Michaels really wanted to help. Rearranging and recording would only be part of the problems we would face. There would be many more things to be negotiated. That led to the next suggestion, that we should meet Michael Crawford's agent, yet another Michael, Michael Linnitt.

So up we went to Michael Linnitt's office, a large open-plan place above the Globe Theatre – now the

Gielgud – in Shaftesbury Avenue, with books and papers scattered all over the place and a dog on the sofa. As amateurs, we had never had anything to do with theatres, actors or agents, so the experience was quite new. It was astonishing to be in a place like this, breathing a heady atmosphere of showbiz, being greeted by this imposing, charming, well-spoken man.

At that stage, though there was no talk of him acting as our agent, we were grateful for the chance to meet him, because he would clearly be involved in any financial dealings over the arrangement of the music.

Thereafter, Michael Crawford became our mentor, helping us to mime trapeze artistes, high-wire walkers and jugglers – it's a circular motion with the shoulders, not just the hands going up and down – teaching us the technique of back-flips, and acting out for us the sort of expressions we needed to project.

We'd never been close to an actor before, and this was a revelation – the intensity of the smile, the steadiness of the gaze, the certainty of belief in what it is you're trying to project. It was no good just smiling, you had to _become_ a smile.

'You have to go out and damn well _show_ them!' he'd say, bunching his fists, throwing his arms wide, zapping us with eyes and teeth.

The arrangement was done, and taped, at first in a piano version which we took with us to Oberstdorf, choreographing for six hours a day, working on steps and sequences in the mirrors, with Betty checking us, encouraging, replaying the music endlessly.

Eventually, to save the cost of a double fare, Jayne

89

made a trip back on her own to be in on the full recording. She returned clutching a master tape and cassette, which we played through in the car on the way back from Munich.

Inspired now by the big sound of the orchestral version of *Barnum*, we went back to work for many more weeks – besides *Barnum*, we had to work on the compulsories and choreograph the original set pattern, a rock-and-roll version by Andrew Lloyd Webber of a Paganini theme. Then, at last, we were ready for the moment we had been dreading, the first – albeit private – performance of *Barnum*.

We were back in England, at Peterborough, because Nottingham had been closed for renovations. Six months of work, condensed into four minutes. A bit like *This Is Your Life*. And what if no one liked it? Courtney was there, with Michael Crawford and Betty. The anticipation was as bad as any competition, because we so respected Michael Crawford's judgement and Courtney had this way of saying, offhandedly, 'No. That's not right,' and you'd feel like yelling, '*What*!? The whole thing? Or just bits? What bits? Why?'

After all the worry and all the work, they liked it, really liked it. We could see from their faces that they weren't just saying it, that the response was genuine.

That gave us all the confidence we needed.

We were ready for the next round of British, European and World championships.

First, the British. For all this time, we had kept our routines as secret as possible. We felt we had something that topped *Mack and Mabel*, and didn't want to spoil it with loose talk and sneak previews.

To sustain that, we broke with tradition. Normally, dancers took the opportunity to run through most of their routines in rehearsal, giving the judges a chance to start their assessments. We didn't. We thought it would dilute the impact. When the music came on, we just let it run, and did our practising at other times without music, keeping the real thing for the night.

It worked. The juggling, the tottering tight-wire walk, clowns making up, the mimed trapeze, the follow-the-band trombone-playing — we didn't have the confidence yet to throw ourselves into it heart and soul. But it was enough. The judges thought it was original and well done. We won.

One move, however, in which Jayne did a cartwheel on Chris's boot, was judged as illegal. So, to prepare for the Europeans, we went back to Oberstdorf to revise it.

Then disaster.

In the new move, Chris, travelling backwards, lifted Jayne from low down. Then she dived towards him, twisted to face upwards at the same time, to be caught again before she hit the ice. The first time we did it in a run-through, Chris overbalanced, and couldn't catch Jayne. She fell four or five feet, crashing on to the ice on her side, cracking one shoulder-blade and ripping all the shoulder muscles.

The pain was excruciating, and she could hardly sleep for days. Back on the ice a few days later, we tried the move again, and it reduced Jayne to tears.

More days of recovery, then another try. This time, she fell again.

Now we knew things were really bad. Because of Jayne's injury, we couldn't rehearse properly, and we had no time to devise new moves, even if Jayne could have skated them. The European championships in Dortmund were in less than two weeks. After days of physiotherapy and agonising about the decision we faced, Betty made us see that we had no choice — we had to pull out.

We learned later we were headline news. But we didn't know anything about that at the time, didn't even watch the Europeans on TV (it was won by old rivals, Natalya Bestemianova and Andrei Bukin). We went off to stay with Clarissa von Lerchenfeld, or moped in town, depressed, and — as usual when dogged by injury — angry with each other.

We had been firmly on a ladder leading upwards to the Olympics, now a year away. If we slipped off a rung, we could easily be replaced. The injury and the withdrawal were like a chink in our armour.

Maybe the judges would say, 'They're not coming because they're not ready,' for no Continental judge had seen either the rock 'n' roll or *Barnum*. No more chances for any feedback or changes. Having not defended our title, we would go into the Worlds at a disad-vantage.

In fact, when we arrived in Helsinki, six weeks after the accident, we were more than ready. Jayne's arm was still taped up, but we had made the Paganini-Lloyd-Webber rock 'n' roll as fast and intricate as we knew how. Jayne's shoulder held. We knew from the audience's reaction how

well we'd done. The judges agreed, awarding six sixes for
artistic impression.

Then, at last, we came to the Free Dance, _Barnum_.
We were not aware of anything but the approaching
moment, hardly a thought for friends and family – or
for our mothers, who had been flown out specially by the
Nottingham _Evening Post_ – certainly no conception of the
millions watching on TV at home. When the music started,
and we caught the first beat, the tension fell away, and we
danced for the sheer joy of it, ending with Jayne's final
back somersault.

When that happens, there is no memory of the performance. You are left only with the emotion: the exhilaration
at something done as perfectly as you know how, confirmed by the applause, and the audience standing, and
the flowers raining on to the ice. And then the ultimate stamp of approval on the choice of music, the
choreography, the months of work: for artistic impression, nine sixes, the first time anyone had received such
a score.

We were world champions – for the third time.

What next? Normally, there would have been the ISU
tour. But to ensure that Jayne completed her recovery
we said we couldn't do that. So we were free to
plan.

Next year would be Olympics year, and we had
music to find and choreography to devise. What would
we do? We had no idea, and were open to almost
anything. The only thing Chris mentioned was a vague
notion of exploring emotions – jealousy, hate, love-hate

— but neither of us could imagine what that might mean.

Still, we had enough people to ask. Michael Crawford, in particular, was keen to help.

One day he invited us to go on a little trip. Where to? we asked. 'I'm going to take you to see someone who you might like to talk to about music,' he said mysteriously, and ushered us into a car.

We sat, wondering, while the car pulled up outside a huge terraced house somewhere south of Hyde Park. Michael Crawford rang the bell. The door opened, to reveal a familiar face. It was Sarah Brightman. We were at Andrew Lloyd Webber's house.

Suddenly we found ourselves part of a little soirée of top showbiz people. Besides Andrew Lloyd Webber and Sarah Brightman, Trevor Nunn was there, and Fenola Hughes of *Flash-Dance* and *General Hospital* fame, all chatting about their next shows, deals, numbers, films, whatever. Michael Crawford was soon deep in conversation with Andrew Lloyd Webber, presumably discussing the possibility of his writing a Free Dance for us.

When Andrew took a moment to ask us about our plans, Chris mentioned that he was thinking about finding an original score and exploring emotions, 'like, all the different aspects of love.' We saw Andrew's face twitch, and wondered why. Later, we realised. It was pure coincidence, of course. Neither of us knew the book *Aspects of Love* existed, certainly not that he was thinking of adapting it.

It was nice of Michael to take us, but nothing came of

it. Andrew was obviously a very busy person, with quite enough on his plate without us.

So with another whole series of championships coming up, including the 1984 Olympics, we still had no idea what we were going to do.

5

Bolero

Jayne and Chris

I n fact, the idea we needed was part of us already, because we had often played Ravel's *Bolero* in warm-ups in Oberstdorf the previous summer. Seventeen minutes was just the right length for warming up on ice.

One day we were sitting with Bobby and Courtney at their house, wondering what we might do. We were going over the sort of things the Free Dance required — the fast start, the slow section, all that — when Jayne said something like, 'Why don't we *start* with something slow for a change?'

'Like *Bolero*,' said Chris.

Tentative nods from the other two. It wasn't an idea that exactly set them on fire immediately, because *Bolero* hasn't the changes of pace that tradition demanded. Also, it was 17 minutes long, and we needed no more than four minutes — well, between three minutes 50 seconds and four minutes 10 seconds maximum.

But as we talked, our enthusiasm grew, and spread to the other two. The drama of the piece appealed, and since we had danced to something specially recorded for us, we thought we might be able to solve the length problem.

Later, we mentioned the idea to Michael Crawford, who found it too serious for his taste, and to Michael Linnitt, who had remained willing to help and was very positive. He represented a composer, Richard Hartley, who would produce the recording, and who knew an arranger. His name was Bob Stewart.

We drove to see Bob in the southern outskirts of London, where he lived with his mother. We were welcomed by this rotund, balding, owlish character in glasses, who turned out to be a brilliant musician — organ scholar to Worcester College Oxford at 16, a First in music at 19, pianist, conductor, teacher and now arranger.

Pouring a glass of red wine — he seemed never to be without an open bottle — he asked us what we wanted exactly.

We explained: *Bolero* reduced to about four minutes, but with no loss of impact, starting and ending as in the original, with the quiet, insistent snare drum leading up to a massive swirling *fortissimo*, with all the instruments.

A classically-trained musician might have been horrified at the suggestion, but Bob was game. Although — as he explained — *Bolero*'s apparent simplicity disguises a surprising complexity of structure, it took him less than a month of intense work to distil it to not much more than four minutes.

The news that he had finished his arrangement meant that we could head down to Oberstdorf, as long as we had with us a version of the arrangement. Bob said he could play it for us, if we could bring a recorder. Fine. We prepared to leave.

That summer, 1983, we were lent two Volvos by a local company, Speeds. It was a good arrangement: we needed better transport, they were happy to help. Our amateur status meant we couldn't accept cash, but the NSA confirmed we could accept the loan of the cars.

The day we left, bright sparks that we were, we started from home about five in the morning, packed our lives into the car ready for six months in Germany, and headed for Bob's house on the other side of London.

Fortifying himself with red wine and cigarettes, he sat down to play it through for us on his rickety old upright with our little cassette recorder placed on top. He played it through with terrific verve, calling out the instruments as they entered – 'Strings! Woodwind! Brass! Full orchestra!'

We could hear that musically it worked beautifully, even if our version did it less than justice, with the sound of Bob whipping over the pages punctuating the tones of his tinny piano.

But there was a problem. Bob simply could not squeeze the revised version into the required maximum of four minutes 10 seconds. The best he could do – the most compression the piece would take – was four minutes 28. We had an 18–second overrun. We could have forced more cuts, perhaps sliced off a few seconds by increasing the tempo, but that would have been to corrupt the music even more, beyond what we all thought was acceptable.

Besides, we were expected at Bobby and Courtney's, so we took our cassette, said goodbye, and drove back into town. There we mentioned the problem of the timing.

'Wait a minute,' Chris said at some point. 'What's the rule about timing exactly?'

We checked: the timing started when the skaters started skating. It was obvious when you thought about it. On the ice, you couldn't start simultaneously with the music, because there was no cue, unless the skater arranged to insert a beep on the tape. Most skaters started a beat or two after the music started.

'So,' Chris went on. 'If we don't skate, the timing doesn't start.'

To put it another way, we could move as long as we didn't skate.

If we wanted to save the music, obey the rules, and not skate, there was only one way to start: on our knees.

It made sense. We had known ever since seeing that little kiss between Christina and Andrew years ago that the performance started emotionally before it started technically. If this idea worked with the music, if it set the right mood of tension and expectancy, it could not help but be part of the performance, even if technically it wasn't.

We still needed to have the original sound of *Bolero*, fully orchestrated. As yet, we didn't know how we would get what we wanted. But that was for later. Right now, we had more things to talk about – like Courtney's ideas for the costumes — before leaving London for the car ferry at Dover.

We arrived in Calais at midnight, and headed into Germany, with Chris driving.

Chris

Jayne was fast asleep. I had been on the go for 24 hours, but was almost unaware of the fact. We were on the almost-empty Autobahn approaching Stuttgart in the early hours when my eyes closed, just for a few blissful seconds.

I woke with a jump, saw the central reservation looming, and hauled on the wheel. The car swerved, caught the metal barrier with the rear, swung back into the road. Jayne jerked awake with a scream as we slid sideways along the road. I turned into the skid, managed to control it, and pulled up safely on the hard shoulder, weak with shock.

We sat there ashen-faced for several minutes, blank and speechless as if we'd been electrocuted. Finally, shaken by our brush with death, and appalled at the damage to the borrowed car, I handed over to Jayne, who drove on all the way to Oberstdorf.

Jayne and Chris

Of course, *Bolero* took time to evolve. Betty, who was technically minded, was not at all sure we were on the right track. She wanted us to win, and with *Bolero* we might not, because it was riskier than anything we had done before. Not exactly meat and two veg for the judges.

But at that point in our development, it seemed to be the best way to go. After *Mack and Mabel* and *Barnum*, we had to do something different, had to take a risk. We might fail, but at least we would have failed on our terms. If we didn't do it, if we reverted to something traditional, we risked failure anyway, and then we'd be left with nothing.

Soon after we started work, we faced the problem of how to get a fully orchestrated version of the new arrangement. We could not contemplate a full 60–piece orchestra, of course, but again we were helped by Michael Linnitt, who already had his eye on producing a record of our shortened *Bolero*.

Another friend of Richard Hartley's, Alan Hawkshaw, who had once worked with Cliff Richard and the Shadows, had a computerised synthesiser, a Fairlight, which could reproduce the sound of any instrument, and combine those sounds.

Breaking off our rehearsals in Oberstdorf, we came back home to help supervise the arrangement. Joined by us and Bob Stewart, Alan, starting with a baseline of the snare-drum, replayed *Bolero* dozens of times, adding a new instrument each time, building up the sound of a full orchestra, layer by layer. It was wonderful, all we needed to continue our work in Oberstdorf.

As we worked out the choreography through the summer of 1983, we built on Chris's idea for the opening. If we were on our knees, this would be a complete contrast to anything we, or anyone, had done before. Instead of a bright, fast, dramatic opening, we would be static and intimate, a couple locked into each other rather than engaging the audience.

From that, and from the ominous feel of the music, we evolved a romantic scenario, a storyline to help us create the feelings we needed in the dance. A man and a woman are in love, but like Romeo and Juliet, they will never be allowed to be united. At first, they don't know this. The lovers are simply there, in love, courting, with no sense of coming tragedy.

Then they realise that their love is doomed, that the only way they will be together is to be united in death, a dramatic, fiery end in the crater of a volcano, an eruption of self-destructive passion.

The woman fights her way up the lower slopes, searching for the path — 'This way,' she says, casting about. 'No, this way.' She steps up, the man helps her by lifting her feet, she becomes tired, collapses.

The boy helps her again — 'Come on! You can make it!' — until at last they reach the summit, and cast themselves into the imaginary volcano, as the music reaches its final _fortissimo_.

If you spell it out like this, the story and the sexual symbolism — the climaxing music, the long-suppressed

103

passion of the lovers, the eruption — sounds completely over the top. But right from the beginning, that took second place to the dance itself. You can't understand the story from the dance. But it was in our minds, and we wanted it to be in our bodies, our faces, our eyes, as we danced. The narrative drive gave us a sense of purpose, and we hoped that the audience would feel it as well.

We had no idea if it would work, no way of guessing how it would be received. Other than the encouragement of friends, we had no real feedback. Even Betty, when she saw us skate it through in Oberstdorf, was not exactly over the moon.

'This could either be fantastic or mediocre,' she said. 'It all depends on the emotion.' Until we performed it for real, we simply wouldn't know which.

Even after Sarajevo, it took years for us to realise what we had invented. There was a time, in our early days as professionals, when we thought, 'Done that. Now we can let it go.' But we found we couldn't. *Bolero* was what people wanted, and they would feel cheated if they didn't get it. So we've gone on doing it. And although the story isn't in our minds when we dance now, the lovers' roles are still there.

We discovered that even constant repetition need not dull the passion, because it is part of the music and the movements, and because the audience is waiting to be moved.

Some performances are better than others, of course. You have off days and unresponsive audiences, and try to force the emotion. But sometimes still, even after about 1,500 performances, you can come away drained, having given everything you can.

*　　*　　*

Bolero, though, was only half the problem. At the same time, we had the compulsories to work on, and the original set pattern, a paso doble, for which we chose a Rimski Korsakov piece, _Capriccio Espagnol_, rearranged again by Bob.

Even the compulsories, in which you do three patterns of the same dance, needed some hint at originality. We decided that if we could not alter the steps we had to perform on the ice, we could at least alter our holds and upper-body positions.

No one had done that before. Originality always entails risk, but Betty, Bobby and Courtney agreed it was fine, that it was actually good for ice-dancing to loosen up the constraints. After all, it was an ordeal for the judges and the audience to sit through dozens of versions of exactly the same music and exactly the same movements.

The paso was a greater challenge. In origin, it represents a bullfighter in action. In ballroom dancing, we had seen the woman mimicking the bull, with the whole dance focusing on the man, the matador, all macho stances, with arched back and head held high.

But when we looked into the roots of the dance, we learned that the woman is the _cape_. This offered the chance to do something original, with Jayne seeming totally passive, blank-faced, the very antithesis of the traditional ice-dancing partner, yet completely a part of the dance.

Jayne would be wearing Courtney's dramatic cape-like dress design, which was so different that we had a practice dress made so we could check the shapes she formed with her arms as we devised the steps.

At one point in the fight, and the dance, the matador turns his back on the bull and drags the cape along behind him in a gesture of deliberate provocation. At another, Chris adapted a 'death-spiral', the move in which the woman is swung head down close to the ice, to make it look as though Jayne were a piece of fabric swept near the ground in a gesture of flamboyant macho arrogance.

If we could capture all that, we would not only have to skate well – to seem totally inanimate while performing intricate steps is very demanding – but we would be doing something different in ice-choreography.

During the build-up to the 1984 Olympics, the tension was something we had never experienced before. It was not just that we were approaching the pinnacle of our amateur career – we were approaching the *end* of our amateur career. Unless something happened to prevent it, we would then be going on to the Worlds.

After that, win or lose, we decided we could not go on being amateurs. We had no money in the bank, no sponsorship, no means of carrying on. With hindsight, this now seems surprising, because becoming a top amateur is a passport to good money. Back then, it meant poverty. As skaters, we couldn't progress any more within our amateur confines.

Of course, we hoped it wouldn't be an end, but a new beginning. The only thing we knew was that we wanted to become professional. What did that mean? We had no idea. There were several possibilities with established ice-show companies like Ice Capades in the USA and Holiday on Ice in Europe.

We made no approaches. Our only assumption was that in some undefined way it might involve working through Michael Linnitt as our agent, because he had been so helpful, and remained so, acting as a buffer for publicity.

Not that he could do much for us while we were in Oberstdorf. There, tabloid journalists took to turning up, eager for stories. There was nothing to stop them wandering into the rink and shouting at us during practices.

'Can we talk to you?'

'Well, no, we're really busy.'

So they would hang around at the rinkside, until we *had* to talk to them just to get some peace. But there wasn't real peace. Practically the only story they wanted, it seemed, was to 'tell the truth' about our 'romance.' With any pictures we agreed to, the photographer would say, 'Put your arm around her . . . Cuddle up closer!' They were forever trying to discover which rooms we had, how close they were, whether we were secretly sharing, and on and on. It was no good saying there was no romance, so we avoided publicity when we could and put up with it when we couldn't. But there was no denying that it was intrusive, and induced extra tension we could have done without.

Once, a photographer snapped us when we fell — it's not uncommon when you're trying new and demanding steps — and that was news: *They've fallen! Are they past it?* And of course, you begin to think, Oh gosh! We must be careful not to fall. And that inhibits you, just when you need to feel total freedom to try some new and risky experiment.

Coping with the immediate pressures was enough, but we knew it would get worse. The looming Olympics filled every waking hour, and many of our dreams.

But first came the British championships in November 1983, the first time we danced *Bolero* in public. Right up until the last minute we still had no idea how it would be received. We rehearsed it time and again, of course, and the press saw it, but their comments were mixed.

'It all depends on the emotion,' Betty had said, and we lacked the one essential ingredient to make the dance live: the audience.

Well, the audience seemed to take to it. Of course, we were performing, as usual for the British, at home in Nottingham, before the most generous and sympathetic of audiences. So there was no feeling that we had achieved something brilliantly original for an international audience.

Since no serious rivals had emerged, we won the British championships again, and won well, with six sixes for artistic impression – more than enough to give us confidence in the course we had set ourselves.

We would need every scrap of confidence, because *Bolero* was now out there, on view internationally, with comments and opinions rippling out from Nottingham across the world, forming the context for our next test, the Europeans in Budapest.

It was there that we received our first proper taste of the politics of judging. A judge present as an observer, but who was not on the panel at the Europeans started to criticise the way we were changing holds during the

compulsories. We can only guess at why this was done —
perhaps to make an impact at our expense and create a
reputation. Whatever the reason, this person's comments
planted seeds of criticism among the judges.

Luckily, this information got back to Courtney in
England. He flew out — quite a gesture, when you
remember there was no spare money to make gestures
like that — and made his own highly respected opinion
felt among the judges.

We weren't involved in this. Chris knew what was
going on, but not Jayne, because everyone was anxious
she would become tense and fail to perform well. Then
we both _had_ to know, because the word came down to
us: it's safer not to rock the boat. So right at the last
minute we abandoned the holds we had been working on
for the last few weeks, and did the conventional thing.

Our main rivals were the previous year's winners,
Natalya Bestemianova and Andrei Bukin, and because of
their status there was no certainty about our winning.
Probably, there would be some bias by the Russian judge
in their favour. Certainly it seemed so, when she gave us
a 5.6 in the technical mark of the paso doble OSP.

In the end, although we were ahead, it all hinged on
the Free Dance, which finished so late that apparently
at least one British paper had two front pages prepared,
one with a black band around in case we lost, the other
proclaiming our success.

Right up until the last minute, we were tinkering with
details. In one run-through, Chris found a ring he was
wearing caught in the hook on Jayne's boot. We had
to stop to untangle ourselves, and decided there and then:

no more jewellery on the ice. Then Betty said she had heard rumours that some judges were wondering about the legality of one particular lift, in which Jayne stepped briefly on to Chris's boot. Only in our last rehearsal did we decide to change the move.

Despite all this *Bolero* went well. Eight of the nine judges gave us sixes for artistic impression, putting us first. The British papers went to bed happy, and so did we.

Naturally, those whose crown we had reclaimed, Natalya Bestemianova and Andrei Bukin, were less happy. There was a bit of fuss, we heard later, at the press conference, when Bestemianova-Bukin's trainer, Tatiana Tarasova, a formidable lady, picked up on the rumours and claimed that one of the lifts in *Bolero* was illegal.

By all the press accounts, she was pretty angry. We couldn't think why. We had deliberately avoided the risk of an illegal lift, and the judges had nothing to complain of. Betty hardly deigned to acknowledge Tatiana's claim.

We were in the foyer of the hotel next morning when a journalist asked her about Tatiana's objection. 'I'm delighted the Russians have found a rule book,' she said, a cutting reference to the way Tatiana's couples had supposedly stretched the rules in the past. Anyway, we'd won fair and square.

It was not only a wonderful reward for the work done and choices made, but also of huge significance for the future, preparing the way for the Olympics. For the first time, we knew we had a chance of achieving our ultimate ambition: a gold medal. After a final month of preparation in Oberstdorf, we were all set for Sarajevo.

To get there, we joined the German team, who were training in Oberstdorf, travelling by rail. It was a rough journey, 20 hours. Chris had the worst of it, because he was in with a bunch of boisterous athletes and was so jumpy about getting some rest that he persuaded the German team doctor to give him some sleeping pills, which kept him feeling drowsy for the next two days.

We hardly saw anything of Sarajevo itself — a grey city, but approaching something like wealth and grace with the influx of tourists and athletes arriving for the games.

Until after the games, we never went to the surrounding peaks, with the alpine skiing, bobsleigh run, ski-jump and cross-country course. Our life revolved around the new Zetra Stadium, and the artificial, sheltered atmosphere of the Olympic Village, a world on its own, with housing, gyms, restaurants and entertainments.

We arrived on February 6, a Monday. We had a few days of practice, except that it wasn't really practice, because the judges were watching, and were already forming their opinions, weighing you up against the others. We treated every practice as a performance that demanded the right look, the right postures, the smiles, the confidence.

The compulsories and the OSP, taking us into the second week, went well enough, and we picked up several sexes, including our first for a compulsory. That was a reassurance.

But the thing that really inspired us was the last practice. We'd not had much of a chance to get used to the main arena, so we decided to take advantage of a practice scheduled for 6:00 a.m. on Tuesday, the day of the final, St Valentine's Day. No dancers but us used to do full run-throughs on the same day as a performance, so the chances were no other couples were going to be on the ice, especially at that hour. There were just we two, Betty, the sound-operator and the 20 or 30 cleaners preparing the seats.

We ran through *Bolero* as if it were for real, putting as much into it as we could – the expressions, the soulful, passionate looks – and as the music ended, we were astonished to hear applause. All the cleaners had put down their brushes and dusters, and had sat down to watch. They didn't have to do that, probably weren't allowed to, officially, so it was quite a tribute. We bowed, and took their applause as a good omen.

That evening, waiting in stillness out of sight, as couple followed couple on to the ice, we heard the roars of applause, but did not take in the marks. They would have been too much of a distraction.

Jayne sank inside herself, switching off awareness of what was happening around her. Chris put his fingers in his ears and hummed to cut out the sound of the loudspeaker announcements and focus totally on the performance to come.

When we skated out, we took heart from the gasps, felt the expectant hush, knew there were friends, relatives, VIPs out there – Princess Anne for one, as President of the British Olympic Association – but neither of us can remember the performance itself. We were but pure concentration, our eyes locked on each other, with awareness of the surroundings and even our own bodies wiped away from the moment the music started. Only mistakes would have stood out in our memories.

That evening, there weren't any. But when the music stopped, and we lay on the ice entranced by joy and relief, everything changed, as we emerged from the trance of the performance. The people stood, the applause went on and on, and Union Jacks waved, the ice became a garden of bouquets.

Drifting round the rink, picking up bouquet after bouquet, Jayne suddenly saw a familiar face, then others, a whole block of people – friends from the Norwich Union who had joined a charter flight. It seemed that all of them were crowding towards her with flowers, and all she could do was take them by the armful and smile and say, 'Thank you, thank you' – not that anyone would have heard above the applause.

Then came the technical marks. Three sixes, six 5.9s. We skated towards the exit, but we hadn't even got off the ice, Jayne still carrying her armfuls of flowers, when the crowd screamed. We looked round. The marks for artistic impression were up:

'Torvill J, Dean C.'
6.0 6.0 6.0 6.0 6.0 6.0 6.0 6.0 6.0

Nine sixes!

So we knew, as we hugged each other, then fell into Betty's arms, that we'd won; that the last four years, our decision to give up everything for our skating, our commitment to our partnership – it had all been worth it.

The memory of the applause, the judges' marks, the delight on the faces of those who were closest to us, the sight of the Union Jack and the sound of the national anthem as we stood on the podium, the flood of telegrams — these are still part of us, reinforced every time people come up to us to tell us exactly where they were and what they were doing when they watched us that day on TV.

And it still happens.

So in a sense the high would remain with us. It didn't seem quite that way at the time, because from that peak of ecstasy there was a quick fall — not in the sense of achievement and the gratitude to all those who had helped us, but in the mood of the evening.

There were TV people eager for comments. First off the mark was an American called Dick Button, a former world figure-skating champion who had become a TV presenter and would later figure prominently in our lives. There was also the doping test, then the press conference.

And then, strangely, we somehow found time had gone by. It was late, and we were almost alone in the echoing corridors of an empty stadium. Laden with flowers and bags, we left our dressingrooms and joined Eileen Anderson, the British team leader, and Betty for the ride back for a party in the Village with our team-mates and Princess Anne.

We were horribly late. Princess Anne was still there, though, gamely sipping champagne from a plastic cup with a small group of British athletes. It was very casual. A brief restrained toast proposed by an Olympic official, a quick word of congratulation from the princess, and she was away.

114

For us, winning the Olympic gold was a strange experience. Like an explosion, its effects spread outwards away from us, leaving us oddly silent at the centre.

Our parents left the following day. Jayne's quiet, restrained father surprised her by bursting into tears. She had seen him close to tears before, but she had never seen him break down. Her mother took it in her stride.

'Take no notice of him,' she said, as she hugged her daughter goodbye. 'He's just sad to leave.' Betty, Bobby and Courtney had to get home, too. We gave Betty our medals for safekeeping.

Then, after the final exhibition, we set off back to Germany, by rail. No grand receptions, no victory parades, no media whirlwind. We wanted to avoid anything like that. It would undermine our motivation and drive towards our next and final amateur competition — the World championships four weeks later.

Sarajevo is a shattered city now, and the Zetra Stadium in ruins, a grim and tragic contrast to the city as we knew it in 1984. Often, charities and articles in the press have suggested we might skate there again one day. It's a wonderful idea. If there was any chance that we could contribute to the resurrection of the stadium, the city, the country, we would love to help.

Arriving back in Oberstdorf, in the company of other athletes, most of them speaking little English, we had virtually no idea of the wider impact of our win, of the press coverage, of the millions who had watched on TV. Our parents told us of the postman arriving with a whole sackful of mail every day for a week, with letters from all over the world, hundreds addressed simply to 'Nottingham,' and a few just marked 'England.'

But it seemed far away. We were back on the ice, looking towards the Worlds, in Ottawa. Definitely our last amateur competition, as we had always planned.

Now, however, there was the possibility of a life afterwards. Dick Button, the TV presenter who had collared us as we left the ice in Sarajevo, wore another hat as impresario of the World Professional Championships, and invited us to compete.

And among the telegrams at Sarajevo had been a one-liner from an Australian impresario whose name meant nothing to us asking baldly, 'Would you like to come to Australia to perform?' Because we were still guarding our amateur status, we passed the request straight on to Michael Linnitt, saying we couldn't do anything right then, but asking him if there was anything in it.

There was — little did we know how much. The impresario was Michael Edgley, who specialised in bringing Russian ballets and circuses to Australia. Now he was planning an ice show. Before the Olympics, assuming that the Russians would dominate as usual, he had already signed up the Russian Olympic skaters. Suddenly, there we were all over Australian TV. 'Jesus Christ!' he said (or so we were told). 'We better get these bloody Poms down here as well!'

Michael Linnitt had contacted Michael Edgley, and came over to Ottawa, eager to tell us we had work if we wanted it. At the time we were still amateur, and still scared of losing our amateur status if we did anything out of line with ISU rules. So we didn't even want to be seen *talking* to Michael Linnitt. He understood, and kept a discreet distance from us, except for a few snatched conversations in his hotel room.

'What would you like to do?' Michael asked us at one point.

'Well, eventually we'd like to create our own show,' we said. It was just a vague thought at that time, something we wanted to do without knowing how or where or anything like that. But it was probably enough to confirm Michael Linnitt's interest. He would certainly handle the Edgley negotiations, if we wanted.

After the championships, we just said yes, in principle, with some relief – we were down to our last £1,000, with nothing at all coming in – and left it at that.

The championship was being held in the afternoon, probably because both BBC and ITV were transmitting live to Britain at peak evening hours.

Just before the competition, about 4:00 p.m. local time, a fire caused the electricity to fail. The lights went, the ice started to melt. It would take hours to repair. They sent us away and told us to report back at 8:00.

Looking back, we can imagine the mood at the rink, and back home. There were millions of people out there expecting us to win, *willing* us to win, because *Bolero* had been so popular, and this was our final amateur performance, a sort of goodbye.

We know now how moved those people were by the occasion, because we read in the papers afterwards, and in hundreds of letters, about the effect we'd had. But at the time, we were not part of that at all. We just sat in our hotel rooms, and

117

did nothing for three hours but sleep, eat and watch the telly.

In Britain, midnight came and went. BBC's and ITV's scheduled programmes ended, but they remained on air, even though there was nothing much to see except the ice slowly refreezing and the Zamboni resurfacing it.

By the time the competition started, half the country was muttering, 'I've stayed up this long. I'm not going to bed until I've seen them!' There are still people who say, as if we had shared an adventure together, 'I stayed up until three in the morning to watch you!'

We won, a fitting conclusion to four years of work, the realisation of all our dreams. Yet permeating the excitement and the elation was a tinge of sadness at the end of the adventure, and a tremor of uncertainty in the face of an unknown future.

Moreover, after four years of ever-increasing tension, we were utterly exhausted. Whatever happened, we would have to have a break. But how, and where, on the amount of money we had?

Michael Linnitt saved our sanity with a beautiful offer: he booked us a ten-day holiday in Barbados. We need have no qualms – it wasn't a gift. It was an advance. He would pay himself back out of the Edgley contract, once it was negotiated.

Then after our break, home at last, to a welcome that we found perhaps the most astonishing thing about this astonishing year. There were press at the airport, still asking about when we were going to get married, but that was something we were getting used to.

It was the reaction in Nottingham that knocked us sideways.

The Council had decided they wanted to give us an official reception in the city's Council House. We were to travel in a motorcade from our homes. We were shy of the attention, but there was no getting out of it. This was apparently the way they wanted it to be, the way they said the people wanted it to be – a parade as if we were a victorious football team. The Nottingham *Evening Post* even printed a map of the route the cavalcade would take.

To our ever-growing amazement, the authorities seemed to have read the mood of the city correctly. The streets were lined for three miles, right the way into the city, with us in an open car like a popemobile. In the central square, we were taken out on to the Council House balcony like royalty, and the whole square was packed. Thousands upon thousands of people. Never had we dreamed of anything like this.

It was utterly overwhelming, humbling, frightening even, because we had no idea we had done something that would release such a tidal wave of affection. All we'd done was work at what we enjoyed doing, which was, after all, only a sport. After the Olympic gold, and winning the Worlds, we had already experienced so much that it seemed impossible to take it all in. Now this. It was very surprising, and very moving.

And still ahead of us, again, was a void of uncertainty.

6

Dream couple

Jayne and Chris

Perhaps the most puzzling thing of all about our life as we began to achieve success was the way the press pursued us, always asking the same question: Were we or weren't we? Did we or didn't we? Would we or wouldn't we?

LOVE ON ICE! shrieked the *News of the World*. TRUE LOVE! claimed *The Sun* after Sarajevo. 'Olympic golden couple Jayne Torvill and Christopher Dean are said by friends to be in love.'

It wasn't as if the attention was unpleasant or incomprehensible. It was intrusive, of course, but we could have tolerated that. The worst thing was the constant attempt to impose on us a false identity. We'd had it in Oberstdorf, and had it again before and after the Worlds.

Just two examples of many will serve to make the point.

When we were at the Worlds in Ottawa, we went back and forth between the hotel and the stadium in a special skaters' bus. In the lobby, waiting for us, was a paparazzi photographer, who had acquired some sort of accreditation and followed us into the bus. It was very weird, because he never smiled, never spoke to us, never asked our permission. He sat on the seat in front of us, held his camera within a foot of our faces, and just took pictures, one after another. We had no idea how to react, were too wary of sparking controversy to tell him to stop, yet couldn't simply ignore him. We just sat there, looking as blank as possible.

On our holiday in Barbados, when we thought we would be away from everything, we reckoned without the tabloids. At least three of them sent reporters down to cover our stay. One local photographer proved particularly dogged, so much so that it developed into a game between us.

Our hotel had its own grounds, with little villas scattered across it. We had one each. He would position himself in a bush, and as we walked unsuspectingly past – *tshk!* – this black Bajun photographer would leap out in front of us and snap us looking startled. Within a day, we could spot him at a distance, and took evasive action. It must have been frustrating for him. The only picture he got published was of our beach shoes, together outside a door, as a symbol of 'unbridled lust.'

Although we couldn't understand the interest in a romance that was non-existent, we recognised that the journalists and photographers had a job to do, and that romance sold newspapers.

Besides, we could see that it served a purpose. To be seen as a dream couple wasn't a bad thing, however unreal. And

Chris, aged five, at the school opposite the Co-Op in which his mother worked.

On our way to another competition in 1979.

Between practice sessions in Oberstdorf, 1980.

On holiday in Skegness, 1975, during our first year together.

Preparing for our first Olympics, 1980.

Dancing Mack and Mabel *at an exhibition performance in 1982.* (Edeltraud Kohler)

The tent made for our Nottingham show during our world tour of 1985 - over 100 metres long and 70 metres wide, it was the world's largest tent and could seat almost 7,000 people.

During our world tour of 1986 - dancing The Planets *in the USA.*
(Judy Eng).

Dancing Oscar Tango *at the World Professional Championships,*
1990, where we won our third professional championship title.
(Judy Eng).

Chris with Colin and Betty Dean outside Buckingham Palace after being presented with an MBE in 1981.

White water rafting during a short break in New Zealand, January 1989 - Chris is sitting front left and Debbie Turner, frozen with fear, is front right.

Debbie, Jayne, and
Rob Hannah turned
out in style to support
Chris at Melbourne's
Calder Raceway, 1989.

All rigged up and
blissfully unaware of
the crash to come.

Recording our ill-fated
album for one of the
most unlucky men
alive. Sydney 1989.

Best frocks on for opening night of the London leg of our tour, May 1990.

A relaxed moment on tour for Chris, Jayne and Phil - Brighton, June 1990.

Chris's birthday, Sydney 1991.

Phil and Jayne, with Betty and George Torvill, at their wedding reception in February 1991 - the marriage actually took place on 21 September in Sacramento, but it was followed by a blessing and reception in Nottingham five months later.

Phil and George Torvill relax at the reception.

Chris and Jill's wedding, 15 October 1994.

The Face The Music company

May 1994, pictured from left to right are :
(men) *Igor Okunev, Tom Dickson, Joe Mero, Alexander Esman, Scott Williams, Martin Smith, Christopher Dean, Russ Witherby, Mark Janoschak &* *Kostantin Golomazov;* (women, middle row) *Marina Kulbitskaya, Jayne Torvill, Charlene Wong, Catarina Lindgren, Michelle McDonald, Jill Trenary;* (women, front row) *Susie Wynne, Tammy Crowson, Jacqueline Petr.*

since the press seldom gave real offence — seldom critical, never abusive — we just tried to ignore the myth, without trying to destroy it outright. Probably it would only have seemed as if we had something to hide.

So we eventually developed a stock response.

'When are you getting married?' we would be asked for the *n*th time in a month.

'Not yet,' we'd say, or, 'Not this week.' Which left open the possibility that we would get married sometime, but it avoided the question of whom we would get married to. We didn't want to second-guess the future.

Maybe after all we would get married to each other, though by the time we became popular we couldn't see it. More likely to someone else. Perhaps to no one. We really didn't know, and for years nothing changed. Until quite recently, we thought we'd just let people think what they liked, but now that we are both married happily, we can see it is worth trying to look more deeply at our relationship, not just to finish off speculation, but mainly because it has always been, and still is, the foundation of our professional life.

It was odd to find ourselves increasingly cast in the role of the fairytale couple. We can see that there is something in our background that contributes to that — ordinary people who become famous. It's the ordinariness that contributes to the image. Working class. Nothing Hollywoodish about our looks or the way we behave. The boy and girl next door.

It was not our background or personalities, however, that marked us out, but our skating successes. There is about skating something magical, which is what attracted us both to it in the first place, a magic conferred by the ease and speed of movement. Skaters seem to inhabit a world apart, like the theatre or film, yet different from both because skaters can also sweep in close to people watching, make them see the sweat and feel the wind as they swirl past, only to fly away again.

It's a magic that retains a hold over all of us who do it. When we no longer feel the magic and want to share it with others, then it will be time to stop.

But still that doesn't seem to explain completely why we found ourselves as a fairytale couple. We know it's not *wholly* to do with our success. That means it must originate with something in the minds of the people who see us.

The word 'fairytale' is probably the clue. In fairy-stories, boy meets girl and eventually the two of them live happily ever after. The ideal of togetherness, of a partnership involving romance, love, marriage, and a happy ending, is part of us from childhood. That's the ideal that people like to see in young lovers and married couples, and that was the ideal that people, and the press, wanted to see in us.

The problem, as everyone knows, is that the ideal has little to do with the way most people actually live, and it certainly had very little to do with the way *we* lived. The romantic myth never had much to do with the realities of our relationship.

When we got together we were so young and naïve that we hardly dared talk to each other. Then, as the partnership grew, we came to rely on each other in almost every way, because ice-dancing was the most important thing to us.

124

In our spare time, we were always together, because all our spare time was taken up with skating, or something to do with skating, whether it was eating, travelling, choosing music, looking at movies, or buying clothes. We had few friends outside skating, and never went on holiday. We never had the time. This may seem strange to others, but to us, even as teenagers, it was normality. We simply never questioned it.

It's true we were thrown together at a time when teenagers who were more outgoing might have started an affair. But we were both very naïve, focused totally on our skating, and shy, not to say prudish. True, we were attracted to each other. But there was never anything physical between us that could have spoiled our friendship and our skating relationship.

A psychologist might say all that teenage sexual energy went into skating. Or perhaps our lack of experience left us innocent, in a way that teenagers today are not. After all we didn't go to clubs, never tried drugs, hardly ever drank alcohol, didn't go to many parties.

Whatever the explanation, by the time we were ready for a deeper relationship, any question of romance had passed, leaving only a deep friendship and mutual respect.

It was never formalised, never a matter of saying, 'OK, we're not going to be a romantically attached; now we can start looking around for other people,' because we stayed together as partners, and there was really no room for anybody else. For many years, it remained a very blinkered existence.

That partnership, which has defined so much of our lives, is hard to analyse. When we started work on this book, we explored ways to describe it, without much success. There is certainly an element of 'best friends', in the way that good friends provide each other with both security and freedom. 'Brother and sister' comes close, because it is a platonic relationship, but not quite brother-and-sister because there was never a taboo between us, and that is important in the way that we dance together.

There is a sense in which we were monk and nun, both dedicated to a way of life to the exclusion of things other people considered normal. Even if we didn't exactly forswear sex, we didn't think about it much, certainly never talked about it.

At the heart of the relationship is trust. It grew from the earliest days of working together, from our experience of our own commitment and reliability, tried and tested time and time again, from the certainty that when one of us arrived to pick the other up, the other would be ready to come, would walk out of the door; that we would go to the rink, and skate together. It was never a question of having to wake the other up or say, 'Do you feel like skating today?' For the present and the immediate future, the commitment was, and is, total.

Only once has that trust been briefly threatened — as we explain in a later chapter — when Jayne got married. That left Chris feeling pretty shaky, wondering if there would ever be the same commitment to skating again. As it turned out, the threat was never there, and the relationship was untouched.

The reason it remained so strong was because it had clear limits.

First, sex has no part in the relationship. We feel that if

126

you are in a sexual or romantic relationship with someone, there is always the possibility – the fear – that the feelings will die, or be changed by an outside relationship.

Fear, jealousy, betrayal, secrecy – all these things form a sort of shadow side to normal relationships, rising up if things go wrong. In the skating world, you see that all the time – couples who skate together because they fall in love and get married split if the relationship falls apart.

With us, there was no possibility of betrayal, at least not in that way. There is no romance to be threatened, no sexual bond that might be broken. That's why we can trust each other so fully.

Second, unlike a marriage, or a new romance, we never made a life-time commitment to each other. It was always provisional. Right at the beginning it was 'We'll give it another week,' then we could look a year ahead, then we embarked on the three-year marathon to the 1984 Olympics, and since then it's been year by year again.

You could hardly run a romantic attachment like that, because it almost always depends on a long-term promise that might prove impossible to keep.

So our relationship is not the dreamy, romantic thing that people see in us when we're dancing. Many times, magazines and papers assume that the way we look on the ice is the way we are off the ice.

'How can two people who look like that, who are that intimate/sexy/erotic on ice, _not_ be lovers off the ice?' The answer is that it is precisely because we are _not_ lovers off the ice that we can focus on each other with such commitment _on_ it. We have learned what works in ice-dancing, and we have had to become actors.

127

When people say things like, 'Surely they couldn't look like that and not . . . ?' we take it as one of the greatest compliments. It shows we are doing a good job.

Actors do this all the time, on stage and on screen. And of course an on-screen love affair often reflects or becomes an off-screen affair. Not so with us. The difference lies in continuity. Actors seldom depend on a single working relationship. Their work, unlike ours, is constantly changing, and the people with it, so compared with *our* working life, there is constant novelty, the regular stimulus of new acquaintance, always a new buzz.

Trust is the foundation. But in practice, the relationship has its complexities and conflicts.

Chris is a strict timekeeper, whatever the circumstances. In the police force you were taught that if work started at 8:00, you were there at 7:30, to be ready for the briefing with uniform and pocket-book. Jayne is the relaxed one. She'll never be early if she can help it.

'You're always late!' Chris will complain, glancing at his watch before some photo-session or interview.

'But never on the ice!' she replies, which is true.

When we were awarded the MBE in 1981, and had to get to Buckingham Palace, Chris white-lied to get Jayne out of the house much earlier than necessary, and we ended up parked in the Mall for an hour, with Jayne in her dark suit and Chris in his hired morning coat.

Jayne is annoyed by Chris's niggling. We'll be coming off the ice after a good performance, usually with Chris leading, and Jayne will hear him say over his shoulder: 'I don't know about this step, or such-and-such a lift . . .'

Niggle, niggle. There's always something. She dismisses the remark with 'Mm, yeah, sure.' Or if he insists: 'Can't stop. Got to change.' Or she pretends she never heard.

As the voice behind her mutters on, her own comments play silently in her head: 'What on earth is he talking about? The people backstage will think we did a terrible performance. Of course nothing's perfect, but couldn't he wait until tomorrow? I enjoyed that, and there he goes spoiling it. Now I feel the whole thing was a waste of time. It's not even worth replying!'

And that annoys Chris, because she _knows_ it annoys him, but she also knows that if he thinks something, he has to say it right then, otherwise it gets forgotten. Saying it is like writing it down. That way, you don't forget. He knows she knows, so why can't she just be a little more helpful?

But these are routine annoyances. They have no effect on the underlying trust, or on the qualities that make the relationship work day by day. Instinctively, automatically, we support each other. If anyone else dares to accuse Chris of being undiplomatic, Jayne cuts in with, 'What do you mean he shouldn't have said it? He was cross! Why shouldn't he say it?'

We complement each other. If Chris is the creative force, never satisfied with what we've achieved, always pushing for more, needing more, _kneading_ more, Jayne is the clay, moulding herself to his ideas, understanding the aims, responding and interpreting.

After all the years together, we have built up a shorthand way of working. Chris will say something like, 'Lay into me, back inside-outside edge.' It might mean nothing to another skater, but she'll know, and do it. He's the artist, sketching a vision in words; she sees it and makes it instant reality.

This involves an additional role, which has emerged since we turned professional and started our skating company. Devising a new show is always pressured, and no one writes down any of the moves. It's up to the skaters themselves to remember, but Jayne provides a vital back-up. While he follows a train of thought, suggesting and coaching, she watches and remembers.

That's the role she's happy with. She never wanted to be the leader, she'd rather stay in the background and deal with whatever comes at her. Any expressions of impatience from Chris — and there are a few sometimes after hours of work on steps that won't come right — bounce right off her. Close friends call her 'the Rock.'

Emotionally, that's how it works. But physically, when we are together on ice, the roles are often reversed. If you added up how many turns Jayne has, you would see that she is often the more active one, Chris the rock.

But it's not that she merely does as she's told or ignores him when it suits her. Often, she rules from behind. She responds to the music as much as he does, and if she disagrees with something, if she feels that it really is not going to work, she can see why, and thinks, 'If I do that, I won't be able to get out of it elegantly.' Then she tells him, and shows him.

'See, it won't work.'

'Oh, right.'

Sometimes, the exchange happens so quickly that anyone else would miss the glance between us. Often, in anything

130

concerned with skating, we know each other's reactions
at once. When we talk, it's usually about skating, and we
constantly interrupt each other to finish off each other's
thoughts. It made transcribing the interviews for this
book a nightmare. Outsiders sometimes think, What is
this? Telepathy?

No, just experience. Outside skating, when we're apart,
there's no telepathic bond. We've each been in trouble –
sickness, injury – and the other has no inkling. Never has
either of us had the pang that twins are supposed to feel:
'Oh, my God! He/she needs me!'

Actually, it's mainly Chris who's in trouble, because he
likes to live dangerously. We'll tell the stories in detail
later, but two examples come to mind. Once, he crashed his
car on his way to the rink. She had no idea that he had
almost killed himself until his phone call. And once, when
we were in Australia, he almost drowned, and was waving
desperately for help. Literally, not waving but drowning.
She just waved back, and walked on down the beach. Fat
lot of use our 'telepathic relationship' was to us then!

Now that we have our company of skaters, the stability of
our relationship has become even more important, because
other people depend on it as well. The show is everything.
Once committed, it _has_ to go on, with us as a rock-solid
centre. True, it's our name on the posters, but we are also
members of a team, a _corps de ballet_.

Let alone the strain of putting on the show, every
tour produces its crop of human problems – injuries,
the strain of travel, inadequacy of hotels, poor food,
relationships forming and reforming – and we need to

be there as parent figures, acting as role-models in a huge skating family.

As a group, we are constantly threatened by the very qualities that brought us together, our collective creative drive, our desire to be rewarded and acknowledged for our dancing and choreography. We stay together only by sticking to a self-disciplined regime. The rules are quite simple and very demanding. Commitment, hard work, attention to detail. Those are the elements that focus us.

Although we had no conscious awareness of what we were doing, we started to live by those rules over 20 years ago, and they still serve us well.

7

Skating the world

Jayne and Chris

After the 1984 Olympics, all the attention, the press coverage and the reception were a surprising and glorious reward for winning the gold medal, but they didn't pay any bills. Our sponsorship money was drawing to an end, and we were scraping the barrel. Very soon there would not be enough even to pay the rent on Chris's little flat.

First of all we had to get back on the ice to prepare for whatever the future might hold. We already had one firm date – a gala in Richmond organised by the National Skating Association. But that was to be a farewell to our amateur life, and would be done for charity.

The two professional offers we had – Dick Button's World Professional Championships in America at the end of the year and the Michael Edgley show in Australia –

both had to be confirmed before we could count on them. That meant contracts, of which we had no experience at all. So our first real task as professionals was to establish a sound working relationship with Michael Linnitt. He was willing to take us on, reassuring us that it need not bind us for ever: 'if we're not all happy,' he used to say, 'there's no point working together.' And we could certainly do with his help, because other people were already making money from our creative talents.

About this time, Thames TV decided to capitalise on all the film footage they had of our amateur performances and interviews, negotiating the rights with the National Skating Association, who made the contracts on behalf of all British amateur skaters and thus retained control. Thames issued a two-hour video, *Path to Perfection*, an amalgamation of almost everything we had done since we started. No one told us, no one asked our advice or approval. Suddenly, there it was, in the shops. It has now sold tens of thousands of copies, making huge amounts for the video company and the NSA, and was reissued in 1994.

In addition, we had collaborated on a book by a *Times* sports journalist, John Hennessy, which spent several weeks in the best-seller list as a result of our success in Sarajevo. When it was published, we undertook two horrible weeks of signing sessions and radio interviews – once, 13 in one day – all over the country to promote it. Again, it was all perfectly legal, we received a small fee, and we had been happy to work with John, but—

But in both cases, a good deal of money was made, but very little of it came to us. Before, while we were amateurs, our hands had been tied, and besides, we had a grant as a financial safety net. Now — as Michael Linnitt pointed out forcefully — things should be different.

By the look of things, Michael Edgley would be our salvation. Michael Linnitt gave us good advice: 'Your profiles are so high at the moment, the pressure is so intense, maybe it would be good to get away, earn a little money, buy yourselves some time and space. Then you'll be able to decide on what you want to do more comfortably.'

So how to proceed?

We would soon know, Michael Linnitt said, because one of Michael Edgley's directors was flying over to see us for a meeting.

We stared at him open-mouthed. This man was going to fly all the way from Australia? Just to see us? Good grief, his air fare alone would be enough to keep us for months.

Suddenly, a mountain of responsibility loomed before us. It was because of us he was doing this. What if he didn't like us? (It didn't occur to us that maybe _we_ might have some right to assess _him_.) And if he did like us, we would be a part of something that would really matter, in a way that amateur shows did not, because it would have a value, and people would be let down if we didn't perform.

Anyway, soon afterwards, we were rehearsing for the Richmond gala at the Nottingham ice-rink, when a figure appeared at the rinkside dressed in a blazer and flannels and carrying a briefcase. His name was Andrew Guild. He watched us skate for half an hour or so, and then we went back to Chris's two-room flat, which was notable for being cold in the winter and breeding ants in the summer. Luckily, this was springtime.

Over coffee, Andrew explained what was on offer. Two weeks in Sydney, and 12 shows. The Russian Olympic team had already been contracted. We would just fit in between their numbers.

'We'd like you to do two numbers in the first half, two in the second, then close the show,' he said.

It sounded fine. He gave us the contract he'd worked out with Michael Linnitt. The amount of money was absolutely staggering to us. Chris thought, 'I could pay off Mum and Dad's mortgage with this! That's it! I could retire on this!'

It never occurred to him that it might have to last until our next professional engagement, Dick Button's World Professional Championships right at the end of the year.

Less than a month later, the Farewell Gala put a full stop to our amateur life. The very next morning, we started a new career as professionals, with all the trimmings. Michael Linnitt saw to that. Bobby and Courtney were there at the hotel to say goodbye when a huge old chauffeur-driven Bentley pulled up. We put our luggage in the boot — just a suitcase and skating bag each — and were waved off like royalty.

Then we found we were flying first class, in a Japanese 747 with a sleeping compartment upstairs in the bubble, all complete with kimono. If the Michael Edgley corporation were out to impress us, they succeeded beyond anything they could have dreamed.

Our first arrival in Australia is still a glorious and startling memory: glorious because of the blue skies, crisp clean air, and graceful descent right over Sydney Harbour, the bridge and the Opera House; startling because we were met by three company people whose main concern was to get us out of there in a hurry. Why?

'There's a lot of press out there!'

No chance. These were heady days down under, with the stock market soaring, Alan Bond at his height, everyone eager to spend and be seen spending. The hotel, the Sebel Town House in the Cross, popular with media folk, had sent a Rolls for us, and there were three TV crews elbowing each other for a glimpse of us, hemming us in, one in front, one behind, one alongside.

Nottingham was no preparation for this. We felt like mice assaulted by hungry cats.

All this came entirely out of the blue. We had not seen any of our Australian posters. We had no idea if the public knew of us. It was only later that day we learned that the _Bolero_ routine had swept Australia, because the TV channels had shown virtually nothing of the Olympic ice-dancing except us. The Sydney Entertainment Centre, which holds 10,000 people, had queues around the block as soon as the tickets went on sale. All 12 nights had been sold out in advance before we even arrived – 120,000 seats.

Every hour brought new surprises. One of the people who met us at the airport was a chaperone, Diana Kelly. One person whose sole job was to look after us! We couldn't believe it.

Then she gave us money.

'What's this for?'

'For whatever you need. Expenses. Whatever.'

A hundred Australian dollars a day, as an advance on our salaries. We couldn't imagine what we had to spend it on. Diana made some suggestions. We would probably need a few clothes, and some luggage to put them in. And how about some sunglasses? Everyone had sunglasses except us.

Jayne in particular learned the new rules quickly, and started to spend all she was given, mostly on clothes.

'Jayne, why are buying all that stuff?' Chris asked after three or four days. 'You don't need half of it.'

'Don't be silly, I have to spend it. If I don't I'll have to give it back, won't I?'

'Oh, Jayne, you don't *have* to spend it!'

The shows at the Entertainment Centre went well. After being used to an amateur life, in which we built to a single all-out performance, we were shocked by the intensity of the schedule – every night for two weeks.

But it was, after all, only two weeks. There was hardly time to accommodate ourselves to the novelty of it when the run in Sydney approached its end. The Russians prepared to leave, and once again, a void loomed. We assumed we'd be home in Nottingham again a few days later.

Then Andrew Guild asked us into the office and made a suggestion. 'Look, this has been great. Could you stay on a bit, and do more shows?'

What, here?

'No, we thought Melbourne.'

Well, yes, OK, we didn't have any plans. But with the Russians gone, what about other skaters?

'We thought, maybe we could get some more in.'

Great. Who did he have in mind?

'Well, we thought *you* might have some ideas.'

So we sat down and made a list of people we knew who

might be interested. Instantly, Andrew got his staff phoning all over the world, making offers and cabling tickets.

We watched, entranced. We had done exhibitions in England for the NSA, and knew the budgets. There was hardly money to give skaters train tickets and petrol money, let alone *fly* them. And here was Andrew slamming down phones and saying, 'Well, they're on. Who's next?'

One surprising thing about Sydney was that it had a superb contemporary ballet, the Sydney Dance Company. We had seen them on TV in England, and now took the opportunity to see them live. The name of the ballet was *Seven Deadly Sins*, and it was like nothing we had seen before – contemporary, but with a warmth and humour we had never associated with ballet. The choreography also involved a lot of lifts, which we at once saw might be adapted to ice.

That visit changed our lives, because after the performance the artistic director, Graeme Murphy, came up to us. We would not have sought him out, because our impression of the ballet world was that the people would be aloof. But Graeme was a mirror image of his choreography: funny, accessible, vibrant.

'Maybe sometime in the future,' he said towards the end of the conversation, 'we could have a chance to work together?'

As we left, it struck us that this could be a way forward, a way to continue in the direction we had established with *Bolero*, trying to make our ice-dancing less a sport and more an art-form.

It was hard to win acceptance as real dancers in

skating-as-a-sport. Others had pioneered this route before us – John Curry and Robin Cousins in Britain, Toller Cranston in Canada – but no *couple* had done it, certainly not in extended, ballet-length form.

A week later Graeme invited us round to his apartment, with a whole bunch of other dancers, all young, all excited by the creative buzz of working with Graeme. That fed into the idea we'd had, to do our own show.

Over the next few weeks, the idea hardened into an ambition – to have our own show, our own choreography, our own dancers, the way Graeme did. Would he be interested in helping? He said yes.

That was a long-term aim. But there was something more immediate that might allow us to work with Graeme. Our next firm date was Dick Button's World Professional Championships in America, in six months' time. To prepare for that we would be spending time in Oberstdorf, working out two new numbers which would not be bound by any of the rules that constrained us as amateurs.

And Graeme was going to be in Europe during that time. Shortly before leaving Australia, Chris called Graeme with a suggestion: any chance he could come to Germany to work with us?

'Wait a minute, Chris, let me see . . . Yes, I can be free for a week.' And he named some dates.

A week! It wasn't enough. We couldn't possibly choreograph anything in a week. As amateurs we used to take two or three months to devise a new number. And Graeme was very busy, and all over the place with his arrangements. We wondered if he would show up at all. Probably not. Probably he'd never even find Oberstdorf.

*   *   *

In Melbourne, another significant meeting.

Mrs Parrish and Mr Bishop had never planned for their creations to be subjected to the sort of use we were giving them. Forget repairs — we needed whole new costumes.

Andrew took us round to someone who specialised in theatrical costumes, Bob Murphy, 'Mr Bob' as his embroidered overall proclaimed. In his youth he had been a dancer, but now seemed — on first acquaintance — to be a sardonic professorial type with glasses on the end of his nose. He made an old-world show of calling us 'sir' and 'Miss Jayne.' In fact, as we later discovered, he was as intense, not to say manic, as anyone we'd met in this business.

He was used to zesty, fast-talking Australians, and it amused him, when we first met, to hear us asking tentatively for a little fix here maybe, and please, do you think, if it's not too much trouble, could we have this sleeve not so full?

We know now what Bob and Andrew were thinking and saying behind our backs. 'They're not very showbiz, are they? We'll all have to loosen them up a bit.' If we'd known, we would have died of embarrassment.

Well, Bob repaired the costumes, with some deadpan references to Mrs Parrish as 'Auntie Florrie up the road.' Soon, he went on to make new costumes. Out went the original *Bolero* outfits, because, as he said, silk was monstrous to maintain and we were making holes in it sliding around on the ice. He made the new ones out of polyester, giving Chris's trousers zips, so that he could change them quickly without having to take his boots off.

The old paso doble costumes also had to be remade, for

similar reasons. Jayne had to spin around on her stomach on the ice, and Mrs Parrish's white front developed a fearful brown stain. Besides, it got wet, and shrank, so every night the costume had to be stretched and dried. With the new material, Bob attached the decorations with 150 press studs, so they could be taken off quickly and the dress tossed in a washing machine.

Halfway through the Melbourne run there came another suggestion.

'How about playing Brisbane?'

'Oh, OK.' Why not? We weren't doing anything else for the next couple of months.

In Brisbane, they took over the open-air QE2 stadium, and sold 14,000 tickets for the opening night. People were flying in from all over, even from New Zealand, to watch.

By now it was midwinter – June 1984 – but still hot, as always in Queensland, with a warm wind that felt like a fan-heater. No one in Australia had much experience of temporary ice-floors. It was the same one we had had in Sydney and Melbourne, but this was the first time they had tried it outside.

They could make ice only in the cool of the day, with the generator turned to its highest setting, with some of the water freezing almost as it was sprayed on to the floor and some lying around in puddles. There just wasn't time to do the job properly.

When we went on for the warm-up, the surface was like the moon, all lumps and dips, with the pipes exposed in a couple of places. We and the rest of the company skated around, avoiding potholes, wobbling like tightrope walkers.

Backstage, as the audience filed in — among them Queensland's controversial state governor, Joh Bjelke-Petersen — we all discussed the decision that faced us. In the end, we said, 'No, it's too risky.' It would be like racing a sports car over a ploughed field. If we fell — if anyone fell — there could be serious injury, which could mean the end of a career.

Bjelke-Petersen got on the address system, and made the announcement: 'Ladies and gentlemen, it seems the weather won't allow this show to go on. Would you all come back again in two days' time?' Which was pretty tough on those who had flown in from New Zealand.

Fixing the ice involved some farcical scenes, as they tried experimenting with polystyrene squares to insulate the ice. The polystyrene kept taking off in the breeze and the arena degenerated into chaos, with everyone rushing around trying to catch these vast, flapping, somersaulting sheets.

At last, we got underway, and we proved a success. So they suggested another extension — Townsville — where we again skated outside, this time in the middle of a dog-track. It was a site with a number of unique features. Surrounded by sand, we were so far from the sound system and the audience that we must have seemed way off beat. The toilets were away in one corner of the stadium, in full view of the audience. And there was no proper entrance.

In our costumes and skates, we trooped on and off over rubber matting, grass and sand like a sort of circus parade. But what the heck, they seemed to like us.

By then we had been seen on Australian television visiting

game parks, and the audience threw not simply flowers, but toy animals on to the ice as if they were giving us a part of Australia — koalas, kangaroos, wombats, teddy bears. It was the start of a tradition of throwing soft toys that has followed us around all over the world. Jayne took a whole trunkful back to England with her. Betty and George Torvill have a room devoted to them.

By the time we finished the tour, we had played six towns, none of it planned much in advance, extending the stay from 12 days to three months.

Sometime before we left, Michael Edgley asked us what we wanted to do next. By now, of course, our reply was beginning to seem like a stock answer: we wanted our own show. That was all it took to set the ball rolling. While we finished our last performances and packed for home, the Edgley people started to talk to Michael Linnitt in London.

Jayne's dad picked us up at Heathrow when we arrived in early August.

Back home, Jayne went back to her parents', but Chris discovered a big change — Tee and his father, who had retired six months earlier after 40 years down the local mine, had bought a house by the coast, at Sutton-on-Sea, and moved.

When we arrived, they came back, staying with Chris's stepsister, Jean, to help Chris resettle in his little flat, the cold one with the ants. Chris felt a twinge of worry when his dad started to haul a heavy case inside. He had always seemed such a tower of strength, and now, with the months of absence, he seemed to be trying to do too much.

'I'll do it, Dad.'

'No, I've got it, Buster!'

Then, perhaps even that same day, we called Michael Linnitt in London, and learned of rapid progress on the show. 'We've set up an office,' he told us, 'and we're starting to interview people about lighting and design. We'll make some appointments, and you can come and meet them.'

A few days later, there was a phone call from Jean. Chris's dad, Colin, had had a heart attack and was in hospital. Jean was reassuring: he was OK, and wanted to see Chris. When Chris got there, he was relieved to find his dad was recovering. A bit groggy, but already joking with the nurses. It didn't seem to have been too serious. There was no need to change plans.

'I wish you didn't have to go to London, Buster,' Colin said when he heard. 'You're always rushing around.'

'We have to go, Dad. There are people to see. Arrangements have been made.' He would be out of hospital in a few days.

Next day, we were in London, staying at the Selfridge Hotel, talking to lighting designers.

Chris

In the early hours, my phone rang. It was Jean, in tears.

'It's Dad,' she said. Dad had had a second heart attack.

There had been no warning. He had died before the ambulance came.

I stood there for a moment, speechless with shock and grief, struggling to comprehend how someone so much part of life could be so suddenly gone. 'I . . . I'll call Jayne,' I said, through tears. 'We'll come straight up.'

Jayne was with me seconds after I called.

For a minute we stood weeping uncontrollably, holding each other, unable to say a word.

'Oh, Chris,' she sobbed at last. 'What are we going to do?'

I drew a breath. 'Pack. We've got to go home.'

She made a little sound of despair. 'I've locked myself out.'

In my mind, I was already at home, with Mum and the family. Her words brought me back to the present, to the practical barriers we had to cross. Packing, checking out, the journey. All trivial, but each one a further delay, keeping me from where I wanted to be, from what was really important.

'I'll call room service. They'll let you in.'

Half an hour later, we were in the car for the two-hour drive north. I was driving – Jayne's new Astra, a nice car. Dad had never had the nice car he had wanted. I heard again his gloomy words – 'She's not going to make it, Buster!' – whenever he had a journey to start. What a time to go and die, just when I had some money in the bank, and he could have had the Mercedes he'd always dreamed of.

There was one last goodbye, at the morgue. I stepped into the room, almost overwhelmed by the power of my grief.

For almost as long as I could remember, Dad had been my only real family, and nothing prepared me for the shock of his absence, or the shock of seeing him like this.

I noticed that his hair was still as full and fine as ever, and that surprised me. I touched his cheek, and was surprised again, by the coldness. It all seemed very strange, as if I was in a void, alone in grief.

The feeling of being a stranger in a strange land stayed with me for weeks. Often at the rink, a glance of sympathy would remind me of Dad's absence and of my grief, and the feelings would come suddenly from nowhere to assault me. Once, in Nottingham, when Sandra was home, we went out to supper, the three of us, and without even speaking of Dad we all ended up in tears.

After the funeral, there was Tee to care for. She had abandoned one life for Colin 20 years before, and now she had to rebuild, in devastating circumstances. She didn't want to stay in Sutton on her own, without friends or family, with only her sandy-coloured mongrel, Buster — Dad's nickname for me — as company. Together, she and I decided to find another house for her and Buster back in Nottingham.

As it happened, Jayne's parents were also on the point of retiring. For the last 10 years, they had been running a newsagent's, and they were ready to give it up. So both families started to house-hunt together, and quite quickly, purely by coincidence, we found two houses in the same rural area on the outskirts of Nottingham.

Jayne and Chris

Meanwhile, the professional bandwagon rolled onwards. The plans for our own show were hardening all the time. We were to go back to Australia in January to prepare for an opening in May. Meanwhile, we had the World Professional Championships to do in December.

That autumn, back in Oberstdorf, we started to work on our two pieces. One was *Song of India*, the other one would either be the panpipes music or a piano piece we'd heard in Australia.

We had been taken to a winery in Petaluma Valley outside Adelaide, and heard the sound of wonderful piano-playing resonating through the wooden floor above. Who was playing? we asked. 'Oh, there's no one playing,' said our hostess. 'That's a CD.'

It was the first time we had heard one, and we were hooked, not only on the sound, but on the piece, played by the American pianist, George Winston.

To our delight, Graeme Murphy found his way to Oberstdorf, and subjected us to an instant transformation in choreography, working first with *Song of India*.

For one thing, he didn't have a skater's inhibitions about using the ice purely for skating. He saw it as a surface, to be used in any way, and suggested we lie, roll, crawl, kneel – anything that could intensify the dance.

It was the same with lifts. In amateur skating, there are all sorts of rules about the type of lift, the number of lifts, the length of time a lift lasts, how high you can lift. He

148

didn't even know the rules, and blasted away our surviving inhibitions — and not just in skating terms.

The moves he suggested recalled erotic Indian sculptures. We felt we were breaking new ground, because we had never heard of anyone doing anything quite so explicit on ice before. Lifting, rolling, intertwining — his demands reduced us to a mass of aches and pains and stiffness, until our bodies adapted.

Secondly, the speed of work was a revelation. After five days, we had sketched out the whole thing, a mood piece, with lots of stylised Indian movements suggested by Graeme and adapted to the ice by us.

Then he said, 'OK. Let's see it.'

What?

'From the beginning.'

How much?

'The whole thing.'

We stared. We had been doing the piece for only five days, could hardly remember what we'd done. We were used to building up a few steps at a time, like writing letter by letter, finding the flow only after weeks of work.

'But . . . we'll make mistakes.'

'Doesn't matter. I just want to get an overall picture.'

So we did it, and made a lot of mistakes, and he was happy. And so were we, because suddenly we got the picture, too. A four-and-a-half minute piece, choreographed and skated through in five days. Impossible one week, done the next.

Those five days were an inspiration — to all three of us, we think. We kept on talking about what we would like to do together. A ballet exploring the contrasting themes of ice and fire . . . an ice-dance version of Holst's suite, *The Planets* . . . Bouncing ideas about, we all became so keen it seemed only right when Graeme suggested we come out to Australia again to work on either the panpipes or the piano piece.

Not so successful, this visit. Graeme didn't respond to the Andean panpipes. But he liked the piano piece, so that was what we went with. Chris had a rough scenario, with us starting at opposite ends of the rink as strangers — something no one else had done before — seeing each other, passing, falling in love at first glance.

It was the story of a whole relationship, which you could read as five days, five weeks or five years. We called it *Encounter*. It was different in other ways as well — it was long, over six minutes, a challenge if we were to hold the audience.

This time, Graeme could not be so involved. He was directing a ballet at the Opera House, and had little time for us. There was more work to do on *Song of India*, which we had to do on our own, because we had been asked to take part in the next Royal Variety Show in the London Palladium, and they wanted to film *Song of India* for the show.

Then, when we did start work on *Encounter* together, we found we were doing as much work on the choreography as Graeme.

In the end, we were left with half a number, which we would have to complete in Oberstdorf.

There was one more engagement to fulfil, the Royal Variety

Show in London. It was an exciting prospect, especially as it didn't sound all that demanding.

Obviously we weren't going to skate on stage, so they had planned a sort of spoof appearance. David Jacobs was introducing us, with good reason, because he had close connections with musicals, especially _Mack and Mabel_, for which he was always getting requests on his radio show.

He would explain that we were in Australia, but had agreed to skate for the assembled audience. Then they would show the film of _Song of India_, as if we were doing it live in Australia. And then, surprise, surprise, we would appear, in evening dress. Nothing to it, just fun.

It turned out to be much more than that. We had last been behind the scenes of the Palladium with Michael Crawford during _Barnum_. That had been our first exposure to a star. Now the place was jam-packed with stars, some we knew, some totally unfamiliar, because we were always outside the mainstream of showbiz.

So we were quite shocked to see a middle-aged man dressed in a beer-stained white dinner jacket, behaving in a terrible way. He was leering, and drooling, his tie was askew, and he kept on spilling his drink.

'Quite honestly,' said Jayne, primly, 'I think that man's drunk.'

She was obviously right. We kept clear, and watched, intrigued by how polite everyone was being, wondering when the management would cotton on and throw him out.

We were even more surprised to learn that this was the Australian cultural attaché, Sir Les Patterson, and that he was actually one of the guest performers.

'Surely', Jayne whispered, 'they're not going to let him on stage in that condition?'

We couldn't understand it. There was royalty out there, Prince Charles and the Queen Mother. It was only during the performance itself that we realised this was Barry Humphries in character as Dame Edna's alter ego.

When it was our turn, it wasn't quite as simple as just walking on. After the mock-live extract from *Song of India*, David Jacobs introduced us, and when the laughter and applause had died away, out of the blue Howard Keele, the baritone hero of *Kiss me Kate* and all those other Hollywood musicals, came on. He handed Jayne a rose, then as she stood there astonished to be on the receiving end of such old-world gallantry from this storybook image of charm and good looks, he sang to her the slow number from *Mack and Mabel*, 'I Won't Send Roses.'

In December, when we were ready with our two new pieces, we flew to Washington for Dick Button's World Professional Championships. Once again, the gamble to be original paid off. We were well received, and won the championship. The win gave us great satisfaction, confirming that the choices we had made with our music and choreography would work, and establishing us for the first time on the professional scene in the United States.

We flew back to Australia on New Year's Day, 1985, to prepare for the first show of our own. We were thrilled by what lay ahead – we'd already made a list of skaters whose talent we had admired in competitions, discussed ideas, had Graeme's agreement in principle that he would help. In four months, we would have a show if all went well.

We didn't know much about the practical details, and we left the financial arrangements — air-fares, hotels, rehearsal space, food, costumes, all the endless costs involved in putting on a show — to Michael Linnitt and the Edgley Corporation. We had money in the bank, enough to see us through the rehearsal period, and a one-third share of the profits from the show itself. We flew in happy, excited by the prospect, confident that we were taking another step upwards in our chosen profession.

The first hint that life was not going to be quite so easy came as soon as we arrived. Before, we'd been invited down for a short time as guest stars. Now we were part of the production, and we were there for a long, expensive stay.

Costs would all be set against the production, months ahead, and had to be tightly controlled. So the hotel was several notches down, a Motor Inn in Sydney's King's Cross area, a red-light district something like Soho.

We gulped, but that was where everyone else would be staying, and the one thing we knew was that we wanted to build a group. Even if it was our name on the posters, we didn't want ourselves or anyone else to act all starry and separate. So we settled in.

In came the other skaters, bringing another dose of reality. We went out to the airport in a seven-seater minibus to pick up the first contingent, three Canadians: Gary Beacom and a dance couple called Jonathan Thomas and Kelly Johnson.

It struck us on the way back that these three, and all the others, had committed part of their lives because of us,

153

yet we had no more than a few ideas. No music for them yet, and no steps. This was scary, because we'd only ever choreographed short pieces for ourselves. Two and a half *hours* for 20 skaters was something else, even with Graeme as joint choreographer.

We couldn't wait to see where it would all come together – a disused warehouse, which had apparently been adapted for us, because there was no permanent rink in Sydney. Next day, even as other skaters were arriving, the minibus took us off to see our rehearsal space.

Sydney's offices and blocks gave way to a dingy suburb. Not a shop in sight. We drew up in front of a huge building. 'Disused' would be a kind description. 'Derelict' is better: broken windows, rubble, dirt, tin roof.

Inside, we had the basics – just. There was running water in two small siderooms we would use to change in, with some old car seats to sit on. There was a kitchen area, even if there was no place locally to buy food. And there, wall to wall on the ground floor surrounded by snaking pipes, and with an ice-plant roaring, was our old ice-floor.

It sounds rough now, but that's because we're looking back after 10 years of professional life. At the time, nothing was going to dent our excitement. We knew that Edgley's were making this up as they went along, as we were. We were all in it together, lucky to be working. No one complained. All of us were saying, 'Great! Let's go!'

Easier said than done. There were only four solo spots and a good deal of company work which demanded mixing and matching. But unlike a ballet company, we were not yet a corps de ballet, with a group identity. These were individuals, all with their own histories, ambitions and

154

ideas, who had fought their way to success alone, or as couples. It had never occurred to us that to create a company meant stripping them of their previous identities and re-forming them. We learned quickly.

Graeme, treating everyone as if they were already part of an ensemble, at once allocated roles on aesthetic grounds alone. But after a month or so, as people started to see the shape of the show and realise what everyone else was doing, we discovered the bugbear of ego.

Allocating the solo spots involved particularly contentious choices, because the tradition in ice-skating was that the earlier you skate, the lower you rank. Resentment spread like a cancer.

'Well, if Chris and Jayne are there, and so-and-so placed number such-and-such in whatever competition, then I'm ranking number three, so why are they asking so-and-so to do this part, and *why is that person coming on after me*? And if I am really better than them, why am I being placed in alphabetical order on the poster? And how do they expect me to dance with thingummy when I've always danced with what's-his-name . . . ?'

Graeme would suggest someone for a solo spot, and we would have to say, 'Um, maybe you shouldn't do that — she's already doing that little spot in the other number, and you'll be taking her away from so-and-so,' because we knew, and he didn't, that the couple had come fifth in the Canadian ice-dance championships two years before. Everyone wanted a solo, no one wanted to be purely a group member.

In the end, we auditioned — just told everyone to dance the same thing, then picked the best, and blamed Graeme for the choice. 'Sorry, he's the choreographer, and I know he doesn't know anything about skating, but, well, that's how it is.'

Later, we came across an equal and opposite reaction. 'If I'm just a member of the company, why are they working me so hard? I know this stuff. Surely they don't need me to go through it *again*?'

And slowly, of course, people began to learn what others were paid, and a whole new area of dispute opened up. 'If I'm doing this solo spot, and coming on *after* so-and-so, how come they're being paid the same as me?'

In the end, we left it to the company managers. There would have been nervous breakdowns and resignations if we hadn't. Finally, the skaters realised they were part of a new and exciting venture, and that we all worked as hard as each other. Egos retreated, a company emerged.

One remaining worry was that Graeme had not yet been formally contracted. That was down to management, not our problem, or so we thought. Now, we would never make such a silly mistake, but then we were all learning, with almost catastrophic consequences come opening time.

But for the moment all we wanted to do was create and rehearse with our dozen or so skaters, for eight hours a day, looking forward to the opening, which would be back in England. We had never worked so hard, and never with such demands.

To match Graeme's balletic standards, he arranged for all of us to start the day with a ballet class, where we met his assistant, Andris Toppe, who would soon play an even more vital role in our lives.

In the 1960s, Andris had been part of Australian dancing

as it established itself internationally. He had worked in Canada, dancing in the rock musical _Tommy_, returned to work with Ballet Victoria on tour with Baryshnikov and Makarova, and had danced in several of Graeme's ballets before becoming his assistant choreographer on this project. Retaining all the litheness of a former dancer, he has a rare combination of composure and clarity of direction, which you feel as soon as you hear his velvet-soft voice and see his direct, blue-eyed gaze.

We did not immediately appreciate the depth of Andris's response to his assignment. Later, he told us why he was so pleased to be asked. Like many people, especially those involved with dance, he had always assumed that ice-dancing, with its mishmash of music, was complete kitsch, a travesty of ballet. So it was flattering to learn from him, of all people, that when he saw _Bolero_ on Australian TV, he found it 'mind-blowing.'

He saw instantly that, although a skater might lack the quick changes of pace that floor-dancers could exploit, the speed and sweeping curves offered a wonderful new range of options to a choreographer. When Graeme asked him to help, he jumped at the chance.

It was now high summer. The warehouse that contained our rehearsal rink, with its ice-floor and tin roof, started to produce its own climate. We would arrive in the morning to a fog of condensation that coated the wall of mirrors we used to check our actions, and had us dripping within minutes. Then, as the sun came up on the tin roof, the heat burned away the condensation.

And melted the ice. By 2:00 p.m. there was a good

half-inch of water on the surface. With choreography that had us rolling on the floor, this was more like synchronised swimming than skating.

To keep cool, and avoid the clamminess and weight of soaked costumes, we all took to wearing shorts and T-shirts. So in our midday break, the company of scantily clad dancers would surge out into the broiling street in this grim industrial neighbourhood, ordering coffee and sandwiches from the 'tuck-truck,' a travelling canteen. It must have been a surreal sight.

That was how it was for two months, five and a half days a week, total commitment, total exhaustion at the end of the day. All you wanted to do was rest, eat and sleep.

In that time we worked out most of the show: an extended company version of *Song of India*, a 10–minute piece called *Hell*, with grimacing punk dancers in black leather and straps, which was eventually to be joined by *Heaven* — both derived from Graeme's *Seven Deadly Sins* ballet — three other solo spots, and our own established numbers, *Paso Doble*, *Barnum*, *Mack and Mabel*, and *Bolero*.

We were particularly pleased with the lights, which are crucial to a show like this. Chris had seen a Phil Collins concert, and been amazed by the lighting. A few calls revealed that Genesis had backed a US company that had developed a computerised, highly mobile lighting system, Varilites, to replace the established fixed lights, which pointed in one direction and were either on or off.

Now, you could have a whole system with all the 20–odd lights individually programmed, so that they could focus in any direction, at any level, and flick to any colour or pattern. It was new, it was exciting, it was expensive.

What was missing was a grand company finale, which Chris wanted to be an adaptation of Holst's _Planets_ suite. In Sydney, we had seen the Moscow Circus on Ice, with some astonishing wire-flying, which gave him ideas for an ending to the _Planets_. This would take more time than we had available in Australia, and would be done in Oberstdorf, just before we opened the show in London.

One weekend, a friend lent us a beach house in Terrigal, north of Sydney, so we hired a minibus, invited a few others, and took off. It was a superb beach, with great waves.

While Jayne took a stroll along the beach with Courtney — he had come out to discuss costumes for the new show — Chris, who was a strong swimmer, struck out offshore, away from a few others scooting around the shallows on boogie-boards.

Chris

Suddenly, as I looked back, I noticed that the shore was receding — fast. I was caught in a 'rip,' an undertow. I began to swim back towards the shallows, but realised to my growing concern that I was making no headway.

I started to do a racing crawl. And continued going

159

backwards. I fought, flat out, not thinking about anything now, except getting back.

Exactly the wrong thing to do of course — you're supposed to let yourself go, drift out to sea until the undertow dies, swim parallel to the shore, and only then, when there's no current to fight, turn inland.

Exhaustion set in. I felt my legs and arms become sluggish. Waves began to slosh over my head. I took a mouthful of water, coughed violently, heaved my head up, gasping for air, and saw Jayne in the distance, wandering along with Courtney. With my fading strength, I waved frantically.

Jayne

It was Courtney who spotted Chris. 'Oh, look, there's Chris, waving.'

'Oh, yes,' I said vaguely, waved back, turned and continued our walk.

Chris

I knew at that moment that I was drowning. The world went into slow motion. I thought of home and

160

family, and then was struck by the strangeness of the situation.

It had seemed such a good idea, to come out here. A vision flashed across my mind: me in a parallel universe, sitting bored out of my mind in a Sydney hotel room. That's what I would have been doing if I hadn't come, and I wished for it with all my being. But only briefly, because then I realised it would be much easier if I gave up all this futile struggling and simply relaxed, and allowed myself to sink.

Just at that moment, I noticed Wayne Deweyert, one of the boys in the company who had been fooling about on a boogie-board some way away. Our eyes met. Wayne saw I was in trouble, and started paddling towards me. At the sight of him coming, I felt a surge of strength, kicked again, flapped my arms, held up my head for another infinite half-minute, and then grabbed the approaching board.

I rested, panting, half on the board, until I had recovered enough to begin kicking. It took the two of us almost half an hour to circle back to the beach.

Jayne and Chris

Jayne had been wondering why he'd taken so long.

'I almost drowned out there,' he said, deliberately off-hand, as he came up to her on shaky legs.

'Oh, yes,' she said, equally offhand, thinking he was having her on.

'Seriously. I was going down for the third time when Wayne saw me.'

'But you waved at me.'

'No, that was *it*, that was me drowning.'

'Oh, that's terrible.' She believed him now, and felt a flicker of the fear he had felt. 'Are you all right?'

'Yes, I suppose so.'

There didn't seem much more to be said, but his words left her shuddering at what might have happened if Wayne hadn't spotted him.

We were nearing the end of rehearsals, looking forward to performing. We almost didn't get the chance. Graeme had been working with us for months, initially inspired by artistic interest, then by friendship and professional commitment. He had an agent, and as we got into the work, negotiations started. But no one in the management seemed to know the rules — everything in Edgley's previous shows had been brought in — and the negotiations dragged on.

Meanwhile Graeme went on devising steps and sequences with us. We had no idea of the legal position, that his creations were *his*, as much as a writer owns the copyright to a manuscript or an artist owns a picture, unless the rights are assigned. So in law we couldn't dance Graeme's steps until he had contracted with the management.

At one point, the management said to us, 'What if we let Graeme go? Can you work without him?'

We were shocked that things had come to such a pass so late on in the day, when we had most of the show choreographed and rehearsed. We *had* to have the steps, not just for what Graeme had choreographed for the

company but for _Encounter_ and our earlier version of
Song of India as well, because the agent now knew we
had received a fee for performing those pieces at the World
Professional Championships, and he wanted his share for
Graeme. Not just an overall fee either – a payment for every
performance.

Eventually, after the agent and the management had
wrangled over clauses and money for three months to
no conclusion, the agent called Graeme in the middle of
rehearsal and told him, 'Leave. Now!'

High drama. We were all appalled, and Graeme was
embarrassed, but there was nothing for it. He left to sort
things out, if possible.

And now we were getting close to an actual performance.
No contract, no performance.

The unpalatable truth was that the agent had the
management in the perfect position, on their knees, hands
tied.

So they agreed the terms demanded, and paid up.

Which meant that in the end _we_ paid, in part, because
that money had to be repaid out of profits, in which we
had a 30-per-cent share.

At the time, of course, we never saw this. All we wanted
was to get on with the show. In fact we almost wilfully
ignored the business and financial sides. The disputes
washed over us, and we had a wonderful, creative time.

Perhaps that was the way to do it. If we had been more
hardheaded, maybe we would never have had Graeme,
never had those great skaters, never had that start at all.

Only later did we understand, and learn. But learning
would be a long, slow process, and doing something about

it – like making sure Chris secured the rights on *his* choreography – would take even longer.

The plan was to finish rehearsals in Oberstdorf, then open in England. But towards the end of our rehearsal period in Australia, perhaps because the expenses were mounting and the management wanted to see an immediate return on their investment, there came another suggestion: 'Before we go to Germany, how about a few performances to try out the show?'

Naturally, we said yes. It would benefit us all to break the show in.

So the first rough and incomplete version of what would become our first world tour was in Christchurch, New Zealand. The town had no rink, and no venue in which to put one. So Edgley's had arranged a huge canvas circus tent – an obvious solution given their circus connections – into which they had built our old ice-rink.

In this strange setting, we previewed our show. The combination of the tent and the commercial success was to be of significance when we finally arrived in England.

Then on to Auckland. Again, there was no arena, so Edgley's had adapted part of the Weary Wool Store, which must be one of the biggest in the world. One of the many vast rooms, with a low ceiling and skylights, had been fitted with an ice-floor and grandstands. Behind the seats though, was the wool, hundreds of bales of it, infusing the whole place with the smell of lanolin. We changed in the offices, moving in as the office staff left.

The strangest thing about the production was the

lighting. In the matinées, you couldn't tell there was any, because the skylights weren't blacked out. But even at its best, there was an erratic quality to it. We didn't yet have the computerised system we had planned, and the lights, hired locally, were under the eccentric command of an ancient white-whiskered character in a woolly jumper whom we called Captain Birdseye.

After the show, when there had been yet another change to the agreed lighting plan, we would say, angrily, 'What went wrong?' And he would say, 'Nothing. I just thought it looked better that way.' In the end, we stopped being angry. He was such a nice guy, and there was no point anyway. They were his lights, and he did whatever he wanted.

Back again to Australia, for another preview in Sydney, where we experienced more than a fair share of teething problems. At the start of the first company piece, _Song of India_, Chris led the way in at the head of a V-formation.

'Now this is really important,' he had emphasised time and again. 'The start of the show. It sets the mood of the audience for the whole evening, so let's get it right.'

No sooner had the full company emerged than Chris got his foot caught in the baggy silk trousers, and took a nosedive, flat on his face, in front of 8,000 people, reducing the skaters behind him to stunned immobility. He got up and carried on, of course, but it's the sort of memory that turns you cold to think of.

Later, in another performance, the Canadian couple, John and Kelly, were dancing a slow, rather deep piece to Janet Baker singing Mahler. About 30 seconds into it,

John raised Kelly in a long, slow lift. There was a fearful ripping sound, and his trousers tore from seam to seam, right under his crotch.

Like a regular trouper, he carried on. But he was wearing only a sort of balletic jock-strap underneath, and for the whole of this very serious piece of choreography he was flashing bare buttocks at the audience. Long before the end, they were both near collapse with laughter.

At the time, these things are the stuff of nightmares, but they also act as tests that temper the company. Steadily, through these shows, the company came together, building cohesion with every setback, until we all looked forward to the opening proper, certain we would be able to produce something stunning.

In Oberstdorf, we worked on the final number, the *Planets*, compressed to 25 minutes by Bob Stewart, who joined us and worked out a version on the piano.

As for the music proper, the Musicians' Union wanted us to have live musicians every evening. Michael Linnitt had a fight to prove this wouldn't work — we needed the music to be exactly the same speed every night, or the split-second timing would be lost, and skaters put at risk of falling and perhaps injuring themselves.

Also, in the case of this show, the range of music was such that no single group would have been able to play it. But the players still had to be paid for each of our performances.

Michael Linnitt's long and complex negotiations ended with the Planets being recorded back in London by the London Philharmonic, backed by a mass of extra players for _Mack and Mabel_ and _Barnum_. Then at the end the tapes had to be destroyed, to prevent the possibility of using them again.

In the _Planets_, our duet was 'Venus', in which Jayne was the Goddess of Love looking after the world. The world was a huge globe, lit up inside, which was suspended from a wire. Jayne, swathed in a huge cape, had to toss the globe, leaving it to swing in a great arc and end up back in her hands.

At first Jayne, with no concept of how it would swing, tossed the globe away like a beach-ball and would stand blankly until it hit her in the back of the head. With practice, she learned to throw it smoothly and receive it delicately back as it completed its orbit.

The number ended with 'Jupiter', the 'I Vow to Thee my Country' hymn-tune, in what would be a wonderfully spectacular company piece, if it worked. We were all going to be spinning like heavenly bodies, most of us in white on the ice, with half a dozen 'fliers' in orbit on wires. At the end, all the lights would go off except for ultraviolet, plunging the rink into darkness, leaving us all apparently spinning in space. For the grand finale, two special-effects men trailing silken tails would become comets, catapulted by bungee cords along wires diagonally upwards into the lighting scaffold.

Rehearsing for all this in Oberstdorf was something of a contrast to our previous visits. Until then we had been the country mice. Now we were bringing the circus to town, spending vast sums of money, and we found the contrast uncomfortable.

The others didn't know the house rules, like clearing

167

up your plates after meals in the *Internat* and asking permission to use the little swimming pool, so we found ourselves on the one hand making decisions that would cost tens of thousands of pounds to realise and on the other acting as Boy and Girl Friday, clearing up after the others and apologising to the staff.

You can't devise something this big without a battle. By hindsight the one that stands out was over costumes for the *Planets*. Inspired by the theme of conflict portrayed in 'Mars, the God of War', the first of the *Planets* suite, Courtney had designed the costumes as two contrasting groups, animals and birds. They had all been made, and looked great. But not to Graeme. When we rehearsed in costumes for the first time, he announced, without apology, 'The costumes get in the way of the choreography.'

What?! All that work, wasted? All that money?

Yes.

Bob Murphy and Courtney were appalled. What the hell did Graeme want them to wear, then?

'I don't know. Leotards.'

'Leotards!' Bob snorted in disgust. 'I've done all that work and you want them to wear leotards!'

But Graeme was the choreographer. He was the boss. And we all ended up in beautifully designed, beautifully made leotards.

And so at last to Wembley Arena, where we were opening. This was totally unlike anything we had done or seen before. In amateur competitions, you finalise everything weeks in advance. In a show like this, some of the really important things would come together only in the final days, the final *hours*.

Crisis built on crisis, until we didn't see how it would ever be ready. The costumes wouldn't be ready, the matting wouldn't be laid, the lights wouldn't be programmed (in fact, after days of marking the sequences and positions of the lights, someone somehow wiped the computer disc controlling them, and it all had to be reprogrammed). Luckily, we couldn't be personally involved in all this. We found ourselves swept up in an army of technical people we had never seen before.

Here we acquired an assistant stage-manager, Debbie Turner, who was to become very important to us. She had been a stage-manager in theatre, and knew nothing about skating – her round, jolly build did not exactly encourage a natural affinity with it – and knew nothing about us personally, except that she had met us once, after a West End production of _The Pirates of Penzance_.

She hadn't been over-impressed. She told us later we had been as quiet as usual, leaving her with the unflattering thought: Blimey, they'd better stick to skating, because they're not much use _off_ the ice.

But she had always loved what we had done on the ice, luckily for us, because she's been with us, in ever more important capacities, ever since.

It was a bit unfortunate that in the presscall, Edgley's man on the spot, Wayne Stevens, suggested that we had to put on something 'specky' – spectacular – for the photographers. One of the most specky things we had were the bungee fliers at the end of 'Jupiter'. Everything was in place, though untested.

'OK, gentlemen,' Wayne said, 'we're just about to test this, so you might want to film it.'

Unfortunately, the bungee cord attached to one of the fliers was under too much tension, and he almost went into orbit. He shot up into the lighting grid and collided with a metal truss, giving himself a nasty injury. Not enough to put him out of the show, but he was still limping weeks later. A nice news item, but hardly a great start to the publicity.

It didn't mar the opening night itself, for which all the 8,000 seats had been sold, with Princess Diana in attendance, and coverage on the national news. At the end, a red carpet was rolled out on the ice, and we all lined up to meet the Princess. Afterwards, the management laid on a huge party with a mass of celebrities.

In such a turmoil, the details blur in memory, leaving only the feeling of relief that the initial decision, the commitment, the artistic choices, all the work – everything had been worthwhile. It was a wonderful start.

But it was, after all, only a start. In the amateur world, the performance is the climax. Now, we had to look forward to seven weeks in Wembley, and then another seven weeks on the road.

We learned a lesson of professional life: after the high of the opening, the hardest show is the next one. That, too, sold out, as they all did.

Quickly, our work over the previous months turned into startling commercial success – eight shows a week for seven weeks, a total audience of almost half a million, a run that may still be a record for Wembley. It was an incredible reward for an investment that had initially seemed ludicrously ambitious to us, and a vindication of the faith placed in our artistic judgement.

170

Then on to Nottingham, not to the ice-rink where we had both spent a good deal of our childhood, because the show was too big for that, and there weren't enough seats to sustain the cost of this production. Instead, we took over the main recreation area, the Forest, where the huge Goose Fair is held every year.

Inspired by the success of the circus tent in New Zealand, Michael Edgley had ordered a tent to be made. Some tent! It was the world's largest circus tent, over 100 metres long and 70 metres wide, 20 tons of startling blue PVC that could seat almost 7,000 people. It was a publicist's dream: 36 miles of planking, 10 miles of cables, eight 80-foot poles and 370 smaller ones, and more.

The tent provided us with another learning experience. It was a cost of the production, paid for ultimately by the profits of the tour, which meant we indirectly contributed to the cost. But it was owned by the producers, who were therefore free to let it out, creating income for projects that were nothing to do with us.

There was nothing underhand in any of this. It was just that we had not figured out — quite possibly no one had figured out — what the rules governing this business were.

If we had known then what we know now, we'd have set it up differently. The lesson, learned only later, was that in every idea, every contract, every new plan, there are hidden implications. There was no one to teach us. We had to learn by experience.

We played in that tent for seven weeks, doing eight performances a week, with Mondays off. The business was incredible, not just for us. Some 300,000 people pouring into Nottingham filled hotels, restaurants and shops.

We couldn't have wished for a better way to thank the city that had nurtured and supported us, turning the council's grant four years before into an investment that repaid itself dozens of times over.

In its turn the city thanked us, by granting us the 'freedom of the city.' It was a lovely notion, involving an intriguing medieval ceremony with ancient keys, but we weren't sure if it had any practical significance. Jayne, the city's first ever 'free woman,' asked, 'Does this mean I can park anywhere at any time, free?'

Er, no, but we were allowed to drive sheep into the central square if we wanted to.

About this time, in the summer of 1985, the Edgley Corporation and Michael Linnitt began to make plans to extend the tour: Canada, Australia again, the west coast of America, the east coast, on and on.

The idea appealed to us, because it would mean keeping the company together. Yet somehow we had to fit in another firm commitment, to the Dick Button World Professional Championships again in December.

We had been working continuously now for over a year, and to go straight on with the tour would have been too much. Sensibly, there was a break planned. So for three weeks, we went our separate ways, Jayne to Australia to see Graeme and other friends, and Chris to Israel.

Chris

The strength of her decision to set off on her own surprised me. This was the first time we had been apart in years. It made me a little nervous, because we had to get back together in Montreal. We had skating commitments, and for three weeks we would not be skating.

Suddenly though, the freedom seemed like a gift. I had the world to choose from. Where could I go? I liked the idea of Egypt, of an ancient land steeped in history far older than Europe's, but couldn't arrange anything in the time. So I opted for the next best thing, Israel.

I became a tourist, on my own, and did the rounds: Tel Aviv, Jerusalem, the Dead Sea, Masada. I forgot about Jayne, forgot about skating, and had a fascinating time until I got on the plane for London, and on to Montreal.

Jayne

Yes, I had changed, become more independent. The success in the Olympics and the responsibility of the tour were part of it. But it was probably Graeme's coaching as much as anything.

It was he, backed by Andris, who continued the

maturing process imposed on me by Zolli years before. They forced me to work out the implications of the roles I was playing – dramatic, passionate, outgoing, and sometimes comic – everything I felt I was not by nature.

Chris and I gave each other everything as far as skating was concerned, but we were very demanding of each other, and had precious little time for compliments. Graeme, though, was generous with praise as well as criticism, and gave me confidence in my abilities, particularly in portraying emotions.

I had never thought of myself as sexy, or elegant, or funny, or intelligent, or any of the things that other people were, the characteristics that awed me and kept me in my place and made me the mousy person I used to be. As a result of all this, I felt I was not just a better skater, but more secure, more self-assertive, and a lot happier for it.

During our break, I flew in from wintry Nottingham to an Australia that was hot, and full of familiar faces. I stayed in nice hotels, visited friends up and down the coast, laughed a lot, sunbathed, and ate well – really well, because I took my diet in hand and gave up eating red meat. I had never liked it particularly and had recently become nervous after reading about all the toxins red meat was supposed to contain. Giving it up made me feel more relaxed. I've never eaten it again.

Suntanned, fit and happy, I left for Canada to do the Dick Button Championships and resume the tour.

When I got there, the temperature was sub-zero. There was no one to meet me at the airport. Once, I would have sat and cried in panic. Now I got a cab to the Ritz

174

Carlton, rang Edgley's in Australia and Michael Linnitt in London, leaving a message saying, 'If anyone wants me, this is the hotel I'm in,' and ordered a terrific meal from room service.

Later, Chris called from the hotel he'd been booked into with the tour.

'What are you doing there?'

'Well, I didn't know where to go. It looked a nice place on the airport advertisements.'

'Are you coming over here?'

'No. I like it here. I'm not moving until tomorrow.'

Jayne and Chris

That left us a week to rehearse for the Dick Button competition. A week! Once that would have seemed impossible. Now, we took it in our stride.

We had to do two pieces, and took them from the show – 'Venus', with the orbiting ball depending on the skill of our company manager, Diana Kelly, as boom operator – and a comedy piece, the _Valentino Tango_, all baggy pants and 1920s slapstick.

It worked, and we won, for the second time, establishing us more firmly in people's minds across North America just at the right time, when we were about to embark on the Canadian leg of the tour.

Those six weeks across a Canada locked in the depths

of winter was a further education. Booked into so many different locations that it's impossible to remember them individually, we became less a traditional ice-show, more a rock-and-roll tour on one-night stands, on a gruelling treadmill of hotels, meals, travel, get-ins and get-outs.

This was followed by another six weeks in Australia, including Tasmania, where we were back in the old circus tent, battered by high winds and almost swamped by rain and mud. At one point, the roof was so leaky that there were umbrellas in the audience and half an inch of water on the ice, making us wonder what would happen if a cable came down and turned the whole place live.

In Melbourne, halfway through one of the shows, just before the interval, there was a power failure. All the lights died. The company were on the ice *en masse* at the time, just about to link into a line. As they did so, someone shouted, 'What do we do?'

'We're going off!' called the lead skater, and led them out like a conga. The music cut, leaving the arena in darkness and silence.

Behind scenes, as we gathered to discuss what to do, there suddenly appeared an apparition. It was Jerry, a wonderful grey-haired old man who looked after the ice-plant. He was like something out of a comic strip, with his face completely black, except for two holes that were his staring eyes, and his hair blown back and frazzled.

Actually, we couldn't laugh, because the poor chap was in shock. The ice-plant's control system had blown as he was fixing something, thrown him several feet across the car-park, and knocked out the power in the whole surrounding block.

After a very long interval, the lights were back on. But the ice-plant was still out, and the ice was beginning to melt.

'Well, can we go on?' Jayne wondered.

The rink already had an ominous sheen. Soon it would be a lake. If we were going on, we had to move fast.

Chris hardly hesitated. 'Yup, we'll do it.'

So on we went, with _Barnum_.

An hour later, as the end of the show approached, there was still no ice-plant. Now there was a good inch of water, and we still had _Bolero_ to do. Our boots were wet through, the costumes were soggy, and as the previous number ended, we knew we were going to have to do the famous slide along the ice into the mouth of a very damp volcano. We would be back to synchronised swimming.

There was nothing for it. On we went, and knelt for the opening, feeling the water ice-cold on our knees. We rose, dripping, and water-ski'd through the number. At the end, we cast ourselves with a passionate splash into a watery grave, sending a tidal wave surging towards the far end of the arena.

We ought to try it again sometime, because the audience loved it.

Then to the west coast of America, in some sort of a tie-up with Vidal Sassoon, on a horrendous schedule, and on the verge of collapse.

Once, briefly, we flew to New York just to have green and orange gel in our hair for a publicity performance in the Rockefeller Center, with its minute rink, where we did a highly compressed version of a tango. We were told we *had* to do it, so we did it, with pretty bad grace, not understanding the significance. There was hardly anyone watching at the rink — but it was on *The Today Show*, and seen by millions, all across America. One vital interview with a terribly important woman whose name we can't remember had to be conducted during a 40-minute drive in a limo. Not much of an interview. Jayne fell asleep, and Chris was almost incoherent with jetlag.

In handling publicity, we were slow learners, but we had the superb, insistent guidance of our publicity assistant, Nancy Saltzer. At her urging, we undertook two days of intensive training in interview technique — the basic facts to bear in mind, how to hold in mind your own agenda, how to get that over in the few minutes you're on air.

'You have to tell 'em times, dates, places. Remember the interviewer's Christian name. Use it. And remember: tell 'em how *great* you are!'

It went against the grain to promote ourselves in this way, but as things turned out, the training took away the fear and made us see the importance of publicity. It saved our frazzled lives many times over.

During this gruelling time, we had a delightful surprise — a wonderful review from Anna Kisselgoff, the respected dance critic of the *New York Times*. It still makes us proud to read her words today.

'Who had ever seen a bull-fighter on ice, much less one who used his partner as a cape to fling toward the ground?' she wrote. 'Passion and performance converged so startlingly in this prize-winning *Paso Doble* that it left sportswriters reeling. This wasn't athletic competition, they complained, it was art. And artistry

is what Miss Torvill and Mr Dean are now offering.'

She praised Graeme Murphy for his choreography, but
also gave Chris due credit. She said we were the 'image
of a couple in total harmony of movement and thus in
perfect emotional rapport . . . As all great artists, they
subordinate technique to expression. The sheer force of
the couple's personality is so great that the eye is often
drawn to the face rather than the legs . . . It is this
concentration that makes their performance so pure.'

In a world dominated by competition and sports writing,
reviews of ice-dancing as an art form are rare, and praise
like this rarer still. Her reactions seemed like a blessing
from on high, proof that we were in some measure
achieving our very deepest ambition — to create a form
of art on ice.

As we look back, this whole period through 1986 begins
to run together in our minds, in a kind of crazy mixed-up
rollercoaster of experiences. There were the shows and the
publicity. Then we were back in Germany choreographing,
rehearsing and filming a TV special, _Fire and Ice_, with
music by Carl Davis and a £1.7 million budget, which we
had devised with Graeme down in Australia and sold to
London Weekend as a Christmas spectacular, and which
we really wanted to do for artistic reasons, because it was
a full-length ballet with wonderful effects.

And then we were back in America, the east coast this
time, doing some nationwide interview with some famous
interviewer called something like Walters or Waters or
Rivers, and being helicoptered to New York to reopen the

Walman Rink in Central Park posing with Donald Trump, and we were just getting ready for a whole further leg of the tour, 60 one-night stands, including Madison Square Gardens, and were back in Portland, Maine, just after the opening . . .

. . . when the rollercoaster came to a sudden, bitter halt.

Our next date, just before the evening show, was a photo session, with the *New York Times*. We had to come into the rink early, and put on costumes and makeup. We had just finished when it happened.

Chris

During the warm-up, one of the men in the company drifted up on skates and said out of the blue, 'Chris, I can't skate tonight. I've hurt my back.'

Oh, please, no, I thought, not this on top of everything else. I was leaving the ice, my mind whirling, frantically planning what had to be done about the cast changes, when I fell. Perhaps there was some unexpected slick on the rubber matting that leads off the ice. I don't know. All I remember is the fall, and a searing pain in my left wrist.

I think I was almost in tears of pain and frustration at this point. I put my whole forearm in a bucket of ice for several minutes, tried a few moves, thought it would be OK, and we went on to do _Paso Doble_, hoping for the best.

It was hopeless. Anything that involved a pull was agony, and I couldn't grip with my left hand at all.

Then _Barnum_ was supposed to follow, with its circus lifts. After _Paso_, I knew I couldn't make it. I looked at Jayne and said, 'I can't hold you, Jayne. We can't go on.'

The company finished the first half without us. Then in the interval the management made the announcement that I had injured myself and that the performance could not continue. Listening to that announcement from behind scenes was the worst feeling in my professional career.

And worse was still to come. We both hoped this was a sprain, involving a week off. But when I had an X-ray later that evening, our worst fears were realised.

'That's not a sprain,' the doctor said. 'You've broken your wrist.' There was a nasty break in the scaphoid bone, which would take two months to heal, maybe longer.

Jayne and Chris

We tried to find a way forward, with a second consultation in New York. But two days later, we faced the truth. There was a company meeting, with the Edgley people, and Michael Linnitt. We came in with Michael Linnitt, who broke the sombre news, to a company that we saw was still unaware of the full damage.

The tour was cancelled, all 50 or so remaining dates. No Madison Square Gardens. All that publicity was for nothing. A year and a half of work together, and now it was all over.

By the time Michael Linnitt had finished speaking, every single person there was in tears.

Chris said, 'If you have to find other work, you must. But if it's in our power, we'll bring us all together again.'

They all wanted to know how long it would be, but what could he say? Part of his mind was telling him there was a possibility that the wrist would not heal properly, that he might have to give up skating completely.

This was a terrible way to learn what we had become. We were not just the two of us any more. We were a part of a company, a whole professional family, that stretched away from the people in that room to their friends and relatives, to all the rinks and arenas relying on us, to all the technical people who were looking forward to another two or three months' work, to the hundreds of administrative people in all the venues that had been contracted – a whole economy, tens of thousands of dollars already spent on advertising, tens of thousands taken on advance sales, millions more at stake.

All gone.

Insurance would cover outright losses, but there was

no recompense for any of us for what might have been.

Only days before, we had the world in the palms of our hands. Now what?

8

Stars with the All Stars

Jayne

Suddenly, all this free time opened up — six weeks, perhaps two months while Chris recovered. I was sure he would, sure we would be skating again fairly soon, so I was quite optimistic.

I decided to do two things. One was to have a minor operation on my right ankle, which had a mild but semi-permanent inflammation — bursitis — and kept on swelling up. It didn't hurt much, in fact not at all in performance, because the boot gripped it tightly and dispersed the fluid, but there was no point delaying any longer.

I had the operation done in Oberstdorf, and went off to recuperate with Clarissa and her family for a week until the stitches were ready to come out. Then I went on holiday with my parents, aiming to doing nothing at all but recuperate until Chris was ready.

Chris

I flew home with my forearm in a cast, very down, and moped around at my mum's house. What the heck was I to do if my wrist didn't heal? I didn't have too many qualifications for anything else.

After a few days, worry and depression inspired a weird idea. I would try my hand at other things in showbiz, explore the sort of life that Michael Crawford had shown us, the world of theatre. I could dance on ice, so maybe I could try ordinary dancing.

I was reasonably musical and had a terrific voice, so I thought, because it sounded so good to me in the shower. I would take lessons in tap-dancing and singing. It sounds crazy now, but I thought I could at least do something positive. Building a foundation for a possible new career seemed like the best therapy.

I was free to go wherever I wanted – I had a Mercedes 190, which I had bought during the English leg of the tour. Through Roz Chatto, Michael Linnitt's partner, I found a singing teacher in London, rented a flat in Victoria, packed the car full of bags, skating gear, stereo, TV, video and tapes, and drove down to make a new life in London.

Next day, I found myself somewhere in Chelsea standing next to my new voice-coach. He was a very nice man, very eminent, whose name I have blocked out for reasons that will become apparent.

'Follow this,' he said, and played a series of chords on the piano. I couldn't understand what he meant. My voice wavered around, searching for something that sounded right. Nothing did. He played a single note. I still couldn't find it. I had no idea how to pitch my voice. I wasn't even sure that I would know even if I hit the right note.

It was a revelation. All this time I had thought I could sing, and when it came to the crunch I found I was tone deaf. I still have no idea how I can listen to music, enjoy it, move to it, feel I understand it, yet utterly fail to reproduce it.

Next, tap-dancing. In this I had some support – Karen Barber. She and her partner, Nicky Slater, had been our greatest rivals for the British amateur championships a few years before. We had always been friends, and she had joined our company when they split up and she turned professional. Now, with nothing else to do for a while, she joined me for dance lessons at Pineapple Studio in Covent Garden.

I found it an intimidating experience. All these people who were clearly dedicated to dancing, with their ripped leg-warmers that had obviously been worn every day for the last 10 years.

Tentatively, we joined the first tap-dancing class. This was not as bad as trying to sing, but still I found myself edging to the back of the class, just so that I could see what everyone else was doing. The problem was that I felt I should be good — I was a dancer, of a sort; I was fit, coordinated, strong, active — and moreover I felt I should be good *instantly*.

But my ankles had been strapped in boots for 15 years, and by comparison with the loose limbs around me I was arthritic. It would take half a lifetime just to loosen up. In a month, I only learned to tap my way through one number.

Besides, I must have been a very unappealing member of the class, because I was still wearing my plaster. I sweated a lot, and there was no way to clean inside it. The smell was appalling. Eventually, I became convinced I shouldn't get too close to people. Once in the cinema I actually moved seats because I thought people sitting nearby might object.

So it was a huge relief when after six weeks the plaster came off, and an X-ray showed that the break had healed perfectly.

There were no other pressing commitments, so I took the opportunity to realise another ambition. I had always loved driving, the feeling of being in control of some fast and powerful machine with lots of dials. The Mercedes was a joy, but I was hungry for more.

I had begun to read car-racing magazines, from which I discovered I could take lessons. So I did, at Silverstone. Naturally, I hadn't the patience to take the full five-week course, and did my first race after two weeks, with four or five more to follow.

It was wonderful to feel the power of the machine and

the thrill of competition, though I soon saw I wasn't going to get anywhere up against the other young guns around, like Damon Hill, who had been at it for years and was just emerging at the top of Formula Ford racing.

Then I decided to hire a racing car, a 1600cc Formula Ford. Of course, all the other young drivers had sponsors. Not me. The maintenance, the preparation, transport to the track and a few circuits — it was like throwing money down the toilet. And that was before the repairs, because I did have a couple of little bangs, nothing serious — 'nothing that money can't fix!' the mechanics would tell me cheerfully, before sending in another horrendous bill. So pretty soon I decided that was that: an ambition realised, a little knowledge gained.

Meanwhile, I was wondering where to live. London seemed hectic and dirty. I had often driven out to see Michael Linnitt, who lived in some style near Henley. That seemed to me to be the ideal: beautiful country, quiet, not too far from London, easy access to Heathrow. One day in his house, browsing through _Country Life_, I spotted a three-bedroomed cottage for sale not far away.

'Come on,' he said. 'Let's go and see it.'

So away we drove, off the main road and down lanes, to this quaint and isolated vision of rural bliss — white-painted plaster, ancient timbers and tiled roof. It was love at first sight.

There was a sign outside saying, 'Viewing by appointment only'; but Michael wasn't the type to take any notice of that sort of thing, and just knocked on the door. A lady answered. She showed us round. Inside, with low beams and inglenook fireplaces, was home.

189

Within a week, I was the proud owner of a 300-year-old cottage.

Jayne and Chris

In early 1987, with Chris recovered and both of us eager to skate again, we received two offers, which together would keep us busy for a couple of years.

The first came from the best-known of the American ice shows, Ice Capades, now under new and ambitious management, wanting us to tour in the autumn for several months. We accepted.

Not only would it give us some immediate income, it was also a way to regain some of our lost exposure in America. And at that moment, wary of repeating our experience as employers, it suited us to be employees, with no further responsibilities.

The second proposal was from our old friend Michael Edgley, who wanted to do another show. Sometime, we wanted to fulfil our promise to put our previous company back on the road, but Michael Edgley had another, more cost-effective idea – to repeat the successful combination of Torvill, Dean and a company of Russian skaters.

Again, we agreed, but that would have to come later, since we had already accepted Ice Capades.

After working with Andris on four new routines through the summer in Oberstdorf, we flew to the US

190

in autumn, 1987, and found ourselves part of a totally new experience.

Ice Capades was part of the same tradition as Ice Follies, founded by the Hollywood star and ice-skating queen Sonja Hennie, who turned the ice show into a national institution of family entertainment. It had long been a source of low but regular income for aspiring young professionals, who were paid about $200 a week and slept four in a room to save money.

We rehearsed to rituals we had never come across — counting endless bars of music to time our entries, checking our positions against markers on the ice — then found ourselves on a gruelling treadmill, playing dozens of cities all over north America, with 'six-packs' on some weekends — three shows on Saturday and another three on Sunday.

We had no time to do anything but concentrate on the job in hand, because the show existed in two versions that toured separately, east and west, and we were in both, hopping backwards and forwards between the two coasts.

We were there, the producers said, to enhance their image. We provided them with a Fred Astaire and Ginger Rogers medley, a Beatles number, _Eleanor's Dream_, based on _Eleanor Rigby_, and a fast-moving, witty 1920s routine called _Hat Trick_, in which Jayne kept on stealing Chris's hat and he kept on snatching it back.

To most of those watching, two-thirds of them children, we were probably the boring bits. What they wanted was the Smurfs, falling about in cumbersome padded costumes and pulling the kids around on sledges.

The balance seemed to work, not only with the audiences. One of the greatest delights of that year was to find ourselves appreciated again, and in even more flattering terms, by Anna Kisselgoff of the *New York Times*. In a review in January, 1988, she wrote about our 'unmistakable aura of romance,' referred to us as 'male and female swathed in passionate rapport,' talked of 'the powerful mix of sensuousness and tenderness that pervades their performances . . . the multi-faceted range . . . the distinct originality of each of their dances . . . the technical ability, pioneering choreography.' She really seemed to understand what Chris was trying to do with his choreography. 'There are no isolated moves, no "unlinked elements" in their seamless skating, no empty spaces in between.' Wonderful words – enough to sustain us through any number of plane-trips and family shows.

Another pleasure about the work was the friends we made, many of whom are still friends and colleagues. So after our final show, in Denver, Colorado, in April, 1988, we planned a surprise party for the company.

Together with Andris, we announced that the theme was Hawaiian. Everyone had to be dressed in things like multi-coloured shorts, shirts, or *leis* of flowers, and after the show everyone would be taken to a party in 'Hawaii,' with the hotel as Hawaii and a double-decker London bus (used for publicity locally) as a 'plane.' The whole thing was extremely silly, but it *was* the end of a long run.

Fine. The show finished. Everyone piled into the bus. Hawaiian cocktails were served. Andris, Chris and Jayne were not with the group – supposedly we were back at the hotel, preparing the party.

In fact, only Jayne was. Andris and Chris were lying in wait, intending to 'hijack' the bus to 'London' — the same hotel as 'Hawaii' — where everyone would have tea with Jayne.

This may not sound the most exciting thing in the world, but there would be a proper party afterwards.

Chris

Besides the driver, only one other member of the party was in the know, and he had a starting pistol that he was supposed to fire to make the passengers jump. So, as the bus set out, Andris and I were hiding in bushes along the way, dressed as terrorists, armed with water-pistols. As the bus approached, we leaped out, pointed our water-pistols and yelled 'Stop!' The bus screeched to a halt, there was a bang from the starter pistol, and we leaped aboard, yelling, 'Nobody move! This is a hijack!'

Unfortunately, behind the bus, purely by chance, there was a police car, obviously checking on this merrymaking rabble. As they pulled out to overtake the stationary bus, the two officers in the car saw these masked madmen pointing guns. In their haste to do their duty, they didn't notice that the guns were lime-green and spraying water. One policeman hauled Andris out, spun him round, forced him up against the bus and levelled his gun.

'It's OK,' said Andris, desperately. 'It's a water-pistol.'

'Shut-up! You're in enough trouble, buddy!'

Meanwhile, the other had boarded the bus, and dragged me out to join Andris.

On the bus, the company had seen the water-pistols and recognised the two 'terrorists'. Some understood what was happening, and cringed in embarrassment. Others were marvelling at the complexity of our plot: 'My God, they've even got the local police in on it!'

'It is, it really is,' Andris was saying, squirting his lime-green plastic weapon. 'Look at it.'

And so, after a long moment, the truth came out, and we were on our way, with dire warnings about what could happen to people who pretended to hold up buses in Denver.

After that, tea with Jayne seemed a little tame. But it turned into a great evening.

The next project was to prepare for the Edgley-Linnitt tour with the Russian skaters. We had six months to work out our numbers and rehearse. Some of this we could do in Oberstdorf, but much of it would have to be done in Moscow, where all the rest of the company were based.

So we made a preliminary five-day visit to Moscow to meet the Russian company.

Ironically, our principal colleague was also a principal rival from the past — Tatiana Tarasova, the formidable coach of both Moiseyeva-Minenkov and Bestemianova-Bukin, both of whom we had defeated several times as amateurs.

She was the one who had made a fuss about our

win in 1984, so there may well be some resentments
to be ironed out. On the other hand, the old world of
Communist support for sport had already begun to change,
and Tatiana — still the doyenne of Soviet ice-dancing —
was now looking to make a living for herself with her
own company, the All Stars. To do so she had to walk
a political and emotional tightrope.

For one thing, she was in intense rivalry with a break-
away group formed by her ex-colleague Igor Bobrin who
had married her former star pupil, Natalia Bestemianova.
For another, it was extremely hard to make a living
in the collapsing Soviet Union. She needed foreign cur-
rency, which meant that she needed to tour abroad,
needed Michael Edgley, and needed her former sporting
rivals — us.

And we all needed her. The management needed her
because the only way to keep rehearsal costs down was to
rehearse in Moscow. And we were really looking forward
to combining the two skating cultures for the first time.
For us, this was the ice-dancing equivalent of working
with the Bolshoi.

With Russian society on the verge of collapse, it was
going to be tough, as we saw as soon as we arrived in
this grey and depressed city. It was the end of April.
We were met by our old friend Andrew Guild, who was
married to a Russian, spoke Russian and had therefore
become the driving force behind the Edgley organisation's
Russian connection. From our hotel, the Intourist, he took
us to meet Tatiana, who was waiting outside.

'Why doesn't she come in?'

'It's a hotel for foreigners only. No Russians allowed.'

We were a little nervous, because we knew Tatiana mainly by reputation. As the best known Soviet coach and choreographer, she was a very big name, with a raft of awards and medals. Moreover, her father Anatoli had been the country's top ice-hockey coach, and was still a living legend, and her husband Vladimir was a pianist of international stature.

Everything about her was big. She was a bear of a woman, with a full face, heavy makeup, and great dangling earrings, with her size emphasised whenever she went outside by a massive fur coat. We were almost overwhelmed by her – her flamboyance, her expansive gestures, her huge beaming smile, her smothering hugs.

'Chr-e-e-es! Jaynitchka! Good to see you!' She spoke some English, not enough for fluency, but enough to get across her meaning.

She had gone to great trouble to prepare a welcome for us – when we got to her apartment, you could hardly see the table for food. With her contacts, life was easier for her than most people, but even so in a city short of necessities, let alone luxuries, it was an astonishing sight.

That first meeting was a little artificial, with Andrew speaking in Russian to Tatiana and Vladimir, who talked in good English to us about Gorbachev, and the new political freedoms and economic constraints being ushered in by *glasnost* and *perestroika*.

Tatiana, consuming quantities of Russian champagne, coffee and cigarettes, was clearly determined to make a go of working with us.

Even so, our collaboration almost ended before it began,

because Andrew Guild had the unpleasant task of trying to rename Tatiana's company.

'The All-Stars,' he said. 'We'll have to change the name.'

She was appalled. 'No, no, no! We are very famous!'

Andrew had touched a raw nerve. Tatiana wanted her company to be up there in the international hall of fame along with the Kirov and the Bolshoi and the Moscow Dynamos.

'Maybe you're famous here,' Andrew explained, 'But no one's heard of you anywhere else. The All Stars — it sounds like a football team!'

No way. She was insulted beyond endurance, and adamant. So that was that: Torvill and Dean and the Russian All Stars, though not necessarily in that order, if Tatiana had anything to do with it.

Andrew was keen to show us the best side of Moscow, but there was no disguising the problems that would face us. In a market on our second day, we saw disturbing sights — women in ragged clothing holding out bits of string, even a single button, for sale. One woman, with an ancient weather-beaten face wrapped in a headscarf, was suffering from rickets. The sight of her — an outcast, tottering on the brink of death — reduced Jayne to tears.

We had little time to see more. The rest of the company were performing in Leningrad. That's where we went a couple of days later, with Andrew and Tatiana, leaving the station on the midnight train for the eight-hour journey. Not a pleasant experience — lots of cigarette smoke, revolting toilets and a grim-faced carriage attendant.

We arrived in Leningrad — not yet renamed St Petersburg

— on the morning of May I. All we had to do was cross the road to be at our hotel, the Hotel Europa. But as we emerged from the station the May Day parade was already passing, miles of workers from separate factories, all with their banners, along an avenue lined with soldiers, trucks and armoured cars. There was no way across, and the parade was due to take three or four hours to pass.

Tatiana led us through, by infiltration. Leaving the luggage at the station to be picked up later, she spoke to a guard, beckoned us on to our knees beneath a truck, and led us right into a mass of marching workers.

'What if we're spotted by an English cameraman?' said Chris as we marched self-consciously along. 'Imagine the headlines: Torvill and Dean defect!'

We walked for several hundred yards, gradually work-ing our way through to the other side of the mass of marchers, then ducked out of the parade, into the hotel.

Leningrad is a lovely place at a distance, all broad boulevards and Renaissance-style buildings, like the hotel itself. Close up, you see the drabness and the decay.

Our rooms were huge — Jayne's had a grand piano in it and a wonderful vase without flowers. But the shower didn't work properly, the bathroom tiles were cracked, and there were no towels. She thought, Why don't they sell the piano and buy some towels?

Luckily, it was a short visit. A quick trip to the rink to meet the company, just long enough to watch the show, shake hands afterwards and say we'd look forward to working with them, and then next morning out to the airport to catch a British Airways flight home. You'd never think a glass of champagne and an English newspaper would mean so much. And that was after only five days.

Rehearsals started briefly in Moscow with a two-week trial workshop in midsummer — and with them problems.

The first piece Tatiana wanted to do was the story of Paganini, portraying two sides to his character. Niccolo Paganini was many things: the greatest violin virtuoso of the last century, a composer, the megastar of his day, and a romantic adventurer devoured by melancholy.

He had seemed to Tatiana and her principal skater and business partner, Yuri Ovchinikov, to be a perfect hero for Russians — a soul in conflict with himself. Yuri would be dancing Paganini's crazy persona, Chris dancing the creative one, with Jayne as the great man's muse. Neither of us took to the number, but restrained ourselves for the sake of a peaceful life.

Chris's idea for the workshop was a version of _La Ronde_, the story of a necklace that is passed from husband to wife to lover to mistress, and on and on, until it finally gets back to the husband.

It dealt with subjects that were not exactly mainstream ice-dancing, like prostitution and adultery. It depended on group patterns and intertwining couples, not at all what the Russians, who were either soloists or couples unused to working in ensembles, were used to.

Rehearsing these two very different numbers was made a nightmare by having two totally different creative people devising choreography from totally different backgrounds. And of course different languages, which demanded an interpreter. At first anything Tatiana said had to be

199

filtered through a friend of hers who was desperate to impress with the depth of her knowledge of English. She improvised Tatiana's ideas into incomprehension. Only much later did we find an interpreter who knew skating terms in both languages.

We swiftly came to realise that Tatiana was no democrat. She was used to being the boss, and if anyone got out of line, she fired a machine-gun of words across the ice in front of them.

She separated the working time into two periods, hers and ours, rehearsing alternately in the mornings and afternoons. But she didn't appear willing to relinquish control and so would arrive and cut in on Chris's instructions with a wave and an imperious 'Niet!' – or 'Da! Kharasho!' if she saw something she liked. Often, we would be startled by yells from across the rink as Tatiana bawled out some unfortunate skater.

It was a tough time. But we could also see her good qualities, her fighting spirit and her commitment to her company, many of whom were no more than kids in Moscow for the first time. We saw the conditions she was working under – little money, food hard to come by, even the most basic things available only by barter – and we sympathised. In the midst of chaos, she was a survivor. So we did our best not to react.

As Chris saw Tatiana storming across the rink and heard her cry of 'Chr-e-e-es,' he would mutter, 'What's she doing now?'

'Shut up,' Jayne would mutter back. 'If you say anything she's going to explode.'

'*She's* going to explode? What about me?'

200

'Just behave yourself.'

This was the beginning of something that was obviously going to be a long, hard struggle, for the management as well as us. We had always known there would be no income for us from this period – any cash had to go to the All Stars and to cover costs. So, as a trial and to help recoup costs, they asked us if we'd put on a performance after the two-week workshop – not the finished show, of course, but at least _Paganini_ and several other long-established routines?

The reception to the first show was astonishing. We had lived apart from ordinary Russians, cosseted in a hotel with taxis back and forth, so we had no idea if we were well-known or not. In fact, as Olympic champions, we were heroes, top news.

The huge Luzhniki rink was full, all 10,000 seats. And afterwards, it was like Beatlemania. There were hundreds of people mobbing the stage door, fans on top of, even _inside_, our car. It took a small army of staff to clear a way for us and haul people out of the car. Then it was 'Drive! Just drive!' and we edged away with people still on the bonnet.

There followed a break while we finished Ice Capades in America, returning to finalise our plans for the All Stars show proper in Oberstdorf.

One thing that required our attention was Chris's response to some Andean music, which reminded him of the terrible things – in particular the officially sanctioned kidnappings – that had been happening in Chile and Argentina in recent years. The subject was very much in the air, after the Falklands War, and more recently the Costa-Gavras movie, *Missing*.

Chris saw in his mind those who had vanished, the fathers, mothers, husbands, wives, lovers, friends and children, and devised a series of movements linking two people who could be seen as friends or brother and sister, confronting authority, cowering before it, searching for lost loved ones, and ending where they started, in limbo. We felt it was something the Russians, too, would understand.

If that was designed to be accessible, we weren't so certain about a second, more demanding, choice. Chris had been interested for a while in ancient Middle Eastern history, and on a trip to London immersed himself in the Egyptian Room of the British Museum.

He liked the feel of the mythology, Isis and Osiris, Pharaoh as god, the idea of dying as a rebirth into the *real* world, the richness of the funerary ornamentation, all that gold and lapis lazuli, the stylised poses in the paintings, the hieroglyphics, and in particular the love story of Akhnaton and his queen Nefertiti. There was so much here to set the imagination on fire. But to what music?

We tried the movies, like Liz Taylor's *Cleopatra*, and found the music too Hollywoody. Then by chance we came across the CD of a new opera by Philip Glass, called, of all things, *Akhnaton*. This is not exactly Top Ten material — minimalist in style, vastly long phrases of repeated notes, but in mood just what Chris was looking for.

All we needed was to reduce a three-hour epic to 30 minutes. To do that demanded total immersion in the story and imagery. It was an odd thing to do, which involved some long negotiations on our behalf with Philip Glass himself, who must have been puzzled, if not horrified, by what we planned. In the end, though, we and Andris did something that seemed to work, starting with a strong image to seize and hold the audience. A huge pyramid of silk, 25-foot square at its base, was being admired by modern tourists. Suddenly, a line attached to the top whipped the pyramid up and away, revealing the world of ordinary Egyptians in the 14th century BC, all in long skirts and sandal-like skates.

Chris as the Pharaoh made an entry carried on a throne, which led into a love sequence with Jayne as Nefertiti, then a rebellion by the people and a royal death, leaving Jayne/Nefertiti in mourning.

If you think this might be strange to Russian skaters, imagine what they thought of being a pack of cards dancing to Scott Joplin's _Ragtime Poker_, or a version of Astaire and Rogers doing _Putting on the Ritz_ from _Top Hat_. This formed part of a tribute to Gershwin, all black ties and top hats and debonair smoothness.

Can you imagine anything more un-Russian? One of the skaters was well over six foot tall, with shoulders like slabs of wood. In evening dress, he was an incarnation of the monster in _Young Frankenstein_. Mr Munster, Debbie called him. It took weeks to loosen him up.

That whole period was as much a struggle with life as with Tatiana. We could get to the rink from the hotel only by cab. But there was no knowing if there would be a cab, or how much the driver might charge. And if you got one, you needed to keep it for the return trip, eight hours later.

But on several occasions, the driver's shift would end

before that. He would sit there all day, doing nothing, then leave just before we finished. Jeannie McPherson, our Australian company manager, would have to run out with bribes of cigarettes to get the driver to stay on.

It was poor Jeannie who held us together. She woke with two principal tasks: to find something to eat at lunch, and somewhere to eat that night. It took her all day to find some fruit or fresh bread (once, bread and jam was all there was – we sat dipping bread into the jam, flicking away ants attracted by the smell of sugar).

'What do you want to eat tonight?' Jeannie would ask at 10:00 in the morning. It didn't matter much what we said. Restaurants were available only with backhanders of dollars or cigarettes, and even then they usually provided potato salad and gherkins, whatever we'd ordered.

Things eased up only when an invitation to the New Zealand embassy revealed an alternative economy. Several embassies used to place orders through a company that flew supplies in from Finland – coffee, tea-bags, milk, toilet paper. Then the embassies took turns issuing invitations to social events.

Later, too, capitalism began to ease its way in. A pizza truck parked right outside the hotel, selling pizza for a dollar slice. The first taste of that was bliss. We stood there and ate like children at a party until our jaws were a mess of cheese and tomato.

It was strange that through it all no one from the British embassy showed any interest in us. No invitations at all. And when we phoned once for advice on a doctor when Chris had a stomach upset we were merely directed back to the Russian authorities. They seemed to exist only for themselves.

Of course, since we were rehearsing there, all the costumes had to be made on the spot. Bob Murphy was brought in from Australia to set up a sweatshop of Russians stitching together material, all of which had to be flown in.

The tensions ran right through to the five shows we did in Moscow and Leningrad in August, 1988, before we left to start the tour in Australia. Hell at the time, funny later.

Once again we took the night train to Leningrad, except that now we had the whole company to rush to the station, and no reliable cabs. It was a question of everyone asking their friends. The only light relief was that the female carriage attendant on the train looked exactly like a grim version of Benny Hill. It took half the night, the giving of many cigarettes and the consumption of much vodka to crack a smile from her.

The Australian tour, opening in Newcastle, north of Sydney, in the big blue circus tent we knew so well, began with a row.

In Moscow, Tatiana had taken the last bow with us at the end. Fair enough, because she was on home ground, and anyway curtain calls are of more significance in Russian shows. But in Newcastle, the Edgley people said it would be different. We had been here before, we were the ones people came to see, we were the stars now – obviously so, from the way the names appeared on the poster, much to Tatiana's indignation. The end had to reflect that.

So we rehearsed a new ending, with the company making a couple of circuits of the ice, then leading off, leaving us to make a final bow, without Tatiana.

After the finale, the company made the circuits in a line, with us last as planned, but then, to our astonishment, just as we were taking our final bow, they didn't exit — just swept on in a third circuit. We stopped, watched in surprise, then retreated, feeling foolish, leaving the company to take the *final* final bow.

Chris

I was in a total rage. How dare she! As I saw it, we'd rehearsed one thing, and she had told them to do another. Still in my skates, I stormed backstage to the caravan that served as my dressingroom, in a blind fury, and suddenly there was Tatiana.

'That was a terrible thing to do!' I shouted at her.

She looked astonished, understandably, because in Moscow we had been so restrained. 'Chr-e-e-es, what you mean?'

'That ending! It was the most unprofessional . . . the stupidest . . . the most ridiculous . . .' She just stood there gawping as I searched for words. 'We just can't go on like this!' I finished, and slammed into my caravan.

Minutes later, still fuming, I told Andrew Guild he had to explain to Tatiana that she couldn't just change things at the last minute, without consultation.

Jayne and Chris

Andrew sorted it out, fast. It couldn't have been too hard, because Tatiana had no option really. If we couldn't work together, the tour might break up and the All Stars could be back on the plane to Moscow with no foreign earnings.

Luckily, Tatiana came and went between Moscow and wherever the tour happened to be. When she went we all got along fine, and when she came back, the tension came with her, as she once again shouldered the responsibility for her skaters.

There were regular outbursts. Once, later in the tour, there was a row over a costume she wanted altering with Kim Bishop, who was in charge of the wardrobe. Kim is a gentle, highly professional character, and he did his best to stall: 'Well, Tatiana, the designer of this show is Bob Murphy, and I don't think . . .'

'OK!' she shouted. 'I fix myself!'

'Tatiana! Stop! Someone get her away from my costumes!'

Kim's yell cut through Tatiana's rage. She looked at Kim, saw murder in his eyes, and fled.

This tour started as a five-month run. In fact, in Moscow we had been told that our popularity in Australia was past its peak. There was no guarantee of success, which would anyway be largely down to the management's promoting skills. That being so, could we drop our share of the profits by half, to 15 per cent?

But in fact, like the previous tour, it began to stretch almost as soon as it opened. Tom Scallen, the myopic impresario of Ice Capades, came over to see the show. Afterwards, when he greeted us, he peered at us so closely through his pebble glasses that we wondered if he actually managed to see us perform at all.

But there was no denying his enthusiasm. He wanted to bring the show to America. At the time we were delighted. Only later did we begin to wonder: could the American market take another ice show? Wouldn't he be taking business away from Ice Capades? Or did he want some control over a tour that he feared would happen anyway, and maybe ensure we *didn't* compete directly with Ice Capades?

We were delighted to discover that Australia still remembered us, and seemed to like us, despite the fact that we had been told we were a declining asset. Eighty thousand people came to the Melbourne show alone. Some decline! When we commented on the success, though, we were told that it was due not so much to us as to the management's expertise in advertising.

But towards the end of the tour, in Melbourne in early 1989, we really did become a declining asset, in a rather dramatic way.

We had been invited to a rehearsal of the Australian Ballet, where we saw a couple of dancers doing a lift that we liked, so in the hour and a half after warming up, Chris suggested we adapt it for the show. We tried it back-stage. It was a complicated movement that ended with Chris holding Jayne with one arm as she twisted across the front of his body. As he took

208

her weight for the final move, he felt a twinge in his back.

'Well, we'll need to practise it a few times,' he said, straightening up and easing himself.

At the time, it seemed like nothing much. But by the end of the show, the back had stiffened up. A doctor came, felt around, and gave Chris some pills, two sorts, one against inflammation and the other to help him sleep.

'Remember,' she finished. 'Take one of the sleeping pills and two anti-inflammatories.'

We called a physiotherapist friend, Rob Hannah, and he promised to come the next morning. Then we went for a Chinese meal. By the end, Chris could hardly stand. Still, no cause for panic yet. Sometimes, you get a painful muscle pull which turns out to be perfectly manageable next morning. Jayne went off to her room, arranging to meet as usual at the rink for the warm-up next day.

Chris

When I got back to the hotel, I opened my pills, and muddled them, taking two sleeping pills and one of the anti-inflammatories. One of those sleeping pills was enough to put a horse down for a day, let alone me. Minutes later, I was fast asleep.

Next morning, I was dragged into semi-consciousness by a distant ringing. I realised after a while it was the phone. I knew I should answer it, but my arms were slow and heavy.

'Mm,' I said into the mouthpiece.

'Chris? Are you awake?'

'Mm.'

'It's Rob. I've come to pick you up for physio.'

'Mm.'

'I'll come up then. Ten minutes.'

'Mm.'

Get up, then. I tried. No good. I rolled out of bed, tried to stand. No good. I crawled to the bathroom, knelt at the loo, hauled myself to the basin, splashed water over my face, dressed . . . leaned against the door . . . fell asleep . . . heard knocking . . . opened the door . . .

'Jesus, Chris.' Rob's voice from a long, long way away. 'How many of those pills did you take?'

At the physio session there was no pain at all in the back — because I fell asleep on the table. Then I went for a scan. One disc was bulging. More therapy: electrodes, ice. It's all very vague, because I was in and out of sleep. By now it was after lunch sometime, and we had to be on the ice to warm up at 4:30. Next thing I knew, I was at the rink, and Jeannie was pouring black coffee into me.

Jayne turned up from somewhere, and looked at me in such a funny way I giggled.

'Oh, hi, Jayne,' I said. 'I sort of can't stand up.'

'Chris!' For some reason I couldn't understand, she started to cry. 'You've got to get your skates on.'

'Skates on.' I giggled again, because people were rushing around and talking to the cast about what to do, and I wondered why, because I couldn't see what the hurry was all about.

Somehow, I found myself standing on the ice beside Jayne in the entrance passageway to the rink.

'Are you all right?' she said. 'We have a show to do.'

'Yeah, yeah. Hold on. I've just got to finish my coffee.'

Jayne and Chris

Through the warm-up, Chris was a rag doll. Then, as the drug began to wear off, he tried to force himself to concentrate, and became cross when he couldn't. Then the pain kicked in. Practising the beginning of _Bolero_, he couldn't even do the first lift. He manoeuvred himself gingerly back to his dressingroom, eyes watering with the pain.

Michael Edgley appeared, worried. 'Can you do the show, Chris?'

'I don't know. I just don't know.'

'Can you do _some_ numbers?'

'Well, yes.' Sigh, shrug. 'We'll try, but we'll have to change a few things.'

Restrained panic. What numbers could we drop, what other numbers could the All Stars insert? They had some other music on tape. There was a quick rehearsal, which went on towards show time. They delayed opening the doors, with the management still wondering what to do and say.

And meanwhile there was a further panic. What about subsequent shows? There were still five to go, 50,000 seats sold.

Chris was lying down in his dressingroom when Michael Edgley came in.

'Look, Chris,' he said. 'I've got this woman coming in to treat you.'

'Who is she?'

'Don't worry about that. Just let her treat you. And don't laugh. Just don't bloody laugh.'

'Who *is* she?'

'She's a faith healer.'

Chris was not in a state to laugh. The woman came in. He can't remember what she looked like, can't remember if she said anything, because as soon as she laid her hands on his head he fell asleep. When he awoke, his back was as bad as ever.

Later, Rob fitted Chris with a brace to support the back, locking him in so tightly he could hardly breathe. With that on, he felt he could risk tackling *Bolero* and *Missing*. But he might collapse, and anyway the audience would feel short-changed if they didn't know what was going on, so Michael Edgley made an announcement, turning potential catastrophe into a sort of success, with sympathetic applause for Chris. With the changes, cutting back our time on the ice, we finished the Australian run.

After Australia, and after a five day break that Chris spent flat on his back, we opened in New Zealand, then

back to Australia again in the new year of 1989 for a few
final shows before a short holiday that would, we hoped,
leave us fresh for our opening in America.

We rented a seaside place in Palm Beach, and were looking
forward to a month of end-of-summer sun, sand and sea,
with nothing else on the cards but for Chris to fulfil an
obligation he'd accepted to take part in a celebrity 'Nascar'
– a race for souped-up saloon cars – at Melbourne's Calder
Raceway. It promised to be a fun way to celebrate the start
of the holiday.

On tour, the insurers would never have sanctioned
his doing such a thing. Now he was free, and could
do something for himself. He had had a day's practice
to get used to the oval track and to the car, lent
by another driver who would be racing after him.
Jayne was roped in to start the race. As Debbie and
a few other supporters from the show, all wearing
specially printed 'Dean Speed' T-shirts, found seats, Jayne
was taken to the start, and Chris went off to get
ready.

Chris

All dressed up in overalls and helmet, I was as excited as
a child by the prospect of racing again. It was a surprise,
though, to learn that in the 'celebrity' race, I was the only

213

celebrity. That meant I would be up against experienced drivers. I was pleased by that.

As I climbed into the seat through the glassless window – the door was welded shut – and strapped myself in, I began psyching myself up for a hard-fought race, something that would be a real challenge. There were only six other competitors, so I could easily be placed.

Jayne waved her flag, and we were off. I revelled in the speed, the roar, the controlled slide into the banked-up bends, the acceleration up to 150 m.p.h. down the straights, and after four laps found myself lying fourth, with a guy right behind me, slip-streaming. We were coming off the bend. Now was the moment to strike, to prevent him overtaking, to gain on the three in front, and at least give myself a chance of a place.

But the moment was wrong by a few yards, by no more than a second, because where the banked-up oval gave way to the flat straight, there was a ridge running at a right angle across the track. As I hit it, I felt a sudden slackness in the back wheels. No traction. The back began to slide.

I turned into the skid, but knew with a horrible empty feeling in my stomach that I had lost control. I hit the brakes, and slid off the track over grass, still travelling at over 70 m.p.h. Ahead was a wall. An experienced driver would have known to take his feet off the pedals at the last minute, draw his feet up and let the straps take the impact. I was still ramming the brakes when I hit the wall.

There was a hell of a bang, my foot jumped off the pedal, the straps cut into my shoulders, and the car stopped dead.

214

Jayne

After waving the flag to start the race, I was struck most of all by the noise. I had no idea what was happening, because I lost track of the laps and couldn't even be sure which car Chris was driving. My next job was to flag the winner. The steward who was looking after me would tell me what to do, because he was monitoring the race on a radio.

The cars were all at the other side of the track when suddenly I heard him say, 'Oh!' Then, 'Oh, he's off!'

'What? Who's off?'

'Er . . .'

I hoped he was just having a problem identifying the car.

'Who _was_ it?'

'Chris.'

'Oh.' I think that was one of the worst moments of my life. The bottom seemed to drop out of my stomach. Chris had crashed, and I was helpless. There was nothing I could do but hope, while they stopped the race and an ambulance raced across to the crash, siren screaming.

'Well, is he OK?'

'Don't know, Jayne.'

'Well, is he . . . alive?'

'They're finding out,' he said. 'Come on.'

Chris

For a few seconds, I didn't move. I seemed to be all sensation: the sudden silence, the appalling change from a world blurred by speed to utter stillness, a terrible pain in my neck, and my shoulders, and my left foot. I sat there, locked in my seat by the belts, in the silence. The first sound I was conscious of was my own breathing.

That's good, I thought. Still breathing.

Then there was a voice at my shoulder, asking how I was.

'I think I'm all right.'

Something quite nasty had happened to my ankle, but the more serious worry was whiplash. In case I had spinal damage, they put a collar round my neck and lifted me out carefully, asking where it hurt all the time. Then I was stretchered into the ambulance and whisked off to the track's emergency room.

Jayne

That was where I saw him, saw his eyes were open and knew he was going to live, at least. I didn't care about anything else, his legs, his arms, I didn't even care whether he would ever skate again, just as long as he lived.

216

I think the first thing he said was something like, 'That poor guy.'

'What?'

'The guy who owns the car. He was going to drive it in the next race.'

Jayne and Chris

Then, while the rest of the subdued 'Dean Speed' support group went off to await developments in a restaurant — booked earlier to celebrate the race — Chris was taken off for a more detailed look at his injuries in hospital, with Jayne and Rob Hannah, our physiotherapist friend, in attendance. Besides bruising from the straps — his chest had a sort of livid crucifix across it — and stiffness from the whiplash, the nastiest injury was to the ankle, which the doctor said had been hit very hard, presumably by the brake-pedal when the impact made Chris's foot slip off it.

There was no telling what the underlying damage was, if any, until the swelling went down, which would take a few days. They gave him some crutches, and sent him hobbling out.

What now?

'If you feel up to it,' Jayne said. 'Come to the restaurant. Everyone will want to see you alive and walking.'

217

Back at the Palm Beach house, set above the sand on a glorious peninsula an hour north of Sydney, Chris rested his ankle. We were joined by Debbie, who volunteered to help out for this brief period, and there was nothing else to do but look forward to a barbecue we had planned for friends.

Chris was already feeling oppressed by his condition, grouchy, and finicky about how the house was being kept, the laundry, the carpets, the kitchen. He refused to use his crutches, but his ankle didn't heal. It was painful, with an unnerving tendency to bend sideways under pressure and make nasty little clicking noises when he walked.

A few days later, a further examination in Sydney revealed the truth. As the doctor, a personal friend, explained, the ligament to the ankle bone had been torn apart, leaving two separate ends like frayed cables. They would rejoin only if they were stitched together. And any delay merely allowed the frayed ends to perish, making an operation increasingly difficult.

'Do I have to make a decision *right now*?' We were meant to be going home in a few days' time. If the operation was done in Sydney, we would be there for weeks.

'There isn't really a decision to be made, Chris. If you want to continue skating, you have to have it done immediately.'

That changed everything. A day later, Debbie and Jayne delivered Chris to hospital. Debbie would remain in Palm Beach to be with Jayne, then stay on as mother hen and chief bottle-washer.

Because it would be better for Chris to stay with the same surgeon throughout, we decided to stay in Palm

Beach for as long as it took him to recover and get back on skates — assuming the operation was a success and he *did* get back on skates. That would be two months, and two *long* months, because it was now April, Australia's autumn, so there wouldn't be much of the sun, sand and sea that had drawn us to the house in the first place.

Well, at least Jayne was off to a good start, because there was the barbecue planned, and Chris wouldn't hear of its being cancelled. Jayne and Debbie left him in hospital for the two-hour operation, and hurried home for the party.

Late that night, Chris received a cheery call from Jayne and a dozen others, all eager to tell him what a great time they were having.

What they didn't tell him was that in some silly joke played on Frank, one of the technical people, a bottle of tomato sauce somehow got spilled over the big carpet in the sittingroom. Out at the house it was a huge joke, because by then a certain amount of wine had been consumed, but Jayne knew what Chris's reaction would be.

'Now, listen everyone, when we call him, *no one mention the sauce*, OK?'

So no wonder they sounded so cheerful: they were all suppressing high-spirited giggles.

Next day, before they went to fetch Chris, Jayne and Debbie cleaned the carpet the best they could and flipped it over, allowing Chris to be brought back to a seemingly pristine house as if nothing had happened.

Then, for the next two months, Chris became a caged lion. Doctor's orders were that for two weeks at least he was not to get up much, because he had to keep his foot elevated. The girls, though, were free enough. Jayne

219

would drive down to Sydney, leaving Chris with his leg up, returning hours later with yet more videos, or CDs, or books, or model aeroplanes for him to make.

'Here,' she would say handing him some intricate game. 'This'll keep you going for a few days.'

An hour later, he would announce, 'Done it,' in a challenging tone.

He couldn't wait to get out again. The first day up was a taste of freedom. Debbie and Jayne drove him to town, where he discovered that being on crutches with a plaster cast on his foot was just the sort of physical challenge he couldn't resist.

He practised extending the reach of his crutches, taking longer swings, moving at walking pace, then faster and faster, urging the girls to get a move on. Back home, when he took a shower, he discovered how to keep his plaster dry: he would stand on one leg, in an arabesque, for as long as he could. Anything to fill an empty hour.

Jayne as usual took no notice of his demands and his moods. Far from being an annoyance, his frustration and his physical problems became a source of huge amusement for the two women. If Chris was awful, so were they. Everything he did became another cause of laughter.

And, because they knew it was so awful of them, they took to hiding their giggles, and that just made it worse. Chris for instance began to berate them for drinking wine. He was concentrating on getting fit again, and all they were doing was having a good time. He couldn't stand it.

'Oh, drinking again, are we?' he would say sarcastically when they brought out a bottle for supper. So they devised a silly ritual of coughing violently in the kitchen to disguise the noise of a cork popping, and then being convulsed with laughter for no reason that Chris could see.

Life became a round of little dramas, which were either incredibly funny or incredibly annoying, depending on who was the perpetrator and who the victim. Know-all Chris, who liked to drive with his plastered leg on the dashboard, insisted one day that they had enough petrol to get himself and Debbie to the gym and back, but ran out, forcing Debbie to walk off in search of a garage.

Another time, she and Chris arrived back to find Jayne had done the laundry – an occupation of which she was lamentably ignorant after a life spent in hotel rooms – put a red T-shirt in with the wash, and turned every item of clothing pink. Debbie banned Jayne from the washing machine after that.

After a while, we ordered a cleaner, whose arrival while Chris was at the gym suggested a way out of a small dilemma that had been bothering Jayne and Debbie. Could he take the sittingroom carpet and clean it? No problem. On his return, Chris was puzzled by the bare front room, but then quite pleased at the apparent onset, at last, of good sense. Then Frank came to visit again, and a chance remark – 'Oh, I see you got the stain out, then' – brought the story of the tomato ketchup and female duplicity to light.

All these minor domestic strains came to a head one wet Sunday afternoon when Chris was sitting in an armchair while the two girls were reading. He was restless, as usual, bored out of his brains by the videos, the games, the books. He started to fiddle and tap.

The girls caught each other's eye. They could feel the

tension building, but knew that if they acknowledged it there would be some idiotic demand for action. So they went on pretending to read, hearing these tense little noises, like an approaching storm.

Chris meanwhile had been struck by a thought.

'Watch this!' he said, grabbing his crutches and launching himself across the room.

The thought was this: I bet I could do a handstand against the wall on my crutches.

It seemed an intriguing and novel idea, just the sort of gymnastic challenge to enliven a dull hour. In silence, he had worked out exactly how to do it, the position of the crutches, the bit of wall he would choose, the spot his legs would come up to, the force needed to swing his plaster that high.

With his cry of 'Watch this!' he went for it, placed his crutches perfectly, jumped off his good leg, swung hard, and to the girls' astonishment stood upside down against the wall on his crutches.

For a second or so.

The one thing he hadn't reckoned on was the slipperiness of the polished wood floor. In slow motion, as Chris fought against the combined effects of polish and gravity, his crutches did the splits, sliding him down the wall and landing him on his head.

No one reacted for a moment.

It was Debbie who cracked first. 'I can't stand it!' she screamed. 'It's like living with a time bomb!'

'Oh, take no notice,' said Jayne. Then she sighed, got up, walked over, peered at the heap on the floor, and said, 'Are you OK?'

'Yup,' he said, without expression. Actually he'd scraped his back against the brick wall, and clouted his head on the floor, but he would never have admitted it even if he'd broken his neck, because he was so embarrassed.

'Right,' said Jayne, and walked back to her book, leaving Chris to pick himself up and return to his settee.

The craziest thing about this crazy time was that we had been asked to make a record. A couple of guys with a small studio wanted us to do a whole album. We were astonished, but if the producers thought they could make it work by capitalising on our celebrity status, we didn't mind. This was not going to be great music, but it could be fun. Never mind that Chris was certain he was tone-deaf — we had said yes. Now, with Chris eager for anything that might bridge the boredom gap, we had six weeks in which to fulfil our promise.

So the producer, Kevin Stanton, who worked from a studio in Sydney, said he'd make trips to Palm Beach to help choose songs — there were to be 14 in all — and to coach us. We knew little about recording, and even less about the way Kevin attracted bad luck.

First off, we had to fetch Kevin from Sydney, because he'd been banned from driving for being over the limit, and then he kept us at it six hours a day accompanying us on his guitar, because of course neither of us could sing much. _And_ we were providing Kevin with a bed sometimes, and feeding him.

Jayne, who began to find the process tedious beyond words, took to making excuses to get out of the room.

'Oh,' she would say, as Kevin was telling Chris to

223

la-la-la a particular phrase for the tenth time, 'I've just remembered. We're out of coffee.' And she'd disappear into Sydney for the afternoon. Or it would be, 'Oh, just a moment, there's something I have to do,' and vanish into her bedroom for a nap.

One evening, after an all-day session, we were sitting around chatting with Kevin and Debbie. Debbie said something about finding it hard to sit comfortably on floors.

'Oh, I used to do that all the time,' said Kevin, remembering his hippie days. 'It's fine if you can get into the lotus position. Can you do that?'

Jayne could easily, Debbie not at all.

'Like this,' said Kevin, rearranging himself. 'Just a bit stiff in the legs.' And he shoved a knee sideways. There was a nasty crack, a little whiplash noise. Kevin yelled, staggered to his feet and started limping round, going 'Ooh, Christ, aah!'

We are ashamed to report that Jayne and Debbie did not even ask him what had happened or if he was all right. He obviously wasn't, and at the sight of him the two became completely paralytic with laughter and had to go to their rooms and put their heads under pillows.

Five minutes later, they had recovered, but Kevin hadn't. Then we all began to feel very bad, because the knee was swelling up alarmingly.

Next day it was very painful and looked like a livid football. We made him go to Chris's doctor, the one who had diagnosed his problem and operated on his ligament. By a horrible coincidence, Kevin had done himself a similar injury — a torn ligament in his knee — and needed a similar operation.

By now we were only days from recording. Everything was booked. And after that we were off back to England. There could be no delay.

The whole thing was already like some sort of black comedy. Now it got worse. Kevin had a row with his partner, the engineer, and there was no one to run the studio. So when we turned up in Sydney for the first day of recording, the first task was for Chris and Debbie to open up the studio while Jayne was delegated to pick up Kevin from the hospital.

Kevin, still groggy with painkillers, had his whole leg in plaster and would need a wheelchair. Jayne packed the wheelchair into the car, and took both invalid and chair to the studio.

There, the two of us and Debbie set up the multi-track, answered phone calls, and made coffee, under Kevin's groggy guidance from the wheelchair, his leg stuck out in front of him so that he couldn't get anywhere or do anything except press the start-stop button, while we were doing voiceovers to the pre-recorded tracks.

We watched him in trepidation through the glass partition, seeing his eyelids drooping. 'No, sorry, that . . . wasn't quite . . . right . . . ' His voice was slurred as it came through the intercom. Then silence. He fell asleep, then woke with a jerk of his head.

'Can we . . . ?'

'Do it again? Yup.' We moved as fast as we knew how. This was our only chance, because we certainly weren't going to delay our flight in a week's time.

'Oh, sorry . . . got to stop . . . need the toilet.'

'Yup. No problem.' Chris would rush out, zoom him

to the loo, zoom him back again, and, 'OK. Let's go!'

Every day, for seven days we did this — 14 songs in seven days, which is fast going by anybody's standards. After a few hours' singing each day, our voices would begin to go. Kevin happened to remark that port was good for the voice. Right. Off went Debbie, returning with a couple of bottles of port, which may or may not have helped when we were singing, but it certainly did when we weren't.

One day, towards the end, we learned it was Kevin's birthday. We were sorry for him, sorry we had laughed at his injury, sorry he was having such difficulties, sorry no one else was giving him a party, especially when we learned that the operation had left him so short of cash he couldn't afford to fly his mother in from New Zealand.

So we bought him a cake. Jayne was carrying it into the studio when she tripped, dumping the spongy, creamy mass on to the carpet. We scraped it up, put it together, and gave it to him anyway. It was like the final proof that Kevin was Australia's unluckiest man.

The last day, it was a question of packing up the house, loading the car, rushing to the studio, recording the final song, snatching goodbyes, and dashing straight to the airport, leaving Kevin to finish production.

The record came out, actually. We never knew how many it sold, and it certainly never made it to England. We weren't surprised. Chris always knew he couldn't sing.

Meanwhile, the serious work had started: the preparation

for the American tour, which was now due to extend into Britain.

The ankle had mended. When the plaster came off, just before the saga of Kevin's knee, it revealed a leg wasted by lack of use, but from Chris's first hobbling steps on a local rink at Narrabeen, the muscles began to rebuild.

There had, of course, been ample time to listen to music. Because we wanted to develop new ideas, we had chosen several new pieces to rehearse for America: two Beatles' songs, _Revolution_ and _Imagine_; a three-part Irish medley; and _Arc of the Bell_, a modern piece by the Estonian composer Arvo Part. These were to be rehearsed in Oberstdorf through the summer, before we opened with the reconvened All Stars in America.

Of these, the most ambitious was _Revolution_. Its inspiration was a Montreal dance group we had seen in Sydney with the odd name of La La La Human Steps, whose rapid, machine-gun, staccato movements were unlike anything we had seen before.

Chris thought the technique might be adapted for the ice, if we replaced the dancers' lifts and throws with quick-fire upper-body movements. He had been listening to a lot of Lennon-McCartney songs while his ankle healed, and responded to the starkness, the force and the aggressive qualities of _Revolution_.

Of course, the Lennon-McCartney piece was more about political change, but it might equally well apply to a man-woman relationship over-strained by tension, collapsing into aggression. The theme was not based on any personal experience but on something that seemed to be part of life for so many of our friends, almost part of the air we breathed in the 1980s. It was long, fast and very testing, not only of our abilities as dancers, but also as actors, in particular for Jayne, who had to go completely against character, with vicious movements and displays of anger. That was new, not only for her. Nobody to our knowledge had done anything like this on ice before.

So, after the longest break in our professional life and another two months of choreographing and rehearsal, we were back into the fray, which is about what it feels like touring the US. We were opening in Sacramento in September 1989, but had to stopover in New York for several publicity dates. Publicity, the bane of our lives, we had long recognised as a necessary evil, but this diversion was worse than usual, not because of the publicity itself but because of the stress of New York.

Our driver was one those people who have no idea where they're going, but won't admit it. After five presscalls in different parts of the city, we were running late for our flight.

'No problem, folks. I'll get you there.'

No way! Manhattan was jammed, gridlocked. At Lexington and 57th, our limo driver diced for a break in the creeping cross-traffic with a yellow cab, inch by inch, until finally the cars touched, unleashing warfare, New York style.

The cab driver leaped out, ranting and raving and bashing our windscreen. Our driver attacked him, then smashed the cab's side window, with us cringing in the back, hoping neither of them had a gun.

Sirens wailed up Lexington – a police car, thank God. But not for us. It crept right past, ignoring the two drivers, now throwing kung-fu blows at each other. A

228

traffic warden broke the two apart, got them to park the cars on the sidewalk, and had them exchange insurance details, while we sat shaking in a nearby coffee-shop.

It turned out our flight was delayed anyway. Several lives had been shortened by stress, for nothing.

In Sacramento, we had the first intimation that this tour was not going to go well. The whole company were presented with expensive leather-and-suede tour jackets. But beyond that, not much.

In venue after venue, there were no newspaper or TV ads that we saw. Very few knew we were coming. Once we booked into a hotel, a whole skating company, and they wanted to know who we were. This was not a resurrection, we decided, but a burial — with serious consequences. Audience figures were down, so eventually it was put to us by the Edgley people, backed by Michael Linnitt, that the only way to continue the tour was for us to cut our fee in half. Not the Russians, just us.

That really depressed us. But in the end we saw that we could hardly expect Tatiana's company to take a pay cut, because their very futures were at stake. So we agreed.

In the end, we gained valuable experience. For the first time, we played to small audiences. It's hard to keep your morale up in those circumstances, but we learned — we learned that you do it as well as you can, not just for the thousands, but for the hundreds. We think that now we would do it for the dozens if we had to, and believe we could do it with no loss of commitment and quality.

It paid off, in an unexpected way. Anna Kisselgoff gave us another wonderful restorative review. Not long before this, we had had our wages cut because we weren't pulling in the audiences, so it was a real delight to read Kisselgoff's words: 'No one interested in dancing, skating, theater, sports, film or glasnost should miss this richly filled study in contrasting styles . . . Mr Dean constantly strikes out in new directions.'

She liked *Akhnaton*, and called the Astaire and Rogers number a stunning masterpiece, '. . . capturing their spirit without any literal imitation and enriched in its variety of invention by the radiant dimension that Torvill and Dean's own elegance contributes.'

There was praise for Tatiana, the Russian All Stars, and Andris. You just couldn't have asked for more.

But the review came too late to forestall another, longer-term effect of the poor showing. There had been a decision to go ahead with the British leg of the tour. The ice-floor was already on its way from Australia and we were into the last week of the US tour when Michael Linnitt pulled out of the British leg. Apparently, according to Wayne Stevens, the Edgley company manager, he had decided it wasn't worth the risk, leaving Edgley's to carry the financial burden on their own, if the tour was to go ahead.

And it *had* to go ahead if the immense cost of setting up the tour − booking venues, shipping the ice-floor, prearranging publicity − was to be recouped. The problem was solved when Edgley's approached the British promoter Phil McIntyre, who came in as co-producer.

Tatiana had problems of her own. On departure from the US, five of her company, on their way to Moscow for a break, were not at the airport. They never did show up, because they had defected. This was a big embarrassment for Tatiana, with additional trouble hard on its heels.

In Moscow, when the company were leaving to come to England, she discovered that two of the company were trying to smuggle dollars out. She fired them on the spot. That left a big hole in the company, to be filled by seven replacements before we reopened.

For all its 14-week British run, opening in Glasgow and ending in Belfast in September 1990, the show worked well — so well that Edgley's came up with another offer. There was a new entertainment centre opening in Adelaide. How would we like to come over for short season? A group from the Ukraine had already been contracted. All we had to do, apparently, was two numbers as special guests. Just a quickie: six weeks, that was all, without the commitment of heading the bill or running anything ourselves.

It sounded good. We said yes.

Through all this however — from the rehearsals in Oberstdorf the previous summer right through the American and British tours — dramas of an entirely different, much more personal nature had been brewing.

9

Tales of love and pain

Chris

For several years, since 1987, the pattern of my life had acquired another strand: Isabelle Duchesnay. She and her brother Paul had become familiar figures in Oberstdorf since we first met them in 1981. I had been attracted to her. But Isabelle was only 18, and nothing developed between us. Jayne and I watched their career from a distance, as they progressed up in Canada, failed in their attempt to break through internationally, and finally decided to make use of their dual French-Canadian nationality to compete for France.

In 1987, Betty, who was still teaching in Oberstdorf,

gave me a call.

'Do you think you might be willing to help Paul and Isabelle by choreographing for them?'

It made sense for both them and me, because they had nothing to lose by trying something new, and there was a piece I was keen to choreograph, *Savage Rite*, almost all African drums, by a little-known band called Mandingo. In my imagination, I saw two people lost in the jungle. I thought it would suit Paul and Isabelle. I could never see them as a romantic couple, but in this they could play themselves, brother and sister.

When we started to work together, I think that they, as amateurs, were as surprised by me as I had been by Graeme when I first turned professional. It took two days to work out 'Jungle,' as we called it. The first day, Paul hurt his back, so a good deal of it I did directly with Isabelle, building in the intensity I wanted, waiting, watching, exploding into action, hiding, surviving.

When Paul and Isabelle danced 'Jungle,' they were brother and sister. When Isabelle and I worked together, it was very different. The attraction I had felt when we first met returned – and strengthened.

Professionally, the new choreography worked for them. Early in 1988, they won a bronze at the European championships in Prague, and came eighth in the Olympics in Canada a few weeks later, with an explosion of publicity, partly because of their dancing, partly because there was a feeling in the press that they should have won a medal and the judges had penalised them – and by implication me – for being 'too innovative' with 'Jungle.'

I was happy for their success, sorry they hadn't made

Jayne, aged 3, on holiday in Cornwall, 1961.

Chris, aged 4, with his mother and Aunt Madge, 1962.

Milford Junior School, 1965 (Jayne is second from the right in the second row).

And another holiday for Jayne, now aged 6, in Mablethorpe, 1964.

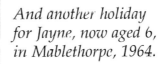

The Nottingham Ice Rink Christmas Show, 1967 (Jayne is second from the left).

Jayne with her parents, 1988. (Auckland Star).

Receiving the Bronze Rose of Montreux - the Palme D'or - for Fire and Ice, *1986.* (LWT)

In Oberstdorf once more - and pictured here with Betty Torvill and Betty Dean, 1985.

Meeting Queen Elizabeth II at the Nottingham Council House, 1984, (Nottingham Newspaper Group).

Performing Fire and Ice *for the LWT Christmas special 1986 with Shaun McGill.* (LWT)

Performing with the Ice Capades in 1987 (Jayne and Chris are centre). (J. W. Reilly).

Performing Hat Trick *in Germany, 1991.*
(Hans Rauchensteiner).

Performing Tilt, *originally choreographed for the BBC* Omnibus
documentary, at a German Exhibition Gala in 1992. (Sven Simon).

Chris's broken wrist, which forced us to cancel the remaining part of our world tour in December, 1986.

During the Ice Capades Tom Cruise came backstage to meet the skaters. He is pictured here with Chris and the mother of one of the other skaters - unfortunately Jayne was manoevered out of sight!

Back in Moscow in 1988 - Chris and Jayne with Andris: not enjoying the boat trip.

Rehearsals with the Russian All Stars in Moscow, 1987 - (from left to right) Yuri Ovchinikov, Chris, Tatiana Tarasova, Jayne.

With the Russian All Stars, on tour in New Zealand, 1987.

A worried looking Jayne and Chris, sorting out glitches while touring with the Russian All Stars, 1987.

Jayne and Chris, 1990.
(Mark Bourdillon).

it this time, certain they could go further.

They approached me again. Time was tight — this was the summer of 1988, when we were also preparing to open with the All Stars in Moscow — and I passed on to them a number Jayne and I had been dancing, _Eleanor's Dream_. Again, the relationship between the boy and girl, with the boy breaking in upon the girl's dreams, did not have to be romantic.

They had further success: early in 1989, they were bronze medallists in both the Europeans and the Worlds.

Onwards and upwards. In the summer of 1989, just after I had recovered from tearing my ankle ligament in Australia, Jayne and I taught them a version of _Missing_. And again, through the 1989–90 season, they were medallists in the Europeans and the Worlds, which I attended after the All Stars' US tour as a guest commentator for the BBC.

By now, Isabelle and I were romantically involved. It was an odd sort of affair, though, because we were apart most of the time. Besides, both Michael Edgley and Michael Linnitt were keen that Jayne and I do nothing to damage our public image, and since Isabelle and Paul were becoming stars in France, we were all wary of the reaction if the press got hold of the story.

We kept it as quiet as we could.

Jayne

Equally quietly, my life had changed, for similar reasons. When we opened the All Stars tour in Sacramento, the company effectively divided into two, Russian-speakers and English-speakers. All the skaters except us were Russians; all the technicians and business people were American, English or Australian.

So naturally we all hung out together. Among them was a quiet, rather good-looking American – a *quiet* American! That was a relief.

His name was Phil Christensen, and as time went on, as interest grew into mutual attraction, I became increasingly curious about him. He had been asked to look after the sound by his production company because the original engineer had gone sick. It wasn't a job he wanted, because he didn't think much of ice skating. His background was rock-and-roll. He had started as a guitarist, but he had had the sense to move into production early on, most recently for Phil Collins.

A few weeks later, after we had played some 35 different towns, he had to leave to prepare for a Phil Collins tour. By then, we were much more than just friends. It was a wonderful time, but not easy, because we were constrained by the need for discretion, not to say secrecy.

Our closest friends knew what was going on, but the managers were keen to keep wraps on the story, so that

236

nothing disturbed the Torvill and Dean romantic image through the tour.

You can imagine that when 20 or 30 attractive, fit young people are thrown together for several months, a glance is enough to set the company buzzing, and then pretty soon the press are on to it.

Actually, discretion suited us. We were not children, so neither of us dared dream of anything long-term yet. All we knew was that we had to see each other again.

At the end of the US leg of the tour, we spent Christmas together in his house in Dallas, while Chris was finalising routines with Paul and Isabelle.

In January, I came back to stay with my parents before the English leg of the tour, while Phil was in Bray, west of London, in rehearsal with Phil Collins. We planned a few days together. I would drive to London in the morning, drop off some things in London, in my house – I had bought it a couple of years before but scarcely had a chance to move into it then go on to Bray.

A simple plan, but it turned into a real adventure, quite a weird experience, like a bad dream in which I was struggling to get to Phil and not getting anywhere.

To the south, unknown to me, gales were brewing. The car, a little Mercedes, was low-profile, so I didn't notice the wind until I saw a lorry on its side a few miles out of London. Then I saw another, realised I might be driving into trouble, switched on the radio, and heard about the gale.

London was jammed, because of roads blocked by fallen trees, I suppose, and I found myself lost. I had no map with me, and knew only my regular routes across London. A sign

237

said 'Barnet,' which I knew was north somewhere. I had to be going the wrong way, back out of London.

Eventually, in despair, I pulled up, and got out into the battering wind, intending to ask my way. Suddenly, I saw a cab, and had an idea. I hailed it.

'I'm lost,' I said to the driver. 'Can you take me to Knightsbridge, if I leave my car here?'

'No, don't do that,' he said. 'Why don't you follow me?'

'Oh, OK.'

'But I can't get you all the way to Knightsbridge. Hyde Park's blocked. I'll get you as far as I can.'

We had reached King's Cross when traffic stopped us, in gathering darkness. He got out of his cab and strolled back to me.

'If I were you,' he said, 'I'd get a hotel. You're not going anywhere this afternoon, and everything's going to be full later.'

I paid him, parked at a meter, and tried the station hotel, but it was already full, because all the trains had been cancelled. So I set off down a side road to find a bed-and-breakfast.

At the first place the door was opened by a man. I was about to ask for a room, when I saw to my horror, because it just seemed so weird, that he had a false arm which ended in a hook. It was like something from *The Twilight Zone*, a bizarre twist to a day that had been like a surrealist dream for hours.

I wasn't going to stay there, but I couldn't on the spur of the moment think of a good excuse for knocking at the door. I stammered, 'I'm looking for . . . um . . . Baker

Street.' It was the first street I could think of that was anywhere near. He gave me instructions, waving his hook westwards, and I hurried off.

I came to another hotel, a small and seedy one. They had a room, for cash, in advance. But there was no phone in the room. Downstairs, I called Mum, to say I was all right, and Phil, who told me I had better stay where I was and come the next day.

I couldn't bear it: the horrible journey, the delay, the strange apparition with the hook, and now the prospect of separation, even if it was just one night. Depressed, I switched on the news. Apparently, the gale was dying away, and central London was clear again.

I decided to set off. Better to be in my own place, if I could make it. I picked up my bag, didn't bother to get my money back, just fled to my car.

I got through to the house, parked, unloaded, and carted things in, only to find the gas had blown out. It was miserably cold, and the house didn't have much furniture, and I was hungry. I thought: 'Blow this, I'm off' – and called Phil, who told me to drive carefully.

I finally reached him later that evening, exhausted, but happy again after one of the strangest days of my life.

After the rehearsals, Phil's tour began in Japan, and I spent 10 days with Phil there, meeting his family in Chicago on the way out. Then, while he went on to Australia, I came back to open the UK leg of the All Stars in Glasgow, where he joined me on April 10. I met him at Glasgow Airport, and that evening we went off to an Italian restaurant.

I wasn't even thinking of the future, so it was a

complete surprise when he pulled a ring out of his pocket and proposed. I was amazed and touched, because I didn't expect a proposal from him right then, certainly not such a formal one.

Apparently on his way back from Australia, he had asked the expert advice of his father, had gone to a jeweller's in Chicago, and bought the ring after much deliberation. He had flown to England with the ring burning a hole in his pocket, checking it nervously every few minutes.

Of course, I wanted to tell the world, but couldn't, not yet. So I didn't wear the ring except in private and told only my family and Chris. He congratulated me, but not all that warmly, because he was as protective of me as I was of him, and he was wondering if Phil was really right for me.

It was only a few weeks later in London, towards the end of the run in Earl's Court, that the story broke. Phil was off to join Phil Collins in Spain. (The 'two Phils' connection was confusing, and we wondered later if journalists thought I was having an affair with Phil Collins.) We were going to be apart for some time, so I wanted to see him off.

'Be careful,' Chris warned us, when we told him we were going to the airport together.

'Oh,' I said, with a shrug. 'I don't think anyone's going to bother with us.'

'Yeah, how could anyone know we're going?' added Phil, who had not yet had much experience of being hounded by the press.

But they did know. At Heathrow, a couple of photographers and a journalist spotted me. Away went any hopes of a quiet, fond goodbye. Suddenly, we found ourselves playing a farcical game.

'Quick. Split up,' I said, so they could only photograph us separately. But they were on Phil's scent. Just before he went through security, one of them asked him who he was.

'I'm her cousin.'

'Oh, right.' Heavy sarcasm. 'Then you won't mind giving your name.'

'Er, Fred Smith.'

'Oh, sure. And where are you from, _Fred_?'

Phil was obviously American, but he didn't want to say so. Since he was on his way to Spain, in desperation he said 'From Barcelona,' and pushed his way on through security.

One paper published Phil's picture next morning, with the caption: 'Who is this "Fred Smith from Barcelona"?' followed by a toll-free number. Luckily, none of our group or Phil Collins's people split on him, so the story died. (The memory lived on, though. After we were married, and moved to the country in 1992, we got a dog whom we named Fred. He's from somewhere in Sussex, not Barcelona.)

It was obviously ridiculous to go on playing this game, whatever the management said. So in Whitley Bay, near Newcastle-upon-Tyne, a month or so later, I made the announcement. Phil was in Germany, and Whitley Bay was the most out-of-the-way venue we had, so it seemed the best time and place to avoid publicity.

There was still quite a storm of press interest, which surprised me as usual because I couldn't see what all the fuss was about. But I was more used to it than Phil. After seeing one headline – something like 'Phil Collins's sound engineer to marry millionaire ice queen' – he called me up, quite spooked by it all, and asked, 'Are you?'

'Am I what?'

'A millionaire?'

'I don't know,' I said.

Actually, as he discovered, the press had it completely wrong. In fact, it was very hard for us to make real money – rock-star, film-star money – because we don't produce anything that can be copied and sold, like a film or a book or a record. It's all in the performance, ephemeral. We didn't even have control over the videos we had made.

I knew that we had a good income, but I was very vague on details, as Chris was. All our accounts, all the company bills and expenses, and all our personal expenses as well, used to go through Michael Linnitt's agency.

We had everything we needed to live: house and car at home, clothes and skating equipment on tour, something in the bank. Since we were on tour most of the time, we didn't buy much, because it all had to be packed and unpacked, sometimes every day. The less we had to worry about the better. I'd had enough such worries while I was administering the Nottingham Council grant, so I was glad to be free of it all, free to concentrate on skating.

Through all this I never really suspected that Chris was getting serious about Isabelle. He would go off to Germany now and then, but I didn't pry. Once, when we were in Birmingham, he said he'd invited a friend over.

'Oh, who's that then?'

'Isabelle.'

'Good. That's nice.'

I thought, I hope this isn't going to get serious. But of course I would never have said anything. If I had, I knew he would go off and do the opposite. My life was quite full enough without worrying about Chris and Isabelle.

Chris

Meanwhile, all through the English leg of the tour, I was seeing Isabelle whenever we could arrange it.

Jayne's engagement had been a bit of a shock. Actually it left me in a strange sort of emotional limbo. All these years we had been together as partners and friends, and suddenly, out of the blue, she was up and off with someone who wasn't from a skating background, whom I didn't have a chance to get to know.

I couldn't help wondering whether she was making a terrible mistake, so I probably seemed a bit cool to the whole idea.

But more than that, my whole future was up in the air. For a time, I really wondered if this was the beginning of the end. Phil was an American. He couldn't just come and work in England, even if he wanted to.

So where were they going to live? Dallas, where Phil's company was based? Chicago? If so, how could we possibly arrange to rehearse?

The old simplicity — just Jayne and me — was going. Already, any decisions concerning the two of us involved three people. And then, what if she had children? This wasn't a conversation I could have with her, because it was only a possibility, and probably she wouldn't know, and anyway it was her life, not mine.

But it *was* my life, as well. Perhaps she would want to give up skating completely. Without her, what would I be?

Again, I could see a professional void before me, as I had after I'd broken my wrist. This time, though, the void somehow seemed bridgeable, if I had a secure future with Isabelle.

All these thoughts slipped into my mind whenever there was a gap in our frantic All Stars schedule. I invited Isabelle to Birmingham from Oberstdorf, where she was rehearsing. Then, in Manchester, I was with her again, developing a new idea with her and Paul, something that seemed to me an interesting way of exploiting them as brother and sister.

Since they look so similar, almost like twins, I took this to an extreme, turning them into asexual beings, two versions of the same persona, dressed in identical black trousers, with identical slicked-back hair. They were to be one person, dancing with his/her reflection in a mirror, probing and releasing inner turmoil, finally resolving it, bending away from each other in a dramatic arc. I called it *Reflections*.

Not long after, at the end of July, when we were with the All Stars in Brighton, I decided that this was the moment. I bought a ring, and booked a flight to Germany

244

for the weekend. No discussion with Jayne, or Debbie, or Tee. It was as if I was being driven by something I had no control over, didn't want to examine.

Debbie overheard me making the booking, and gave me a look. 'Not going to do anything silly are you?' she said.

'No,' I said, flatly.

So I just went and proposed. Isabelle said yes.

Jayne

Phil, Debbie and I were in the bar of the Grand Hotel in Brighton when he came back. He didn't say much. Had a nice time? we asked. Fine, he said. Then he ordered a bottle of champagne.

'Well, actually, I've got something to tell you.'

The three of us exchanged glances, and waited in anticipation. As he poured the champagne, I still had no idea what he was going to say.

'I've got engaged,' he said.

For a few very long seconds, there was a deafening silence.

'Who to?' I asked, hoping against hope.

'Isabelle.'

'Oh, Chris!' we all said. You could almost hear the hearts sinking. 'Congratulations! That's wonderful!'

Phil and I wanted to get married at the first opportunity,

as quietly as possible, though I didn't want to disappoint Mum and Dad, thinking they would want a traditional wedding. I needn't have worried. Mum was now very aware of media attention and was as shy of it as we were. Besides, she had just seen a TV programme about a couple who had married on a small tropical island, and it had struck her as a romantic gesture.

'You should just go off and enjoy it,' she said. 'Have some time to yourself.'

It was a lovely idea, but where? With all the media attention, there was no chance of a quiet wedding in England.

Our chance would come at the end of the UK tour, while Phil was with Phil Collins in Sacramento. It seemed like fate – this was where we met, and this was where we would marry. But there was just one day we could do it on, because the tour was going straight on to Los Angeles.

It had to be planned down to the hour. Towards the end of the All Stars tour, I flew over from Belfast, met Mum in London and spent all day choosing a dress, finally settling on a knee-length pink one from Versace, very simple with long sleeves. A week later, I flew to join Phil.

He had booked us into the Sacramento register office in the Town Hall, and until the night before we thought it was going to be just ourselves and a couple of guys from the Phil Collins tour as witnesses. But then, at the concert in the Arco Arena, Phil said, 'The crew have all asked if they're invited. What do you think?' So from four we jumped to 20.

That night, they were all given black shorts and black

T-shirts emblazoned with a Phil Collins tour logo. And that's what they all turned up in next day, September 21, 1990, as if they were in uniform.

I think they had already been celebrating, because when the registrar – a rather attractive lady – came into the little room with its tacky pink altar she got a raucous reception. It was the greatest fun.

Afterwards, back at the hotel, everyone who couldn't be there – Chris, Debbie, Phil's family, my family – were all calling, and had all sent flowers and wedding cakes. We had five of them, and enough champagne to float us to LA.

That evening, we flew to LA, and the very next day, believe it or not, I had to fly to Oberstdorf.

Jayne and Chris

By now, in the autumn of 1990, we had several things to prepare for. The BBC's _Omnibus_ team were making a documentary about our choreography, for which they had commissioned new music and a new dance. Chris had already started work on the music with the young, up-and-coming jazz composer, Andy Sheppard. Now he was ready to start on the steps.

We had also agreed to do two numbers in the Dick Button World Professional Championships in Washington again just before Christmas. Beyond that, Dick Button had expanded his operations internationally, and had persuaded us to dance two further numbers in his World Team Championship, to be held in Barcelona immediately after the Washington show.

And Chris was again choreographing for Paul and Isabelle, who had set their sights on the World championships three months afterwards, in March, 1991.

So in the space of six weeks, we had to devise and rehearse five numbers on our own, with Chris devising and rehearsing two more pieces for Paul and Isabelle.

At the best of times, this would have been more than flesh and blood could stand, even with Andris there to help. Added to this was the fact that Chris had just got engaged, plus the fact that Jayne and Isabelle were finding each other increasingly hard to take, plus the fact that Jayne had just got married, and had had to abandon her husband after two days of marriage. It all added up to a recipe for catastrophe.

Jayne

I arrived in Oberstdorf in shock, first from getting married, second from the sudden amputation from my new husband, even if it was by choice. To cap it all, I couldn't relate to the stark, modern music that had been commissioned by the *Omnibus* people. To be frank, I couldn't understand Chris's ideas for the music, couldn't understand what he was trying to get me to do.

There seemed no way out, though. He was under such pressure that he couldn't accept any delays, alterations or criticisms. And of course, there was less chance to talk to him off the rink, because he was with Isabelle. And it made me sick at heart that he was with the person he wanted to be with, and I wasn't.

'Chris, I can't do it. I don't understand.'

'Yes, you can do it. Just _do_ it.'

But I couldn't. After a few days, I broke down in the middle of rehearsal, walked off the ice, and sat on a seat, in tears.

Andris knew this was not like me at all. He came up to me and said in his soft, understanding voice, 'Now, darling, what's all this about?'

It all came out in a rush. 'I've just got married to this really nice man, and I'm dancing to music I can't stand, and I'm never going to be able to do it, and _this is driving me crazy!!_'

Chris had joined us by this time.

He sighed. 'What do you want to do then?'

'I want to go home,' I said through my tears. Home in London would be a haven, because Phil was due in shortly, having completed his arrangements to move.

I must say that then, Chris was very understanding. 'If that's what you want,' he said, at last. 'You must go.'

He booked flights, and took me to the airport next day for a two-week break.

Jayne and Chris

We had to find a way forward, and of course we did. Jayne returned to Oberstdorf, reassured by her stay with Phil. We delayed *Omnibus*, with the BBC's agreement, and for the Dick Button shows we decided to do three existing pieces and work out only one new one – *Oscar Tango*.

But there was no way to resolve the emotional tangles that caught us all. Chris was trapped between Isabelle and Jayne. Isabelle couldn't understand why Chris had to spend so much time with Jayne. Off the ice, Jayne was on her own, excluded from Chris and Isabelle's company, missing Phil. Even when Phil came to Oberstdorf, it didn't work out for long. Because we were training most of the day and the town was dead, he almost died of boredom.

'Why do you *have* to be here?' he wanted to know. 'They have ice in London, don't they? Ice is ice, isn't it?'

And that rattled Chris, because perhaps Jayne would want to give up skating to be with Phil, which would certainly have made Phil happy at that point. A very fraught time.

Well, we came through, winning both of the Dick Button Professional Championships. *Oscar Tango* proved strong enough to justify our decision to do only one piece. And winning this, our first competition after six years of absence, was proof that we could still compete on the world stage, that we could, almost certainly, be current in both amateur and professional worlds at the same time.

250

Now, though, Chris chose to focus on the new direction his life had taken, with Isabelle.

Chris

After a Christmas spent with Isabelle's family in Canada, _Reflections_ was much admired at the European championships in Sofia, Bulgaria, but not admired enough by the judges to win. They placed it second, and we were told in no uncertain terms that there was no hope of winning the 1991 Worlds less than two months later with it. 'Too contemporary,' was the message. 'Don't be too avant garde!'

We had six weeks to come up with a solution.

The solution I chose was imposed by the pressure of time, but it also turned out to be an original idea. I proposed a sequel to _Missing_, which Jayne and I had taught them the previous year. No one had ever done a sequel, but it made sense.

We had the music, the costumes, a basis for the movements. Enough people, and enough judges, would have seen _Missing_ not to feel threatened by it. Any originality could be contained within a safe context.

And it worked. In March 1991, Paul and Isabelle became world champions.

Of course, they were ecstatic, and the win gave me a joy I had never experienced before, that of seeing one's

251

own creation performed with passion and energy, and then appreciated by both audience and judges.

It was an odd experience, though. Again, I was commentating for the BBC, but could hardly comment in detail on my own choreography. And the Duchesnays were surrounded by a sort of court – their official coach, Martin Scotnicki, his wife who acted as an adviser, a ballet master, an agent.

So just at the moment of glory I was assailed by two conflicting emotions: happiness at success, sadness at feeling an outsider.

Jayne and Chris

Now we still had to come to grips with the *Omnibus* piece. To be close to home – on Jayne's insistence and for the sake of the BBC – we would rehearse in north London, in Alexandra Palace, the huge glass-roofed Victorian pile which crowns Muswell Hill.

The BBC would provide the scenery, planning for a six-week rehearsal period and a two-day shoot.

Living so near home, relieved of the tensions that had tormented her in Oberstdorf, Jayne found she was now receptive to music and choreography that she had found so difficult before.

Even so, it seemed the project was doomed. On the very first day of rehearsal, we were practising a jump.

'Jump into me!' Chris ordered.

'Are you sure? You really want me to jump?' Jayne was nervous, remembering his back injury in Australia.

'Yes! Jump!'

So she did. And his back went again.

We had seen enough of the filming so far to know that this was something we really, really wanted to do. It would give our choreography a cachet, helping to establish ice-dancing as an art-form. And _Tilt_ itself, a demanding, original piece, would become an important element in the body of our work. We couldn't conceive of postponing yet again.

So to save Chris the agony of hours of driving every day, the BBC hired a van, in which he lay flat, commuting morning and evening, for all the six weeks of rehearsal.

After that, Chris turned his attention once again to Isabelle.

Chris

We planned to marry in May, 1991, after a long separation – while Jayne and I had been working on the _Omnibus_ film, Paul and Isabelle had been on the traditional post-Worlds tour.

Isabelle's family was very well known in Aylmer, Quebec, as I knew from my stay the previous Christmas. Her mother ran the kindergarten, her father was a retired businessman, and Paul and Isabelle were like royalty locally, especially now, as world champions, with an Olympics in France coming up.

Their experiences – the competitions, the media atten-tion, the pressures – rivalled mine and Jayne's in 1984, with one major difference: Paul and Isabelle had profes-sional advice, and some extremely powerful commercial interests behind them, in particular one of France's biggest corporations, Bouygue, a construction company linked to dozens of other companies, with a turnover in the billions and corporate jets on tap.

So there was huge interest in the wedding, as I discovered with growing horror when I arrived, four days before the ceremony, right in the midst of negotiations with *Paris Match* and one of the French TV channels. This was Isabelle's territory and Isabelle's wedding, with a flowing white dress given by a French haute couture house, Nina Ricci. I was just the bridegroom, with very little influence on events. Only once did I put my foot down when I said, 'No cameras in the church!' but no one took any notice.

Aylmer is an old town of brick and clapboard houses that runs along the Ottawa River, with a view across to Ontario and, in the distance, to Ottawa itself.

There is a small Catholic church, St Paul's, where the wedding was held, a lavish affair, with 270 guests for the service and the reception. Among them, somewhere, were some from England – Jayne, Phil, my mother, Betty Callaway, Debbie, a few other friends – but they were almost lost among the other guests.

I had never felt so exposed, yet also strangely removed.

When we walked out of the church, past the peering cameras, the street was packed with thousands of people.

It took minutes for the Rolls to force a way through to the reception in the hotel, its foyer full of pictures of Isabelle and Paul. Press reports described me as Isabelle's choreographer, as if she was marrying her hairdresser.

In the church, an orchestra had played the music from _Missing_, with which Isabelle and Paul had achieved their first great international successes. I was there in body, but in spirit I felt that I was the one who was missing.

You would think that as skaters, knowing each other for so long, working together as we had, we would start off on the right foot. Not at all. Right from the first, within days of the marriage, we were living in two different universes labelled 'his' and 'hers.'

For Isabelle, this was to be the beginning of a new life, in that I would be beside her as husband and choreographer. She and Paul were beginning the gruelling schedule that would take them through the 1991–2 round of championships: French nationals, Europeans, Olympics and Worlds, with me (she imagined) firmly on board as a vital emotional and creative support in the ascent to the Olympic gold.

But it was not like that for me. Jayne and I still had a professional life together, and it never occurred to me to set that aside. Trying to combine the two worlds landed me with a horrendous set of practical and emotional demands.

Soon we were back in Alexandra Palace. That was where Jayne wanted to be, near Phil. Since we had our own work preparing for the Australian trip, that was where I had to be as well. And so, of course, that was where Paul and Isabelle had to be, to work with me on their preparations for the 1992 Olympics.

The circumstances were not ideal. Paul, Isabelle and I, living together in my house near Henley, were two hours' drive away from a less-than-full-size rink that was available for only four hours a day — four hours that had to be divided between work with Paul and Isabelle and work with Jayne.

As usual, I wanted to involve Jayne, and found myself trapped by the growing antagonism between Jayne and Isabelle.

If I choreographed with Jayne, that annoyed Isabelle. If I tried to demonstrate something on my own, Isabelle would often say, 'I don't like that!' If I had asked Jayne to demonstrate the move, it would have sparked a row.

Even so, I was spending too much time and energy and consideration on Jayne, as Isabelle made blindingly clear in one outburst. Why was I so pro-Jayne, so anti-Isabelle? Why couldn't I be more this, that and the other? If I told Jayne that I could choreograph without her, she would give a hard little 'Hm' of disdain. I could see no solution. Both women seemed spring-loaded with resentment, ready to fire off at me.

For the sake of peace, I simply abandoned some new moves with Paul and Isabelle rather than fight my way through the emotional tangle (opting, of course, for old moves that drew a cutting 'That's *our* move' from Jayne). Sometimes, I just wanted to go into some quiet room, and shut the door until the problems had gone away.

Then, in July, I was off to Australia with Jayne to join the Edgley people for nine weeks, leaving Isabelle and Paul to continue their training in Oberstdorf. Given Isabelle's character, to leave her two months after the wedding was not a wise thing to do. But given *my* character, any other action would have been unthinkable.

I *had* to fulfil my contract, could never have conceived of changing plans made with Jayne, Michael Linnitt and Edgley's.

Jayne and Chris

It was to have been a simple little tour, a couple of numbers fitting in with the Ukrainian company brought over by Edgley's. As we understood it, we would just be guest stars to add some lustre to the show.

We began to wonder how much lustre we would add when it was put to us — again — that we were no longer popular enough to justify our agreed fee and agreed percentage cut. Would we drop our profit share from 15 to 10 per cent? Oh, and to help cut costs, would we fly Jugoslav Airlines rather than Qantas or BA?

We weren't happy, and didn't agree at once. But since we were 'only' guests, we did insist that we would do only three numbers. That caused a bit of a stir, probably (we realised later) because we had already been billed as something more than guests. Wayne Stevens, Edgley's

257

company manager, called to tell us how important we were to the show.

'But your name is on the poster! People are coming to see you! If you only do three numbers, people will complain and you'll suffer.'

But if we were so important, how come they were dropping our percentage?

'What? Where did you get that idea?'

We never fully understood the details, but we kept our 15 per cent.

A good job too, because when we arrived, we found, to our horror, that the show was plastered all over Sydney as 'The Very Best of Torvill and Dean,' on a glitzy, circus-style poster, a slapped-together mishmash with feathered showgirls who weren't even wearing skates.

Of course we had not been shown it. If we had seen it, the design of the poster would have been a minor worry. Our biggest concern was that the show was billed as ours – Ukrainian folk dances and circus-turns! – when we had no idea what was in the show or what the standard was.

In the end, there was nothing to be done. We allowed ourselves to be persuaded into doing four numbers, intermixing with the circus acts and folk dances.

It ran in Sydney, Adelaide and Melbourne for six weeks, and did well, with the result that Edgley's suggested a UK leg.

No way, we said, not if the show carried our name. But if it wasn't our show – no disrespect to the Ukrainians – it wouldn't have enough appeal to be worthwhile. There's just so much Ukrainian folk dancing on ice that a British audience could take.

We said the only way to make it work for us, and probably for the audience, would be to make it *completely* our show. That would mean new numbers, weeks of rehearsal, new costumes, expense, expense, expense. But it was the only way.

To their credit, Edgley's agreed, and scheduled rehearsals in Kiev.

Throughout this year, Phil had been coming to terms with the huge step he had made in marrying Jayne. In between touring in his own business, he had moved countries, acquired a British work permit, and then started to remake his career in England. For someone at his level of expertise and achievement, this was not so easy. On top of that, Jayne kept on disappearing, for reasons that he could not fully understand.

For many months, he would have been quite happy if Jayne decided to give it all up and focus on him and the marriage. He was thinking, It would be nice when I come home if you were there — be nice to actually see my wife once in a while.

But as he understood Jayne better and saw more of the strange business he had married into, he also saw that Jayne would not and should not be parted from skating. And increasingly, he also saw that there were ways she and Chris could be managing their lives better.

Slowly, over the course of the year, he saw what had to be done if the marriage was to work: if you can't beat 'em, join 'em.

It started after he moved to London with an odd feeling that something was missing. There was a good deal of mail, mostly fan mail for Jayne. But never any bills. No electricity, gas, phone, or rates. No brown envelopes.

Why not?

'Michael Linnitt's office does all that,' Jayne said.

'You mean they have your cheque book? And sign in your name?'

'Well, yes. Because I'm always away.'

That struck Phil as crazy. He had managed his own budgets for tours, and it was weird to find himself in a house and marriage without even having a sight of a phone bill.

So he arranged to take the household accounts back.

Then, on the Australian tour, Edgley's needed a sound engineer. Michael Linnitt suggested that Phil do it. It was a good idea, easy work for Phil, and it would mean spending that time with Jayne.

It turned out not so good, from his point of view, because he found it odd working in that role as husband of the star. And in a strange way, she was still not quite there. On tour, all she did was sleep and skate. If he was to be with her, he would have to find a way to work *with* her all the time, not *for* her occasionally.

After the tour, Phil asked to see all our accounts, and went through them with us. It's almost incredible to us now, but this was the first time we had actually seen the financial details of our own professional lives. He didn't have to tell us that we had been naïve. We could see that. But he did tell us, in no uncertain terms.

'I can't *believe* you guys!'

'Oh, you know . . .' one or other or both of us would say, embarrassed. 'We wanted to do the work

260

'. . . we didn't have the time . . . we just wanted to skate . . .'

Anyway, in the end, it was quite obvious that if we could only take responsibility for our own affairs, we would do much better. Michael Linnitt had been a father figure to us both in the early days, when we were kids straight out of our parents' homes. But in the past 10 years we had grown up.

Now we knew our business from the inside out: ice, skaters, dance, music, costumes. No one had more experience of making their own ice shows.

It was ridiculous of us not to complete the task, take control of our own business lives. We had the experience, the appeal and the power. And with Debbie now working full time as our PA, we had a good in-house organiser. It was just a question of seeing our way clearly, and taking action.

That took time, partly because we dreaded breaking with the man who had given us such a good start. Would it have been better to have made the break earlier? Perhaps we would have made better deals — but on the other hand perhaps there would have been no deals at all. Perhaps everything had been for the best. Perhaps if we had acted sooner — been greedier, if you like — we wouldn't have had the opportunities. Michael Edgley might have decided from the start that we weren't worth it. Perhaps there would have been no world tour, no All Stars tour. Perhaps it would all have been very different, and far less of a success.

In the end, after Phil had explained several sets of figures, and pointed out different ways of working with managers and agents, and Debbie had been handling our affairs for a while, we gathered our courage and went to see Michael Linnitt.

It was a painful meeting. We reminded him of his words right at the beginning – that if we were unhappy we should leave – and said we thought the time had come to move on.

He seemed disappointed. But in the end, what else was there to do but accept? He gave a sad shrug, and said goodbye.

With the Moscow experience behind us, we would not be spending much time in Kiev if we could help it. That would be up to the long-suffering Bob Murphy, whose unenviable task it would be to set up another local costume-making sweatshop, and Andris, who would be directing three new group numbers into which we would eventually fit – we hoped – with the minimum of trouble.

For the couple of weeks we were in the Ukraine – we went back and forth three times that summer – rehearsing in Kiev was considerably better than rehearsing in Moscow had been. True, it was a huge company – 60 people – and Andris, who bore the brunt of the rehearsal work, was driven to distraction by the length of his stay and the problems of working through an interpreter.

But rehearsing this group was a dream compared with the experience in Moscow, because there was no conflict over choreography; their artistic director was more business manager than choreographer.

And living was marginally easier. The end of Commu-nism had had an effect. Though the place seemed to be

262

run by black-marketeers and young mafiosi in designer suits and some things were very basic — at the rink, the ice was scraped by a man pushing a piece of tin — at least there were vegetables and fruit in the market, for those who could afford them. Even for those who couldn't, there seemed to be hope in the air.

We liked the company — those we got to know — and the show came into shape well.

Chris

Meanwhile, Isabelle was in Oberstdorf, angry and hurt at my absence. So it was partly my fault, as I was later made to feel, that because of the strain she was under she turned her foot over while walking, giving herself a hairline crack that forced her off the ice for several weeks.

Then, immediately after I returned, Isabelle, Paul and the whole family were struck down by tragedy. Her brother, Gaston, died of cancer. It was not unexpected — he had been ill at the wedding — but a devastating blow nevertheless, and an additional emotional burden.

After the funeral, there was nothing for it but to focus on their new numbers, locked away in Oberstdorf, behind schedule now, with just a few weeks to prepare for the French Nationals in November. They couldn't afford mistakes this time around, couldn't afford to be too avant garde, and couldn't afford either to be too conservative.

263

I had suggested *West Side Story*. It seemed the best way to capitalise on their power, with a twist added by choosing to focus not on the usual Tony-Maria love story, but on the story of Maria and her brother, who gets killed.

Now, something had shifted in the relationship between Isabelle and me. I was no longer the great teacher, she no longer the eager, compliant pupil. She was an international star in her own right, and I was her husband. She was fighting a new corner, and had no qualms about telling me if she didn't like a move, or saying 'I told you so,' when something wasn't working.

Besides, I didn't have the certainty I needed. In my new role, I could no longer say, 'Fine – don't do it then,' and walk away. Now it was 'OK – we'll try something else,' just to keep the peace, even if it meant doing something less challenging, less interesting.

Artistically, I felt I was being forced into compromise, not only by Isabelle. She and Paul were champions, and had to walk a fine line between originality and the conventions of amateur ice-dancing. Both of us were edgy and argumentative (even though Jayne was nowhere around) with poor Paul in the middle.

Then there were all the entourage to consider, and the demands of continuous publicity. Every day there was a row of some sort: between me and Isabelle, Paul and Isabelle, Martin and Isabelle. Too much time was spent massaging egos, calming, compromising, and not enough on skating. I felt beaten down.

In the end, we genuinely ran out of time. Isabelle's cracked foot had not mended quickly enough. At the last minute Paul and Isabelle had to withdraw both from the French Nationals and the Europeans. For Jayne and me, years before, to cancel an appearance at the Nationals would have been a setback. To miss the Europeans as well would have been the end. But Paul and Isabelle, as world champions could go to the Olympics anyway.

Then the tension really began to tell. They were competing for France and the Olympics were in France, in Albertville. Courting the media yet also suffering as its victims, they were caught up in a vicious circle of heightening expectation and increasing stress.

Isabelle, who had trouble sleeping anyway, became an insomniac. Then she got a cold that left her physically and psychologically drained. Every minute she wasn't skating, she was in bed, resting.

Looking back, I understand. I had endured similar pressures, and sometimes I had cracked, in my own way. This was Isabelle's way of cracking. There were rows, shouting matches, blame, stress, stress, stress.

At the Olympics, I was commentating again. I realised well before the end that they couldn't win, when they were lying third at the end of the OSP. They did well to win the silver, behind Tatiana's couple Klimova and Ponomorenko, but when you're aiming to be the best, being second-best is no substitute.

When I saw Isabelle immediately afterwards, she was in a photo session with _Paris Match_. She seemed a shell of her former self, incapable of reaction. In a sense this was understandable. The stress and the workload had been enough to drain anyone.

But there was something else as well. She had never

really seemed to enjoy the fight, or take it on as truly *her* struggle. Now that it was over she did not want to see the failure to win gold as her responsibility. Everyone else had somehow let her down. It was as if the sport had been her enemy, and we had not fought hard enough in her defence.

So we parted again, she to do the post-Olympics tour organised by Tom Collins, me to the Ukraine and then to Davos, Switzerland, with Jayne.

Jayne and Chris

While we were still rehearsing for the Ukrainian tour, in June, 1992, we were asked to fly to Davos to celebrate the 100th anniversary of the International Skating Union. It promised to be a grand occasion with a specially commissioned film about the history of skating and a mass of skating people.

It was wonderful. The film, shown in the cinema, was a superb recollection of past events and great skaters. For us, it was more than that — most skaters were given small extracts, but in the section devoted to us the director had included all of *Mack and Mabel*, uncut.

And after the film, and during the dinner that evening, masses of people — past champions, past judges, current judges — kept coming up and congratulating us, telling us in the most forceful way possible that we had not been forgotten by the amateur world, and that the work we had done as amateurs had been influential in the development of the sport. You gave us what we needed, they said. *Mack and Mabel* would be ideal for ice-dancing now. It represented what ice-dancing should be. Back to basics! Away from unjudgeable ballet-style dances!

That was when we heard about a coming change in the Olympic rules, to allow professionals to regain their amateur status, something that had occurred long since in other sports like tennis and athletics. News of the change planted the seed of an idea in Chris.

It had been a long evening the night before, so on the way back to Zurich airport, on the little train that goes up and down to Davos, stopping at every station, we dozed.

'Jayne,' Chris said at one point, gazing from under heavy lids at the mountains, 'Do you realise we could do the Olympics again?'

She opened her eyes. 'Yes, sure,' she said, and closed her eyes again.

'No, really, we could,' said Chris, fully awake now.

'Well, how?'

'You heard. They're going to open it up to professionals.'

'Mm-hm.' Still only half listening.

'Really. We could.'

'Well,' said Jayne, responding at last. 'I suppose it's only a few minutes of dancing. Not much, compared with what we perform in our own show.'

'Yes. How many minutes?'

We worked it out. Four minutes for the free dance, two for the original set pattern — the original dance as it was now called – and four compulsories of a minute or so each, of which two would be chosen prior to each competition. Ten minutes maximum – nothing compared with a tour, on which we might have to dance an hour a night for weeks at a time. Of course, psychologically it would be a huge commitment, but in purely physical terms it sounded relatively easy.

By the time we arrived in Zurich, we had begun to talk about routines, and rehearsal times. We could feel the adrenalin flowing already. The timing was right – with the Winter Games rescheduled for 1994 to give a two-year separation with the Summer Games, we wouldn't have to wait for four whole years.

The practical demands would be minimal compared with what we had been through over the past eight years. We would both be working from home. We wouldn't have to cope with the pressures of a commercial tour, agents, hotels, and a company of other skaters.

The more we talked the more we liked it. It would be exciting. Our whole skating life had thrived on challenges, on our need to find and leap new hurdles. After 10 years of professional life, the single, dramatic challenge of the Olympics was just what we needed.

Chris

The next crisis came when Isabelle, after a stay at home

in Canada, was due to come to England to join me in Nottingham – where we were rehearsing – before we left together for a brief, final trip to Kiev. After that she was due to start rehearsing in Oberstdorf for a series of shows in France.

When we spoke on the phone, I could hear her unhappiness and turmoil, could almost feel the coming crisis. She said she was coming, and named a day, then cancelled, rescheduled her flight, only to cancel again. When she eventually arrived to join me at Tee's house it was only a few days before we were due to leave for Kiev.

As the time approached for us to leave, the crisis reached fever pitch.

'I can't go,' she said, over and over. 'You have to cancel.'

'Isabelle, we can't cancel. We have to go.'

My refusal turned her into a soul in torment, unable to face the flight, sleepless, pacing around, applying then tearing off false fingernails. Watching her, I was in despair, trapped by my inability to do anything to help, blaming myself.

Finally, at 2:00 in the morning the day before our departure, panting in distress, she demanded a doctor. I persuaded her we could wait until the morning. But when the doctor came, all he could say was that she was in crisis.

'I can't go,' she said again.

'Well, I have to. The tour's booked. This is the last rehearsal before the tour.'

But she didn't want to fly, didn't even want to leave the house.

269

In the end, I had to go, leaving her with Tee.

Looking back, I think now that my refusal to change my plans, my insistence on leaving her, finally killed something in her, perhaps the hope that she could have me on her own terms.

When I came back, she kept on asking what we were going to do, where we were going to live after the tour was over.

By now she knew of our vague thoughts about competing in the Olympics, and that increased her distress. Her roots were in Canada. Clearly, for her peace of mind, for the sort of emotional stability she needed to continue her career, she would need to be near home.

I could not imagine making that commitment. I didn't know what to do or say, and the conflict between the need to do right by Isabelle and the need to follow my own destiny was like a noose tightening round my neck.

I would have blamed myself more, but she was still capable of pursuing her own career when it came to the crunch. She had not been able to get on a plane to be with me. But she managed to get on a plane to go to Oberstdorf, to fulfil commitments she had made with Paul.

Jayne and Chris

The most dramatic incident of the Ukrainian tour came about because of Edgley's introduction of a circus element, nothing to do with skating. The act they really loved was a brilliant Russian high-wire walker, Adam Visitayev, who would back-somersault, skip, jump through hoops, all without a net or safety harness. Sometimes he would carry his wife, who would stand on his head. (For the company, they made an exotic combination – she was an extremely beautiful Tartar girl whom he had bought for cash.)

His speciality was a mock falling off. He would fall, grab the wire, hang on, and haul himself back up. Wayne was convinced the audience loved it. We weren't so sure, because people seemed genuinely fearful. From backstage you could hear the screams and indrawn breaths. There were no tricks, and there was real danger, so the crew had been told: If he falls, don't move him in case he has spinal injuries. Just leave him and wait for the ambulance.

We were in Glasgow, where the high-wire act was not performed over the ice, but off to one side of the rink. It was a matinée, and we were backstage, getting ready in neighbouring dressingrooms, listening to the oohs and aahs from the audience at Adam on the high-wire, when suddenly, five minutes into his act, there was a huge, communal scream.

Debbie was in with Chris. A voice came through on her radio. It was Phil, out front, so shocked he could hardly bring himself to speak clearly.

'Adam's down.'

'What did you say?'

'Adam's fallen to the ground.'

Chris shouted to Jayne. We all stood, shocked, for a few seconds, knowing there was nothing we could do, except what entertainers do at such moments – move, get out there fast, and keep the show going.

Even as we rushed to the ice, with Debbie shoving the company forward, the girls in tears of shock, Adam's Russian assistant, unaware of the instructions not to touch him, appalled probably by the lack of action, ran up to Adam and just dragged him off. A corpse, for all the audience knew. Even if he wasn't, he could have been seriously injured by the move.

Thankfully, he was not dead, though he had nasty injuries. He had landed with his face on his arm, and broken both the arm and his cheek-bone.

And – would you believe it? – Wayne Stevens went and hired another high-wire act, a Portuguese. We were mortified. This was supposed to be an ice-show. But it was out of our hands. As Wayne said, the audience loved it. Who were we to say he was wrong?

As the tour ended, we had already floated the idea of another one among ourselves. We knew even then that if the idea came to anything, the ground rules would be different. Total artistic and financial control. Our routines, our choice of skaters, our producers, our agents, our finance, our everything.

Now *that* was an inspiring thought. Phil was eager to make a start. There was not all that much he could do, though, before we knew our own minds. Were we really going to do the Olympics? Given Chris's marital crisis, was there anything firm we could say about the next year or two?

Chris

It was Christmas again, the end of 1992. After cancelling a tour in France, Isabelle had got herself back to Canada with Paul, and I was to join her. This surely had to be make or break time. I was ready now to do my best, ready to commit myself to Isabelle, if we could find a way forward. I was hardly aware of what I might be doing to Jayne and Phil – leaving them in apprehension, not knowing if the Olympics was on or off, whether we still had a career together, whether I would be back at all.

I remember driving down from Tee's in Nottingham to the cottage outside Henley, knowing that the next day I would be on a plane to Canada. It was twilight. The first stars were sharp in a clear winter sky. In one of the lanes near the cottage, I stopped, got out, and stared out, over the hedge, across the fields, feeling the cold bite, breathing in the country air as if I wanted to pack it away inside and take it with me. A typically English scene, made vivid by the possibility of loss.

I thought of other losses in my life: my mother going, my father dying. I saw distant trees, whose bare branches were nothing more than shadows against the darkening sky, and thought, Is this the last time I'll be a part of this?

It seemed a real possibility. If Isabelle and I made up our

273

differences, if there really was the certainty of a happy marriage, I would stay.

I arrived to find Canada in the grip of 20 degrees of frost. Isabelle had rented a house in Aylmer, not far from her family home. But we used the house as a dormitory, because for much of every day Isabelle wanted to be with her mother. That was her emotional anchor. We would wake up, have some breakfast and Isabelle would say, 'Let's go round to Mom's.' So it didn't give us much time to be alone.

Restless as ever, I passed the time skiing a little with Paul (who as usual seemed to preserve an amazing equanimity), skating on the local rink, working out in the gym, wondering what the future held. Clearly, there were possibilities locally. Mr Duchesnay – Henri – was involved in planning a new rink complex, and there was a good chance I could help run it and teach in it.

But the longer I stayed, the more I could see what I could become: an appendage of Isabelle and her family. Increasingly, I came to believe that she didn't just need me, she needed to control me. And the more I thought about it, the more I realised I was not ready to cut myself off from the life I had built up with Jayne. I wanted to do the Olympics. I wanted to go on developing interesting projects, devising original choreography for myself and Jayne, not just for other people.

I tried to discuss the Olympics idea more seriously with Isabelle.

'I don't think you should do it,' she said. Then, when I mentioned it again, her opposition hardened: 'You don't need to do that again.'

In turn, my resolve strengthened: 'I _do_ need to. It's my last chance.' Nor would the Olympics be the end of my commitment. Afterwards, we hoped, would come another world tour, our own show.

My ideas seemed to drive her into a state of confusion. In one breath, she said she understood, but in the next she said she couldn't accept what I wanted to do, because it meant a very different sort of marriage from anything she had considered. The Olympics would take a year. Then probably there would be the world tour. So it was going to be two, perhaps three years, before we had a 'proper' marriage.

Eventually, we came to the nub of it: a proper marriage meant Isabelle pursuing her career with Paul at the expense of mine, and of course Jayne's. Their time had come; ours was past. Either I gave up my skating life – Jayne, the Olympics, the world tour – and committed myself to her, or that was that.

'Chris, can't you see? I just can't go on living like this. If you go and do these things, we may as well say goodbye.'

She put it as if it was my doing. Obviously, in a sense, it was. But the idea of splitting up was not my decision.

'It doesn't have to be like that,' I kept saying, still hoping for compromise. 'We can work together, we can travel together.'

In fact, an opportunity had just arisen – all of us, Jayne and I, Isabelle and Paul – had recently been invited to do a post-Worlds tour run by the impresario Tom Collins in a couple of months' time. It was a well-paid, straightforward exhibition with top skaters.

After that, we would see each other quite easily when she came to Europe to rehearse for a series of Holiday on Ice shows in France. I couldn't accept her way of seeing things, her determination to make my continued presence such a black-and-white issue.

But the truth – clear by hindsight – was that we couldn't work and travel together, not in the long term. I had seen how threatened Isabelle was by my work with Jayne, and I knew now I couldn't give that up. I couldn't be what I felt she wanted me to be, her personal choreographer, because I was left feeling caged in, unable to pursue my own destiny. She, with a stubbornness and a volatility that more than matched mine, was as anchored to her life – with Paul and her family – as I was to mine.

Her way, my way. There was no middle way.

The crunch came when, after almost two months, I insisted the time had come to fulfil an arrangement I had made to meet the cellist Yo Yo Ma in London, to discuss an idea for collaboration. Beyond that was a conviction that we should both get on with our lives. She had her commitments – the Holiday on Ice, the tour in France. Jayne and I had ours, most immediately the Yo Yo Ma meeting and our preparation for the Tom Collins tour.

'Don't go,' she said, over and over. 'Don't go.'

'I have to. I can't stay here for ever.'

When the time came for me to go, she refused to come to the airport.

Some weeks after I got home, I received a letter from her lawyers: 'If your attitude and actions do not change, my client will be forced to initiate divorce proceedings.'

Now, of course, Jayne and Phil were hanging on my

decision, their lives as much on hold as mine, wondering whether we were going for the Olympics or not. When I came back, I said enigmatically that I was 'on the yes side of maybe.' But we didn't have much time – a couple of months – if the application to regain our amateur status was going to be in, and the implications for planning the World Tour were pretty dramatic.

Isabelle's letter put the decision in the starkest terms.

I made my choice.

We would do the Olympics, come what may.

The next two months were ones of black despair. I felt weighed down by guilt, at having committed myself to an impossible marriage, at having been in part a cause of Isabelle's distress, at not being able to do anything about it.

One further attempt at reconciliation – a trip to Paris – collapsed when I got stuck in a rail strike on the way in from Charles de Gaulle, got lost, arrived at the hotel hours late, only to find myself locked again into the same closed circle of recrimination. I left after two days.

The cottage was no comfort now. I was alone, in deep depression. Once, when Jayne heard something in my voice on the phone, she became concerned for me.

'Do you want me to come and stay?'

'Oh, no. I'm all right.'

But she knew better, and drove up to be with me. It was good to have the sympathy, but there was no answer in her. Whatever she felt, she never told me what I should or shouldn't do, except to keep me focused on our skating, on the immediate task – a contemporary percussion piece,

Drum Duet, for the Tom Collins tour — and on the long-term task we had given ourselves: to show everyone that we were still up there with the best, even if we were now the oldest in the profession. That was the real purpose of the Tom Collins tour: to carve a foothold on our way to the Olympics.

It may have been the stress, or just my habit of always testing life to breaking point, but I almost put paid to everything just before we left. It was the Bank Holiday, just after Easter, and I was due at the ice-rink. On the way to the main road from the cottage was a hump-backed bridge which led into a sharp bend. I drove too fast over the bridge, took off briefly, couldn't make the bend, and ran slap into a tree.

It was a heck of a bang. I climbed out. There was no one around, of course. Bank Holiday. So I called Jayne on the mobile phone. She arranged for a garage to haul the car away — it was a write-off — drove up, collected me, and took me to Stoke Mandeville Hospital to check for whiplash and bruising.

I was skating in a collar for two days, and it took weeks for the pains to go away.

With the injury and Isabelle's threat hanging over me, I was tempted to back out of the tour. Jayne said she would understand. But besides offering proof of our talent, it was well-paid work that would help finance our Olympic year. And I also saw that I would have to see my marriage through somehow, either to reconciliation or divorce. This was as good an opportunity as any.

So in April and May, 1993, we were all on tour together, stressfully, and very publicly. Despite the lawyers' letter,

278

despite the fact that she actually had the divorce papers with her, as she told me, Isabelle was not committed to divorce. She seemed to live in a constant flux, switching back and forth between parting and reconciling.

For my part, I experienced her efforts as an emotional rollercoaster. One day I was in favour, and we were sharing a hotel room. The next it was all over, and we were apart.

The company rooming list gave nightly snapshots of our relationship to anyone interested. Of course, everyone was, and everyone saw what was happening. They had little choice. On the buses between venues, sometimes we were sitting together, sometimes not; sometimes talking urgently, sometimes in stony silence.

One morning — after one of those nights when I had been assigned my own room — I decided I couldn't stand it any more. It was like a cat-and-mouse game. I called her.

'OK,' I said. 'Let's sign.'

We met down in the lobby.

'Shall we give it one last chance?' she said.

I was at the end of my tether, not willing to accept any more of what I saw as manipulation. 'I think I'd rather just sign,' I said.

So we did, and posted the document to the lawyers.

As far as I was concerned, the decision was made. I could at last contemplate a new life.

It was not quite so cut and dried for Isabelle. She had anyway been due to leave the tour to fulfil an engagement in France with Paul.

In Paris, she gave a press conference. Her reason, so she said, was that the press were hounding her for details, so

279

she decided to deal with them all at once. The first I knew of what she had said was when I read the headlines. Thank goodness I was still touring far from home.

SHAM! ICE LEGEND CHRIS NEVER TREATED ME LIKE A WIFE, SAYS BITTER ISABELLE.

She went on to call me cold, distant, totally obsessed with work to the exclusion of her. No privacy, no married life, no chance of children ('She wanted babies, he craved glory') and always the bitterness towards Jayne – 'I know that Jayne hates me because she was afraid I'd take Chris from her . . . Jayne only smiled at me once – when my love failed.'

It was hurtful to read, but at least a confirmation that my decision to go ahead with the divorce had been right. Of course, I was asked for my comments, but I didn't want any more publicity, certainly didn't want to get into a slanging match, so all I did was confirm the fact of the divorce.

Apart from that, I felt a great weight lift off my shoulders. I had been struggling to make something out of a relationship that hindsight now told me was doomed from the beginning. Although we had known each other for years, we had somehow never had a chance to get to know the real person. We had each married a false image. Recognising the truth had been a long and painful process.

Now it seemed to me that I was fully awake again. For the first time in a year, I could raise my eyes and begin to look around me.

And there, waiting, was a new life.

I had been unaware of it, but through the tour Jayne, sharing dressingrooms with the other girls (including Isabelle), had made friends with one of them, Jill Trenary.

Jayne began to talk to Jill as a friend, and it was natural that I should eventually do the same.

I knew about her, of course, because in 1990 she had won the World Figure Skating championships in Halifax, where I had been commentating. Originally from Minneapolis, she had shown prodigious skating talent as a child, becoming the US junior champion, and at 14 moved in with friends in Denver, where the US Olympic Training Center is.

We had been touring together for weeks, but when our friendship developed, it flowered very quickly into something much deeper. Of course other people must have thought it unrealistic, foolish, a rebound on my part, a crush on her part.

But I saw in her qualities that answered a deep need in me, an inner strength, a generosity of spirit and a sensitivity that balanced my volatile nature. We seemed to have an instinctive mutual understanding, and knew, with utter certainty, that we had to be together.

And so we were, from the end of the tour onwards, as we began preparations for the Olympics. We tried to keep our lives as private as possible, but eventually, after we were photographed at a concert together a few months later, it came out.

For days, the press camped on the doorstep, hungry for pictures and quotes, while we peeked at them through curtains. Then came more unsavoury headlines, as the press descended again on Isabelle:

'DEAN HAD A STRING OF LOVERS, SAYS WIFE.'

This time it was easier to ignore, an echo of a past pain already overlaid by newfound happiness.

Jill was with me, supportive and understanding, with her own career on temporary hold, through the build-up to the Olympics, the national championships, the Europeans, and the Olympics themselves.

We were engaged in the New Year, just before the Olympics, and married on October 15, 1994.

10

Going for gold, again

Jayne and Chris

With Chris's arrival back at the end of January, 1993, we made our decision: to compete in the Olympics, and also do the World Tour.

From that decision, which had been on hold for the best part of a year, flowed a whole train of consequences. The Olympics were in February, 1994. That meant there could be no World Tour until after that. All the groundwork would have to be laid, but with Phil now our acting business manager and Debbie our assistant, much of that work could be done with only occasional thoughts from us.

Phil, with his contacts in the rock business, already had ideas for an agent and promoters. On the basis of Chris's first ideas, and with many of his own, Andris would start to plan out company pieces and research music sources. Bob Murphy would be contacted to do costumes.

Eventually, the whole venture would be financed by promoters' advances, but for almost a year the cost would be ours, and any income delayed by our decision to compete in the Olympics.

We had two months to get our application in. But there was no point even applying without being certain of how exactly we would go about it: choosing music, arranging for recordings, rehearsing, designing and making costumes. This was no small undertaking. It would cost us over £100,000. It would be good if the Olympics somehow boosted interest in the World Tour. Certainly, we knew what an Olympic success could do for us financially. But there was no guarantee of success. We might fail completely, with no commercial benefit for the tour. In fact, if we made complete fools of ourselves, we might achieve quite the opposite of commercial benefit: we could end up doing ourselves a fatal disservice, with no money and no further career.

So we had to go into the Olympics for its own sake, risking everything financially and professionally, each of us responding to gut-feelings. Being at the 1992 Olympics, Chris had had a reminder of the ecstasy that champions feel when they are the best, and acknowledged as the best. Though more subdued and circumspect, especially now that she was happily married, Jayne was still susceptible to Chris's enthusiasm. We were not ready to have people ask

cach other, 'Whatever happened to Torvill and Dean?' as
if we were about to draw our old-age pensions. Going for
gold was not all there was to professional life – there were
still new frontiers of choreography to be explored – but
there was no denying the thrill of setting ourselves such a
challenge, or the satisfaction we knew we would get from
competing, let alone winning.

Of course, we also risked losing. That too was part of the
excitement, providing the bitter-sweet edge involved in any
high-risk decision. Win or lose, we wanted to do it.

But there was no point in doing it unless we did our
best to steer a true course through the murky waters of
amateur ice-dancing – to ensure we did everything we could
to appeal to the judges in the four competitions before us:
the British, the Europeans, the Olympics, the Worlds. To
achieve that, we had to have guidance from within the
amateur world.

We went to see our old friends and advisers – Bobby
Thompson, British national coach; Courtney Jones, a
member of the International Skating Union; and Lawrence
Demmy, vice-president of the International Skating Union
– to ask what they thought.

They were unanimous: 'You have the ability. You would
be in with a good chance.'

And it was something they would like us to do, because
it would give ice-dancing in Britain a lift it badly needed.
Since 1984, the sport had slipped in popularity. Our
return, they said, would generate huge interest and be
a wonderful boost for the sport. They would provide all
the help they could.

The application was easy – all we had to do was get

it in on time, before April I, commit ourselves not to take part in those professional events not sanctioned by the International Skating Union, and establish a trust fund to administer any income from professional sources.

More important, support from Bobby, Courtney and Lawrence meant we had access to the advice we needed on the things that would appeal to the judges — how to strike the magic balance between originality and conservatism, how to delight them without challenging them.

We would have new rules to obey. But ice-dancing is notorious for its subjectivity. To have a chance of success we would have to be aware of the different interpretations of the rules, the quirky attitudes towards music, costume and presentation, and above all the hidden currents of friendship, rivalry and influence within the world of ice-dancing administration and judging.

As we ventured out, first to Europe, then to the Olympics, and as the stakes got higher, it would be harder and harder to be certain of anything. We needed all the help we could get, and there, in Bobby, Courtney and Lawrence we had the best we could hope for.

We made our decision public on March 30, eager as schoolkids, believing we knew exactly what we had undertaken.

If only . . .

Once the decision was made, we had to design a game plan for the whole year.

First, we needed to ensure continuity of advice. As President of the British National Ice Skating Association, a member of the ISU Ice Dance Technical Committee and a long-established judge, Courtney gave advice that was crucial, especially on costume design. As the national coach, Bobby would be able to offer a lot of help and we also wanted to work with Betty Callaway, who had been such an important part of our amateur life up to 1984. Finally, of course, we wanted to continue our relationship with Andris, with whom we had grown up over the last 10 years.

We already had an idea of the music we wanted. Long ago, looking at Fred Astaire and Ginger Rogers routines, we had watched the video of *Follow the Fleet*, and loved *Let's Face the Music and Dance*. Ever since he first mentioned the idea of the Olympics, Chris had been mulling over the number.

Now, as we discussed what sort of music and style might impress the judges, Bobby, Courtney and Lawrence reminded us of what we had been told at Davos: back to basics, no more of the way-out modernist balletic dancing that judges found so hard to assess.

For that reason, a new rule specified no classical music.

The Russians wouldn't be able to adapt a Tchaikovsky ballet, we couldn't do anything in the *Bolero* line. This struck us as perverse. How odd to exclude a vast range of material that had nurtured ballet dancing, and should be available to do the same for competitive ice-dancing.

Remembering the reactions we had heard in Davos, we would have to give them something that looked back to the origins of the sport, something ballroomy, with two people simply dancing with each other in ways that didn't seem pretentious.

287

Well, we could aim a little higher than that. What could be more suitable than something in the style of Astaire and Rogers, who had lifted ballroom dancing to a new level of sophistication and romance?

The music would not work as it was, of course. The original was partly vocal. The changes of pace did not provide enough variety. We would need rearrangement, as usual, but one that accentuated the back-to-basics ethos by providing all the different ballroom rhythms that the judges had been used to in the old days, before we messed everything up for them with *Bolero*.

Normally, this would have been a huge expense. But luckily, with Phil's involvement, there might be a way to avoid this. Through Phil Collins and Genesis, Phil had got to know their British booking agent, Graham Pullen. Smart, young, and streetwise in the music world, Graham was a man with many ideas.

He pointed out that whatever happened we would generate a fair amount of publicity. The music we danced to would automatically receive huge exposure. If the arrangement was original, then a record of that music would have huge free publicity.

He was sure he could get the music done free, by finding a record company willing to pay for the arranging and recording as an advance against sales. Later, he came up with other ideas, talking about sponsorship, advertising, merchandising, and many other angles we would never have thought of.

Through the spring and summer, the music worked out exactly as planned. Through Graham we met Andy Ross, the well-known conductor on *Come Dancing*, and his arranger, Cy Payne. Cy worked with a keyboard sequencer to tailor a version of _Let's Face the Music_ for us, starting with a quickstep, moving to waltz and tango, with a big-band swing-time finale.

It took for ever, because we involved Bobby and Courtney, whose opinions slowly evolved with the music. It became increasingly fascinating to work with Cy, because, as the arrangement was nearing completion, he would come into the rink with his keyboard, computer and speaker, and he would be able to tweak the combination of instruments, the rhythm, the pace, the transitions, everything, right there, matching music to steps. This was interactive choreography of a type that would not have been possible for us in the 1980s. Later still, when we had our final version, Cy would have it transcribed, played by a studio orchestra, and recorded.

With this process underway, we turned to rehearsal space. The natural choice would have been Oberstdorf. But Oberstdorf was now Germany's main Olympic training area, and we weren't keen to expose ourselves to rivals before we were ready. We wanted seclusion.

Even before going on the Tom Collins tour, Chris had had a wonderful idea: why not use the Olympic ice-skating arena itself, in Hammar, Norway? It was finished – Lawrence Demmy had been out and seen it – though the village itself wasn't. This, surely, would guarantee seclusion, with everyone else working on administration, music and costumes flying in and out as necessary.

A quick visit confirmed what we'd heard. The village was still a building site, but there were two maisonettes we could rent for the next six months. A paved road led to the arena. We could hire a car and drive back and forth. Perfect.

But when we got there to start training, it was not perfect at all. It was too secluded, even for us. There was no one else around. It would be just us, joined if we were lucky by Phil and Jill, but basically skating for hours a day, with nothing to look forward to but *Neighbours*, *Eastenders* and *A Country Practice* on the English channels of the TV. This was not seclusion, it was isolation.

After just one day, we saw our mistake. After two days, we were both phoning home to say so. Why pay a fortune in rent and car-rental and food – the food was horrendously expensive – when we both had perfectly nice houses and loved ones at home?

After a week, we knew that six months of this would drive us crazy. Within two weeks, we were home again, grateful to be back in safe, familiar places with the people we loved, able to call friends and find a pint of milk and a newspaper on the doorstep every morning.

We returned to find new rehearsal plans almost in place. Debbie had started to research the possible rinks. There were not many Olympic-sized rinks to choose from, and of the ones that were available, some, thinking we had unlimited funds, priced themselves out of our reach immediately.

Milton Keynes, though, proved ideal. The Olympic-sized rink had just been modernised, and was about to reopen. It could do with some publicity, and in exchange its management were prepared to guarantee seclusion at a price we could afford. We did a deal: £20,000 bought us four hours of ice a day, six days a week, for six months. It may sound a lot of money, and it was certainly one of our greatest expenses, but £30 an hour for a whole arena, dressingrooms, ice, upkeep and all, was astonishingly good value.

Besides, we were still hoping that we would not have to fund the whole venture ourselves. Graham and Phil between them tried a hundred or more possible sponsors. No one was interested. We wondered why, and could only guess at answers. Perhaps the companies thought we were past it. Certainly we could offer no guarantee of success. Probably, no one wanted to risk being associated with failure.

So in the end, all the investment, and all the risk, was ours.

It was already midsummer when we started to rehearse at Milton Keynes, driving an hour and a half from our homes every day, working with Bobby and Betty twice a week, and Andris, who kept a watchful eye on us every day working with a video, with which we could also keep an eye on ourselves.

The arena was perfect, as secluded as we could wish, sparkling with fresh whites and blues. At once, though, we found ourselves landed with a human problem. Still in search of sponsors, we needed all the publicity we could get, and agreed to any number of newspaper interviews. Naturally the journalists were particularly interested in Betty, whom they remembered well from 1984. Bobby seldom got a mention. After a couple of weeks, we found ourselves nervous of arriving in case there had been another interview in which Bobby had been ignored. Anyway, he and Betty had different comments about our skating, so it was soon obvious they shouldn't both be there together. They agreed to alternate.

Luckily, they knew each other well, and weren't going to argue, but the mistake – our mistake, as we saw later – pointed up a dilemma. We had landed ourselves with too much advice, too much of it contradictory. In other circumstances, we would have relied solely on Andris, with his sharp eye and the video. That arrangement had been fine for almost 10 years, until we chose to re-enter the strange world of amateur skating, taking decisions not because we thought them best for our dancing, but because we had to fit in with the rules and regulations. We were no longer just ice-dancers. It was as if we had a journey to make, could see our destination clear enough, but suddenly found ourselves with soft ground underfoot.

Ahead, as yet unseen, were quicksands.

At the time, that was not a major problem. We were among experts and friends, as passionately committed to our success as we were. The four compulsories – the *Starlight Waltz*, the Blues, the Paso Doble and the *Tango Romantica* – with their exacting technical demands, came on well. It did not take long to master the flow of moves, displaying inside-edge and outside-edge turns, forwards and backwards movements, all in a variety of holds and positions, performed in absolute unison.

It was a frustrating business, skating prescribed steps to the same degree of perfection day after day, and the constant repetitions of music and steps almost drove Andris mad. But Betty and Bobby forced us to look ever more critically at ourselves, and after several months we all felt there was no way to improve further.

In the original dance, the rumba, that problem was less-ened, because at least there was some degree of flexibility. Once Courtney had emphasised to us the importance of stressing one particular beat in the sinuous, syncopated rhythm, we moved forward confidently to create something that we and our critical coaches were happy with.

In the free dance, we choreographed a basic outline within a couple of weeks. Our approach was 'back to basics,' back to ballroom, as we had been told, away from balletic athleticism, away from aesthetic upper-body work, and back to footwork. _Let's Face the Music_ is pure ball-room, two dancers holding each other, working together, without the 'highlights,' nothing obviously flashy.

You are allowed up to five lifts, and we had only three. We concentrated on devising intertwined body-positions and rapid, intricate, angled footwork, a flow of quick-change, inside-edge-to-outside-edge steps, and lots of turns. All this can cut down on fast-over-the-ice movement, so the challenge was to maintain flow and speed.

Normally to build speed you do quick running steps, which, if you lead up to a trick, looks good to the crowd, but it is easy and clichéd. Our aim was to base our routine on flowing and intricate transitions, accelerating as naturally and in as technically interesting a way as possible, building speed by varying edges or body positions.

That was the thinking behind the concept: intricate footwork, no runs, few lifts. At that stage, there was no thought of the lift that would cause so much fuss later, Jayne's final over-the-head somersault. It seemed to us that our concept took the required approach to a new level. We thought people — especially the judges — would appreciate the purity and the technical difficulty.

That part was quickly done. The actual work — which was all about detail, the exact height of a leg, whether there should be a lift here or there, the position of the head, the expression, the eye-contact — would be done over the coming months.

And gradually, the original choreographic concept became diluted. According to the advice we were given, the judges would *expect* the five lifts allowed, so it might hinder our chances if we used only our intended three. We put in five. It felt wrong to go against our instincts in this way, but what else did we have expert advice for?

Once training was underway, we turned to costumes. Courtney knew of a company, Chrisanne, who specialised in supplying a huge variety of fabrics to ballroom dancers. Aware of the demands being made on our finances, he suggested that they might sponsor us with free costumes. That would save us thousands.

They agreed, without knowing what they were getting into. Jayne would have 10 costumes made for her, free. It sounds a lot, but we needed a good range for the four competitions ahead, and we would also need costumes for practices. To follow established procedure and have practice costumes seemed silly to us — we wanted to be in simple black warm-up clothes — but everyone assured us that, since the judges came to the practices, every practice was in a sense a performance that would help pre-form the judges' opinions for the final.

The trouble was that instead of Chrisanne doing a job for us — driving to the rink, measuring, going away, bringing the costumes for trying on, all that — we were cooperating as equals.

So it was up to Jayne to go to their place, in Mitcham, south London. Half a dozen times, she drove to the rink early, then drove back for two hours through London to Chrisanne, finally getting home after a 12-hour day, about five hours of which had been spent in cars. It was enough to make her pine for Mr Bishop and Mrs Parrish.

Chrisanne had taken on an immense task, which they were keen to do because this was a new direction, as well as good publicity. But they had not made skating costumes before. They were learning as they went along, which made it a frustratingly slow process, especially as the original designer left to have a baby. Once, Jayne found herself driving all that way to try on one leotard, which wasn't right. And they didn't understand Courtney's sketches, which had to be completed in the making, with zips, poppers, and hooks-and-eyes inserted in the right places. Then Jayne's skirts were wrong. We knew exactly what we _didn't_ want, and must have been horribly demanding.

In the end, it worked, just about, for us. We got several thousand pounds' worth of costumes free, not all 10 because time ran out, but enough to see us through. It placed a lot of pressure on them. We hope it was worth it for them, but fear it wasn't.

What with the training, the music, varying advice, hours of driving, and frustrations over the costumes, we already had quite a bit to cope with. But there was more.

In July, when we had been in Milton Keynes a month or so, it occurred to us that it would be a good idea if the whole process could be recorded on film, because we had always regretted not having any record of the preparations for the 1984 Olympics.

Our tour promoter, Phil McIntyre, picked up the idea. From his point of view, it would be good publicity. He called the BBC, and was put through to a well-established documentary film producer, Eddie Mirzoeff, who invited us in for a meeting.

Eddie Mirzoeff turned out to be something of a star in his own right, with dozens of documentaries to his credit, three of which had won BAFTA awards. He gave us a little lecture about how he worked, and how tough it was to be the subject of his documentaries, talking about the need for commitment, trust, mutual regard. He mentioned problems and pain. 'Once you say yes,' he told us, 'you have to go on saying yes. I just want to make sure you understand what you're letting yourself in for.'

Oh, sure, we said. We had worked with film crews before. Of course we knew what we were in for – we had been delighted by the technical excellence of the *Omnibus* film. We even had some warnings of our own. Things happened very fast sometimes – steps being explained, rehearsed, or changed – and if he wasn't ready for instant, spontaneous filming he would lose it. We couldn't repeat things or wait while he put up lights, because we wanted it to look real.

'That's very much the way we work,' he said.

'The fly on the wall.'

'Absolutely.'

What we should have said was no many times – no, we had not been the subject of a documentary like this; no, we had no idea what it was like to be under the scrutiny of a demanding, experienced, committed, top-class director; no, we had no experience of the pain involved; and no, we certainly wouldn't want that on top of everything else, so thank you very much and goodbye.

But it seemed a good idea at the time. So we said yes, and left happy.

Eddie started filming in September. At first, during training, we found his occasional presence no imposition. But as the British championships in January approached, his warning became a reality. He was not so much a fly on the wall, as a giraffe on the wall, with his camera craning over, round and into us.

It seemed that he would turn up whenever it suited him. At every turn – at the rink, behind scenes, in our homes, at the dressmakers – there he was, probing for deeper insights, complaining that we weren't giving enough, trying in vain to get us to wear radio microphones – 'They're only little things, they won't interfere with your movements.'

We understood. We knew what he wanted. We knew he was one of the best. It was all our fault – our initial approach, our 'yes.' We knew we were driving him crazy, as well as vice versa. But that didn't help. In the end, as the tension increased, we became increasingly wary even though we knew he was doing a difficult job the best way he could.

To others, it must have seemed as if we were returning breezily, perhaps even arrogantly, to reclaim a crown that we thought was rightfully ours. To us, it felt exactly the opposite, as if we were entering unknown territory without a compass, wading ever deeper into a morass. We hoped the British championships, at the Sheffield Arena in January, would give us a sense of direction.

As the British approached, we should have been buoyed up by confidence, because when we skated the whole programme through for everyone involved, it went perfectly. Betty, Bobby, Courtney and Lawrence, who knew our rivals nationally and internationally, and understood the judges' expectations as well as anyone, agreed: 'We haven't seen anything better than that!'

We couldn't be sure, though, and were more nervous going into this, our first amateur competition in 10 years, than we had been in Sarajevo. Experience brought with it a burden of awareness we hadn't had then. The fears kept on surging to the surface. What if we were too ambitious, not ambitious enough, too slow, too old? One competitor in the British hadn't even been born when we started our career.

This was not only a national championship – it was being televised, and would be seen worldwide, by judges as well. It was in effect the first round of the Olympics, and we had to come through unscathed. We not only had to win – we had to win *well*.

So on the day, we should have been in good shape. But were we? In the practices at Sheffield, in the new arena set out of town in a huge open area near the football ground, Bobby suddenly didn't seem quite so sure.

We should smile more. We had to make everything 'bigger,' whatever that meant. We had to be seen to be the old fairytale couple, always look happy.

And there was Eddie, wanting his footage. Before a competition, you need to grab moments in which you can sink into yourself, find some inner peace among the turmoil of emotions. Resting between the final practices; sitting quietly in dressingrooms applying makeup before the actual competition; standing in the echoing corridors while the sound of music and applause for other competitors comes tinnily through the tannoys – these are sacred moments, vital if you are to achieve the relaxed concentration needed in the minutes and seconds before the music sweeps you away.

Yet there, just when all emotional reaction should be draining from you, was Eddie – demanding reactions. It didn't help to know we had encouraged him in the first place. It was as if we had released some darker aspect of our own personalities that kept appearing round corners to haunt us, threaten us, perhaps even undermine our chances.

We started well. In the compulsories – the waltz and blues – we averaged 5.7 and 5.8. For the rumba, all the marks but one were 5.9s and sixes. We were well ahead at that point, but the free dance, _Let's Face the Music_, amounts to half the competition. If we fell, if the judges disapproved, we could easily go down.

We gave a safe performance, nothing more. We waited for the verdict, knotted up with tension, sitting in the 'kiss-and-cry' area as it's called, with Bobby on one side and Betty on the other. The marks began to come up. It looked good: eight 5.9s and a six for technical performance – then, suddenly, excellent: nine sixes for artistic impression.

We'd won.

The tension broke. All four of us collapsed into delighted smiles, Jayne into tears of joy and relief.

At this point, we should have been able to relax into final preparations for the Europeans, two weeks later, knowing that we had got it right. Unluckily for us, there was someone in Sheffield who was about to pop our delicate, new-found confidence. He was Hans Kutschera, who as head of the ISU's Dance Committee, had been invited as an observer.

Since he was so influential, British officials tended to treat him like royalty, so when a message came through that he wanted to see us back at the hotel, we were happy to oblige, looking forward to some official congratulations, perhaps, something that would match our euphoria.

Now, Hans Kutschera was not an athletic-looking man. Once he must have been, because he had been an ice-dancer himself.

We went in with Betty, Bobby and Courtney, expecting formalities, and found ourselves on the receiving end of remarks that we found increasingly hard to take. He told us in his dense Austrian accent that in the Blues, we had to be 'like a cat.' We exchanged glances. Why a cat? Then, as we stood there with fixed, puzzled smiles, he criticised our free dance in terms we couldn't quite grasp. This, he said, was all to help us.

We smiled some more, and thanked him, and left, with puzzlement giving way to baffled fury.

'Goodness!' Jayne exploded. 'Our whole life is skating, and he thinks he can step out of some office and tell us how to do it!'

'That man!' Betty, normally so restrained, said angrily.

We should not have been affected as we were. After all, it wasn't _what_ he said – he could have any opinion he liked, and he had experience enough to back it – but how he said it, as if we were newcomers who should feel grateful for his opinion. We had no reason to think he was being deliberately hurtful. We should have just been able to set it aside, forgive him, forgive ourselves our petulance and forget it. Certainly we expected Bobby and Courtney to say, 'Oh, take no notice.'

It was a surprise, then, when they took his comments seriously. Kutschera was a very senior figure. He would be a referee at the Olympics. They pointed out there was something about our programme he didn't like, and his opinion (they implied) could infect the international judges at the Europeans and the Olympics.

'You have to listen to him,' they said. 'Couldn't you just change a little bit at the beginning? It would look better, look as if you'd followed his advice.'

Change a little! With us leaving for the Europeans in a week's time!

Half an hour before, we had been ecstatic, sure of ourselves and our course. Now, we were depressed and uncertain.

The next day, back in London, we planned to practise

as usual. Eddie wanted to join us. He'd been complaining that the film lacked tension and drama. We talked on the phone and decided we couldn't stand the idea, didn't want to be nudged and prodded when we were already feeling so depressed about the previous day and nervous about the Europeans, two weeks hence. There was nothing much we could do to improve things anyway.

We told him we were having the day off. And then went to the rink anyway.

Later that day, Debbie received an angry call from Eddie:

'We can't go on like this, you know.'

'Oh. Er, what's the problem?'

'They lied to me! They're training, aren't they? Someone saw their cars. Just tell them I really don't know if we can go on with this project, if they're going to do that sort of thing.'

That evening, Phil called Eddie to explain as well as he could. But that didn't change anything. We felt we were in a belt of tension, and the belt had just tightened another notch.

By the time we got to Copenhagen, with Phil, Jill and our coaches, it tightened further. The whole competition would be carried live on TV, the press were hungry for interviews. We had not regained a scrap of confidence, and could find nothing to reassure us, no spirit of welcome. We felt as if we didn't belong, like outsiders.

Our main rivals were two Russian couples, the current world champions Maia Usova and Alexandr Zhulin, and the silver medallists, Oksana Gritschuk and Evgeny Platov.

Everyone had seen our free dance, but neither Bobby nor Courtney knew much about what the Russians had to offer. Our jitters increased.

In the practice, we put on our black training costumes and found ourselves in what struck us — after 10 years of professionalism — as a madhouse. We were one of six couples skating their compulsories at the same time, starting at different positions on the ice. This was the second session, and the ice was already ploughed and rutted. Of course, it was the same for everyone, but we felt we were in a unique position, with all eyes upon us.

And in this crowd of skaters, on these tramlines, feeling painfully exposed, we were skating as if for the championship itself, because the nine judges were all there watching, assessing form, chatting with each other, and inevitably coming to conclusions that would affect the final marks.

There had to be a consensus — if anyone was way out of line, it would lead to an inquiry — and a consensus could emerge only in the practice. You could see the talk and the exchanged glances, imagine — for the imagination begins to work overtime in those circumstances — the nods and winks, the friendships forged, the conclusions agreed.

There were to be several practices, so there were other chances to impress, to secure our position as much as possible in advance. And Bobby's advice was: 'You've got to make everything bigger.'

The truth was that he was as nervous as we were, and there was nothing he could say to help us. Betty didn't seem her usual calm self either. The message we got was that something was wrong. But what?

We all began to twitch with rising, badly suppressed panic.

The practice outfits! We were wearing our black practice outfits! Too dull! For the rumba practice, Bobby said, Jayne had better wear something else. Not the rumba costume, of course — that had to be saved for the real thing. Just . . . something better. What did she have? Well, there was a short skirt she'd brought with her. Wear that. It could act as a rumba skirt, couldn't it? Yes, fabulous.

But after the first rumba practice, there was a comment from one of the judges. So then it was, 'No, the skirt's not right. Don't wear it again.'

It was no better off the rink. We still had this image, Bobby said, of the squeaky-clean couple, whiter than white, and nothing must touch the image. We should always be together, always smiling, always eating together, avoid being seen with Phil and Jill as much as possible — a suggestion that Jill, on her first trip in public as Chris's partner, found distressing.

Certainly, we were told, avoid being seen with our loved ones in the restaurant, because the ISU people ate at the top table, and they would see us, and maybe they'd think — what? No one knew.

All we could do, it seemed, was play games, project an artificial image left over from 1984, and spin downwards into a pit of paranoia.

As we worked through the compulsories, our fears were confirmed. We skated well, yet found ourselves placed second after the first dance, the Paso Doble, with one astonishingly low mark of 5.2 from a Swiss judge. The Blues went even better, according to Bobby, Betty and even a couple of judges who congratulated us later, yet we still placed only third. That made us joint second overall with Gritschuk and Platov, behind Usova and Zhulin.

Both Betty and Bobby were puzzled. Betty had spotted an error in the leading Russian pair, yet they had not been penalised. We had skated error-free, yet not been rewarded. We did not know what was going on. All we knew was that the British press and our contingent expected us to be out there in the lead, and we weren't.

It didn't look good, because in the past the ultimate winner was almost always in the lead after the compulsories.

All the newspaper and TV people would want to know why we were doing badly, and each one of them would want to ask us personally. However forthcoming we were, we would not be able to respond to all of the approaches. That might make us seem evasive.

So we decided to call a press conference. There, we expressed our surprise, saying that obviously we were not doing what was wanted. But it wasn't over yet. We would fight, and come back in the final, if we could.

The rumba went well. The crowd seemed to like us. A 5.5 in composition from the Austrian judge was balanced by two sixes (Britain and the Czech Republic) for presentation. We won, which put us first equal with Usova and Zhulin.

So it all hung on the free dance, on the last day. Usova and Zhulin were on before us, Gritschuk and Platov after us, in the strategically dominant position, because the judges always tended to hold back in marking earlier contestants in case the last ones deserved higher marks.

Usova-Zhulin averaged between 5.7 and 5.8 for technical merit and a little higher — seven 5.9s and two 5.8s — for artistic impression. We were in with a chance, even if a slim one.

Our marks were fractionally ahead on the technical, and exactly the same — seven 5.9s and two 5.8s — for artistry. But we were not fractionally ahead, because according to the judging rules, the position is based on the judges' place-marks, not on score. In fact, five judges placed Usova-Zhulin ahead, and only four voted for us. We were behind.

Even as we left the rink, after Jayne had swept up bouquets of flowers and a huge white teddy bear some British supporter had thrown on to the ice, someone had worked out the result.

'You're lying second,' shouted a reporter as we walked off. 'How do you feel?'

'Great,' said Chris. How did he think we felt?

Depressed. Horrible. That was how we felt. We had lost. We even congratulated Usova and Zhulin on their victory as we walked past them. That was that. We felt we'd let everyone down. Let ourselves down. And already, in the seconds it took us to walk along the corridor, with Jayne carrying her flowers and her teddy bear, the questions were starting. Was this really all our fault? Or was there something else going on, something we could not understand, some sort of feeling against us for making a comeback?

And there, in the boldly painted corridor with its blue runner and red piping, was the BBC sports producer Alistair Scott, and Eddie with his cameraman, eager to capture every nuance of our depression and humiliation. A horrible moment, sitting there, listening to the echoing sound of Gritschuk and Platov doing their rock-and-roll number, the applause, and then the rollcall of marks.

They were good, too good (three sixes, four 5.9s, only two 5.8s). Jayne was in her dressingroom, finding places for the flowers and the teddy, slipping on a jersey. Chris slumped on to a bench.

It was impossible to assess on the spur of the moment where we had come, but as far as we were concerned it was just a question of whether we were going to be second or third. In any event, the Olympic gold looked like a vanishing dream.

In fact, there was a possible reprieve. The actual marks, remember, were only a refinement of the position allocated to a couple by the judges' place-marks. If Gritschuk and Platov, who were lying third, won the free dance — as they obviously had — there was no clear winner. The final result would depend on the tally of second and first places, which in these peculiar circumstances were treated as identical.

It was a long shot, and anyway no one with us at that moment had access to the right information, even if they knew how to work it out. Alistair was listening intently to what was happening in the arena on a radio earphone, ready to pass on any information.

There was a pause.

Then he reached forward, and shook Chris's hand.

'You've done it!' he said.

'No! You're kidding!'

'No, you've won.'

Chris, almost speechless with surprise and happiness, hugged Bobby and Betty, who broke the news to Jayne in her dressingroom. Her reaction was close to schizophrenic: Joy and doubt, in equal measure.

Lawrence Demmy came by to congratulate us as Jayne came out. 'I told you how it would go,' he said.

'By default, but what the hell,' said Chris smiling as Jayne hugged him.

But it was a very modified form of happiness. We had lost two out of three sections, winning only by a quirk in the marking system. Gritschuk and Platov had been condemned by their third place, leaving us as winners 6:5 – six judges had placed us second, while five had placed Usova and Zhulin second or first. It was not a result the judges could possibly have intended or predicted.

For an hour, we could pretend we were triumphant, but underneath we knew differently. As we looked forward to the Olympics, it seemed the odds were already stacked against us. If we wanted a chance at gold, there had to be major changes. But we didn't know why we had lost, or what we should change to have a chance at victory.

We had just two weeks to decide, and act.

Two days after we came home, we held a post-mortem in Jayne's London house, with Lawrence, Courtney, Bobby and Betty. We were as eager to question them as they were to offer advice.

First of all, what was wrong with our compulsories, when we had followed all the advice to our coaches' satisfaction? No real answers, just sighs and wild guesses.

Betty said she had never been sure about the compulsories

— they seemed old-fashioned, needed bringing up to date. We weren't 'big' enough — Bobby's word again. The costumes were wrong, they said, Jayne's skirt too short, Chris's trousers too heavy. We had to be more flamboyant. The Russians had thrown their legs in the air more. We would have to out-do them.

But we had been told to get back to basics, avoid flamboyance. It was so confusing. All that work, over six months, and now to be told we had taken a wrong direction — it was almost more than we could bear, especially as we felt we had been persuaded to do things against our own judgement.

Next, the rumba. No problems there. We had won anyway, so we could leave that.

So it was all down to the free dance.

'I'm not sure about the music,' Courtney said. 'The middle section . . . it doesn't build in the right way. I think that's what Mr Kutschera was getting at.'

That touched raw nerves. You can change steps, but not the music. The rearranging, the re-recording, the time, the expense — it had already cost many thousands. For all these reasons, it was just impossible.

At one point, Chris even said, 'Is it even worth going on?'

'Oh, you must!' said Lawrence. 'You'll come back with a gold medal, I'm sure you will.'

He became quiet, assured, focused, making us face the practicalities. What choice did we have? Go in as before? Or change things, and give ourselves a better chance? We couldn't change the music, nor did we want to, so we had to change the steps.

'You have to put in more highlights, maybe elements you've used in the past.'

What — rechoreograph from scratch? It seemed impossible.

'Isn't there *anything* you can use from the past?'

We showed videos of old routines, and spotted some movements that we could adapt.

A starting point, at least.

Next day, we were back on the ice.

When we arrived at Milton Keynes, we were the lowest either of us ever remember, shell-shocked and seething with frustration. We were disillusioned with ourselves, disillusioned with everything and everyone. Jayne, normally so controlled, so willing to take on whatever needed to be done, could hardly bear to drag herself to the rink and put her skates on.

Jayne

There seemed no point in being there, because I didn't want to skate, and felt nothing would be achieved. But I *had* to be there, trapped by the clock ticking away towards the Olympics.

I felt as if there had been a death in the family. In a way there had — the joy of skating, my sustaining passion, had shrivelled to a near-corpse within me. All I wanted was

310

to nurse myself and my spirit back to life, in privacy, over a long, long time.

But there was no time, no privacy.

Jayne and Chris

In addition, we were embarking on something in which we had lost confidence. There was much in our programme to date that we had compromised on, but at least at heart we had believed in it. Now we were changing – taking out intricate steps, inserting highlights – for reasons that felt wrong. We had lost faith, and there was no guarantee we could regain it in time.

Finally, even if we did make the changes and regain our faith, we had no idea whether it would do any good, because the impression was growing in us that we were actually being undermined by factions within the skating fraternity. Perhaps this was completely false, perhaps such thoughts were the consequence of stress-induced paranoia because, as with most conspiracy theories, there was no hard evidence. But there was plenty to fuel speculation.

Look at it from the point of view of our amateur rivals and the judges. The judges are selected to judge international competitions – with all the related kudos and perks – if amateurs from their nations are among the top 10 internationally. Over a period of a few years, a certain status quo is established, with amateur champions of certain countries linked to the careers of judges and coaches from those same countries.

By suddenly returning to the field, we injected a wild element into this cosy, usually predictable system. Would it be so astonishing if there was some resentment against us? Would it be impossible to imagine resentment hardening into outright antipathy?

Here's an example of how it might work. Years before, in 1981, we had taken the European title from a Russian couple, Linachuk and Karponosov. In the intervening years, they had established themselves internationally as trainers of many couples.

One of their couples were Gritschuk and Platov, which offered one set of contacts through whom influence might be exercised. But there were more subtle connections as well. Among their protégés were a Swiss couple, who were competing in the Europeans. As a result, Switzerland had a judge, and this judge gave us our lowest mark: 5.2.

Was this coincidence? (Probably, because he gave us a 5.9 in the free dance.) Or was it the result of antipathy towards us, based on loyalty to our former rivals? We have no idea. All we know is that, among amateur skaters, scenarios like this are commonplace, especially when you lose. In fairness, we should say it works the other way as well: judges often boost the chances of their own nationals. One of our sixes in the rumba came from Britain.

Our paranoid mood favoured conspiracy at this point. The idea would grow almost by the day as the Olympics approached, but for now it was no more than a further shadow, adding to the misery that burdened us that first morning back on the ice.

And there, waiting for us, were Eddie Mirzoeff and his camera crew. The problems were worse than after the British, and we felt much, much worse; but we wouldn't – couldn't – have avoided him as we had before.

Once again, Eddie urged us to wear the little radio microphones, which Jayne was convinced would inhibit her movements. This day, though, there was no fight left in her. She agreed. When we drifted out on to the ice to work on the leg-positions in the compulsories, with Andris watching from one side, everything we said was being recorded loud and clear.

Since both of us were in despair, each isolated by anger and depression, there was no real feeling of partnership that day. After an hour, as we repeatedly tried wide backwards curves, with alternate right and left leg raises, trying for an extra few inches in foot-height, Chris, feeling the constant, growing pressure of time, began to lash out at Jayne with stinging words.

'You're not trying . . . we don't need to try anything if you're not going to _do_ it . . .'

We broke off, and drifted over to Andris at the side of the rink.

There was a silence while we stared at each other, accusingly.

Jayne broke the silence. 'Don't look at me like that.'

'You're just acting as if to say, "It's not my responsibility, I'm not changing it, I'm not going to do anything"—'

313

'I *am* trying to change it.'

'No, you're not.'

'I am.'

'You're not.'

This was silly, squabbling like kids. Jayne shrugged and turned away, driving Chris into scathing sarcasm. 'Hands up, eyes to the ceiling. Yup. Great. Good attitude, Jayne.'

Back we went to try again. Still not right. Over to Andris again.

Jayne

Normally, I can take his mood, whatever it is, accepting the good, letting the bad slide away like water off a duck's back. At any other time, confrontation would eventually have sparked a sharp response, enough to regain the balance between us. And in an extreme case – it had happened only a few times – I would have simply said enough was enough.

But today there was no escape. Chris could vent his mood on me, and was doing so with an intensity that fed on my passivity, but I had nowhere to turn. Knowing that every word was being recorded, that Eddie wanted drama, that we were giving him precisely what he wanted when we felt at our most uncooperative, that I could say nothing except useless

314

little 'sh' noises at every new criticism from Chris, that he would go on and on if I didn't say or do something – it was too much. Despite myself, the pressure broke through.

'You just don't want to be here, do you?' said Chris.

I didn't, but what choice was there? 'Yes,' I said, but without conviction. 'Do it with me.'

'I've been doing it, Jayne. The problem is, you haven't even _bothered to try._'

At this point, I gave up, stopped responding, stopped listening, and wept, unable – because everything was being recorded – to do anything but struggle to restrain tears that would not be restrained.

'It's no good crying! I've got no sympathy!'

That was it.

Without another word, I walked away, past Andris, who was watching in silence as all this unfolded, back to the dressingroom, tore off the horrible little microphone, and threw it down on the table. It must have made the sound-man jump out of his skin.

Chris pursued me.

'We have to work,' he said, coldly.

I looked at him, and snapped back bitterly, 'Don't you ever have an off day? I always have to be OK, and just for once I don't want to be here. Just give me a bit of support, can't you?'

Jayne and Chris

Chris was at a loss. He shrugged, and walked back to the rink, to Andris, who was standing patiently waiting for a resolution.

'I don't know what to do with her,' Chris said.

'You're trying to make her do something she doesn't believe in.'

Which was so obviously true that his mood softened. He apologised. And Jayne, on her own, freed from the constraints of the microphone, found her emotional balance returning.

Chris was right. There was no escape from the task we had set ourselves. Every second counted. We had to find a way forward, and so we did, abandoning the compulsories, starting work on the free dance.

When Eddie's documentary came out, it was seen by millions and much praised. It irked us though that the few minutes of tension and tears were intercut through the film to suggest this was a key to our working relationship, when it was the presence of the camera and microphone that contributed to both the tension and the tears.

What followed that moment was truer to us, though less dramatic — two solid productive hours of work as we tackled the revisions to the free dance. But those hours, like so many others, found no place in the film.

It wasn't just a few steps we had to revise. To insert 'highlights' — jumps and lifts — into the free dance

316

meant also revising the movements that led into and out
of those elements. Eighty per cent of the whole piece would
eventually be newly choreographed and rehearsed.

But there were so many other changes we were advised
to make as well, all taking precious hours and days of travel
and talk. First, the costumes. Jayne's skirt had been short,
whereas everyone else had been wearing long ones; so hers
had to be long now. And Chris's trousers needed to be less
heavy, so that they ruffled in the wind, to intensify the
impression of speed.

Jayne's hair was another issue. She'd had long hair for
10 years. In the Europeans it had been in a ponytail. Was
there perhaps a better style, something that would make a
better impression? Up? Curled? Braided? Who knew what
was best? A decision had to be made, and Jayne made
it, booking a hair appointment and opting for a simple,
dramatic solution: cut it short. Luckily, everyone approved
– not that they had much choice because no further change
was possible.

On top of this, as part of the deal by which the music
had been recorded free, we had committed ourselves to a
commercial that was to accompany the record of _Let's Face
the Music_. There would also be a publicity shoot. All this,
when every hour counted.

In the end, everything else – costumes, commercial,
documentary, hair – was subsidiary to the new-look _Let's
Face the Music_, with its extra lifts, assisted jumps, bigger
and more impressive leaps. This had nothing to do with
our original conception. When you see Astaire and Rogers,
their dancing is not about feats of strength, high legs, or
stunts to make an audience applaud and dazzle judges. No

317

time now, though, to fret about betraying our principles. Lawrence, Bobby, Courtney and Betty all advised us: 'Put everything in – within reason.'

One addition, for instance, was in the compulsories. With all the steps specified, there's little room for manoeuvre. But you are allowed seven steps to get moving, and the tradition had grown up that skaters used these seven steps as a mini free dance, doing little flourishes, even a lift, to impress audience and judges. We had decided to emphasise 'basics' by omitting the flourishes. Now we were advised: give yourselves bigger and better starts. In went the flourishes.

But it was no use just following fashion. There had to be something more. It was now, in the four days that it took us to map out our new movements, that we came up with a spectacular ending, a final flip that carried Jayne from a piggyback position clear over Chris's head in a somersault. There was nothing original about it – it was adapted from a move we had included in *Barnum* after we turned professional.

In view of the fuss this movement generated later, it's worth looking at it in some detail. Of course, we had to be within the rules, and the rules were clear enough: the man was not allowed to lift the woman above his shoulders. The crucial word is 'lift.' There was nothing in the rules about the woman travelling, vaulting, flying, leaping above shoulder-height by some other means, if she could get up there.

It was not hard to obey that. The new conclusion was in fact only a small, low-level lift, to help Jayne on to Chris's back. Lifting ceased well below shoulder-level – it would be a very strong man indeed who could lift another person over his shoulders from behind. For Chris, to lift Jayne that way would have been impossible. Jayne's momentum came from a combination of movements, in part from a thrust from Chris's back, but mostly from Jayne's legs as she swung them in an arc that carried her up and over.

Once we had finished re-choreographing, we performed the whole dance for the 'Committee', as we had taken to calling our advisers. They were unanimous. It would make a terrific ending. It didn't infringe the letter of the ISU's laws; nor did it test their spirit, as _Bolero_ had done in 1984. Now that we were including so many other 'flashy lifts,' it would be in character with the rest of the dance, providing a good, dramatic conclusion.

With the moves decided, we had just over a week to perfect them. To put this in perspective, we would normally have given ourselves a week to choreograph, a week or two to rehearse, and then a final two weeks to iron out any imperfections. On our current schedule, we scarcely had time to learn the dance, let alone be confident that we could dance it to perfection.

This was a challenge we knew no other pair would have considered attempting. It was the toughest, riskiest thing we had ever done. As a result, as we approached departure for Lillehammer, we lived a contradiction. On the one hand, we had devised and rehearsed in record time something that was technically as demanding as any programme we had ever done. On the other hand, artistically, we had compromised ourselves. The original idea — the back-to-basics concept — had gone. We were caught by a dreadful irony. We could go for gold only by doing something we had originally sought to avoid.

By now, we believed we could at least put on a creditable performance, and had a good chance of success. But there was more to success than being good. We needed to understand what else we were up against — the loose network of interlinked friendships and interests that tends to produce a climate of opinion favouring certain couples.

It's important to emphasise the word 'favouring,' because skaters also believe that individual judges cannot distort reality very far. Leaden performers cannot reach the top through influence. But Olympic medallists emerge by fractions of points that depend on judges' opinions. The opinions may be held in all sincerity, but even if they are not, no one will question small distortions. It is here that the possibility for exerting influence lies, for small distortions can produce large consequences.

In the Europeans we had felt as if we were lost, not because of our dancing, but because of the politics, or what we imagined to be the politics, the hidden world of innuendo, glance and whispered comment. If the Europeans had inspired paranoia in us, it would be worse at the Olympics, where the panel of judges suggested any number of conspiracy theories in suspicious minds.

Take three scenarios suggesting how Eastern European skaters might find particular favour, within wider circles of influence.

I. The Olympic panel would have four judges from the old Soviet Empire — Russia, Byelo-russia, the Ukraine and the Czech Republic (the others being from Germany, Finland, France, Canada, and Britain).

320

In the old Soviet empire, ice-dancing, like other sports, had once been a microcosm of Communist ideology, and the same people were still up there, administering and judging. As a result of the break-up of the Soviet Union, they represented different nations, yet shared similar backgrounds and loyalties, and had an interest in forwarding each other's skaters and coaches.

2. Let's say that a former skater from Eastern Europe is now the national coach of a western country, and also teaches a couple representing yet another western nation. Besides the fact that his influence would naturally extend into at least the first three countries, he could also — as a member of the old Soviet skating fraternity — retain influence within the four nations of the old Soviet empire on the Olympic panel.

3. Influential figures within the skating hierarchy often offer advice. What if one person's circle of friends happens to include national coaches in Eastern Europe? And what if his advice is selectively offered to favoured skaters, and particularly well followed?

Exploring such scenarios, it is not hard to imagine a climate of opinion favouring Eastern European couples. Then along come Torvill and Dean, outsiders returning from the professional world threatening this climate. Was that how we were perceived? It is at least possible. If so, no wonder there was some hostility towards us.

Whatever the truth of our speculations, it would be good

to know how our new routines would appeal to the judges. It was Chris who suggested the way forward. He noticed an advertisement for the Russian All Stars, who were touring Britain with a version of *Sleeping Beauty*, still under the direction of Tatiana Tarasova.

Why not approach Tatiana, invite her to the rink, and ask her opinion?

After the rows and tensions that had characterised our tour with the All Stars, you might think it a crazy idea. But in fact the tour had worked, despite the dramas, and at a very deep level we had tremendous respect for Tatiana. She was difficult and demanding, but she was also creative, generous-hearted, passionate about skating, and a survivor, who had endured, with success, in circumstances that would have utterly defeated us.

More to the point right now, she was vastly experienced, perhaps uniquely so, in the politics of Eastern European amateur skating. She was not herself part of that world any longer, but she, if anyone, might know what was expected.

Her response was typically generous and enthusiastic. She had no couple of her own competing, so she was free to offer any help she could, and did so eagerly.

We danced it through for her. Even though we were still concentrating like mad to remember the new moves, she was enthusiastic and supportive. She knew almost without being told what we had been through, and why we were so worried. It was a good routine, she said, offering sensible advice. We had to go for it, focus on the dancing, forget the politics, and *enjoy* it. 'Chre-e-es, Jaynitchka, think only of the skating! It is for you!'

Chris

Meanwhile, every day brought new horror.

On the Monday morning with a week to go, I awoke with food poisoning, probably the result of eating some old salad dressing the previous night. I was wrung out, dehydrated, too weak to do anything except phone Jayne, and then lie in bed, tended by Jill, take the pills the doctor prescribed, and worry about the amount still to be done, the moves to be perfected, the costumes to be finished.

That night, after a day of misery, unable to eat anything, with Jill downstairs, I heard a heavy knock at the door. Who would come calling unannounced in the depths of the country at this time of a winter's night? The security light popped on. I heard voices. Jill appeared in the doorway.

'Chris,' she said. 'Just when you thought it couldn't get any worse, it just did.' She had nervously opened the door to find a man in a suit, carrying a bag. He was a doctor, who said he had come to perform a random pre-Olympic dope test. He wanted a sample.

'I can't,' I said. 'Tell him I just can't.' I was dehydrated, doubled up with cramps, and knew I couldn't produce anything.

Back downstairs, the doctor was sympathetic, but he had a job to do. Jill came up after he'd gone. 'He said he had to put it down as a refusal, but with mitigating circumstances. He'll be back in two days' time.'

323

Jayne and Chris

Chris was back on the ice the next morning, not feeling much better, and a day later Jayne got it. The bug must have spread through the skin. Luckily, she didn't suffer so badly, but enough to leave her near collapse at the end of the day.

Pressurised by ill-health and lack of time, we decided to fit in as much training as possible, so we arranged not to accompany the rest of the team to Lillehammer, delaying our departure by several days. By the day of departure, we had managed to get through our new routine just three times.

To squeeze in one more practice, we planned to set off at 5:00 a.m., drive to Milton Keynes, and train for three hours, while Andris, travelling out from London by rail, would make final comments before we set off for Heathrow and Lillehammer.

We awoke in pre-dawn darkness to find it was snowing. With Chris and Jill setting off from the cottage, and Jayne and Phil from Knightsbridge, we drove to the rink through snow, only to discover that Andris's train had been cancelled. He didn't arrive until 10 minutes before we left, by which time we had finished the run-through, and were almost ready to head for Heathrow. Four full run-throughs, that was all, and no final chance to see ourselves in action on the video. Never had we been so unprepared for any competition.

In Norway, all six of us — we had been joined at Heathrow by Bobby and Betty — were picked up by a British team car, and driven through snow-covered landscapes to Hamar, sadly dropping Jill and Phil off at rented apartments, while we were taken on to the Olympic village.

Settling in was no simple thing. We were wearing British team uniforms, with leather shoes, and the paths were like ice-rinks in the -25 C. cold. There were forms to fill in, security passes to get, an X-ray machine for the luggage, all details, but at that point every little thing seemed another hurdle thrown up to frustrate our progress in this doomed journey.

We walked off gingerly through the cold, carrying our bags over the icy pathway. 'Just our luck to slip over and break an ankle,' muttered Chris. And finally, we got to our rooms. They were the size of prison cells: a bed, a sink, a desk, a wardrobe. Chris's room was freezing, literally, even though the heating was full on. He had to sleep in his clothes. Next morning, staff discovered an air vent that had been left open.

Later that day, we did a compulsory-dance practice in the main arena, inevitably in front of a battery of cameras, judges scattered round the auditorium, and a crowd large enough to make it seem like an actual performance. But no feedback, no smiles or nods of approval, none of the warmth we remembered from Sarajevo.

Then, at the free-dance practice, if we had followed our normal routine, we would have run through the full four minutes. That's what everyone else was doing. The judges liked it, because it gave them a familiarity with what they were judging.

325

But given the days of sickness, and the demands of the dance, and the fact that we had been through it only four times, we did not want to risk testing our stamina and our memories in practice run-throughs that might end in very public disaster. We would keep as much as possible for the performance, praying that we would rise to the occasion.

So in this and later practices we just did sections. And now, each time, the public responded to us, giving us the greatest cheers when we were announced, and foot-stamping applause afterwards.

Our spirits rose. Every day, Jill and Phil were there to support us, along with a team of people – Debbie, Bobby, Betty, Courtney, Andris – who helped us back up from our pre-Olympic depression. Every day, in the few days before the competition itself, the crowds at our practice sessions were appreciative. We began to feel that success might, after all, be within our grasp.

First came the compulsories, on Friday, with the choice falling on the *Starlight Waltz* and the Blues. Of the four possibles, we felt these two were our strongest.

We skated the waltz for all we were worth, with the high leg raises and the smiles, and we thought we had done it as well as we could have done.

We watched the marks with dismay. Some were worse than those of the Finns, Susanna Rahkamo and Petri Kokko, who had never come close to us before. Usova-Zhulin and Gritschuk-Platov bumped us into third place. Then, in the Blues, we were third again. It was little consolation, and only added to the mystery, that a good part of the crowd booed the judges and whistled their derision as our marks came up.

Afterwards, as we changed, and our imagination got to work, we wondered: had we been placed third just to make absolutely sure we had no second placings that might lead to the same quirky upset that had occurred at the Europeans?

The draw for the order for the next day's competition, the original dance rumba, was about to take place. It was a very public event, with all the judges and press present, at which the placings for the compulsories were read out before the couples made their draw.

'Oh, I'm not going to the draw,' said Jayne when we met again after changing. 'I'm not going to stand there looking happy when I feel so disappointed and disillusioned.'

We asked the British team leader to draw for us, which was perfectly within the rules, but Bobby and Betty said they thought it wouldn't look good if we weren't there. That annoyed Jayne, who said sharply, 'You think they'll stop us winning just because we didn't go to the draw?' They said nothing, but their looks said yes.

Later that night we — Chris and Jill, Jayne and Phil — gathered at Phil's apartment to discuss the day's events. Consoling ourselves with several glasses of wine, we were quite ready to believe we were being blocked. True, we could probably win the rumba — 'they wouldn't want to make it look too obvious,' said Chris cynically. Since the rumba carried 30 per cent of the total marks, as opposed to 20 per cent for the compulsories, we would then be in the lead going into the free dance. But what if the conclusion was already decided?

'Oh, it's not really sewn up, surely. It can't be,' said Chris.

'It is,' said Phil, 'I heard.'

'Heard?'

'From our friend.' Phil had made it his business to form a contact with someone in the know who does not wish to be named. 'They said they had had a conversation with a judge who said there was a move to put you fourth or fifth.'

We sat in stunned silence. All the talk of prejudgement was not merely the product of our imaginations. The cards had always been stacked against us.

'So you did pretty well,' said Phil, 'Coming third today.'

(Later, we heard a similar story from an entirely different source. One of our family members had a friend who by chance had a friend with good contacts in the skating hierarchy. In a post-Olympics phone call, relative and Friend A chatted about how we had done at the Olympics. Referring back to a pre-Olympic conversation with Friend B, Friend A, still furious, remarked what a pity it was that 'they were always going to be placed fourth.')

Was there any point going on? What with the depression and the wine, we started to make cynical suggestions. Why not just . . . pull out? Or go out and dance *Bolero*, just to show them?

Just bitter jokes, of course, nothing serious. We wouldn't let down an audience of millions like that. But the thought of those millions added another layer of depression – all those people to whom we were champions, and now we would not be champions any more.

We felt we bore a nation's dreams, and now almost

certainly we knew that we could never make those dreams a reality.

The next day, Saturday, we decided to take time off. It was a day off for practices. We agreed we wouldn't do the first practice, which was to be in the secondary rink.

We just planned to do a later practice session in the main rink. It seemed a decision without significance, yet such was the press interest that great significance was read into it. Bobby and Betty had been there at the first practice, and all the judges. Why hadn't we? Had we given up?

The storm died away as quickly as it had blown up. Later, we practised on the main rink, dancing the rumba through and doing part of _Let's Face the Music_. The applause was good for both.

Next day, the rumba. One of those occasions when everything goes so right that you can't remember it, except for the audience beginning to clap before we started. It flowed easily from start to finish, earning us 5.8s and 5.9s for composition, and 5.9s and two sixes for presentation, enough, as we had hoped it would be, to place us within sight of the gold.

A final practice the next morning and we were as ready as we could be to 'Face the Music' in the evening, eight hours later – eight very long hours. There was nothing to do but sit and agonise, both of us in our separate rooms.

Jayne was able to sleep some of the time away, but not Chris.

Chris

To dull the ache of anticipation and fill the emptiness I felt in my stomach, I sat in my prison-cell bedroom and read *Schindler's List*, feeling like a condemned man, finding security in the little room, not wanting the time to pass, not feeling — as I should have done, as I had so often in the past — any thrill at the coming challenge.

The words passed unremembered before me. I kept closing my eyes, not sleeping, but rehearsing. The only images I saw were the dance, step by step . . . a page . . . eyes closed . . . the dance . . . eyes open . . . another page . . . eyes closed . . . the dance — a waking nightmare, until at last the book was nearly read, and the hour approached.

Jayne and Chris

We showered, dressed, and went together to the arena. The event had already been underway for a couple of hours, and it felt strange, coming from isolation and fearful anticipation into the bright, noisy warmth, hearing the sound of music and applause and marks being read, all echoing around us in the concrete corridor.

'Sounds like the Coliseum in there,' said Chris.

'What?'

'Lions. Christians. You know.'

'Oh. Yes.'

We dressed, Jayne in her silver white, Chris in his dinner jacket costume, and made our way to the corridor backstage.

Fifteen minutes to go.

We stretched, moving back and forth on our skates, guards on, in silence, with Eddie's camera peering at us all the time, trying not to think of what awaited us out there, where our parents, Phil, Jill, many friends, and hundreds, maybe thousands, of supporters waited.

Usova and Zhulin danced, got good marks, all 5.9s and 5.8s, then Rahkamo and Kokko.

Four minutes more, then us.

A gasp from the arena. The Finns had fallen. That put them out of the running, and improved our chances.

Chris remembered a former occasion, what was it? Where? Washington, perhaps, three or four years before, when Jayne had muttered to him, 'My legs are shaking.'

Fear.

It had struck him then because it was so unlike her. Was that how it was going to be here, now, in a few minutes? Fear that would freeze us both?

We weren't nervy people, but right then, we simply didn't know what was going to happen to us until we stepped out there. No matter how many times we told ourselves, 'We've done this before, we know it, of course we can do it well, of course we'll be OK,' we couldn't make ourselves believe it, because this was still new, still skating by the seat of our pants. No good thinking it through step by step.

There was still the fear that the *whole* did not hold together, that somehow, as in a nightmare, you would seize up half way through, not be able to breathe, pass out, anything, and simply find yourself still and exposed in front of the 6,000 people in the arena, the millions watching at home, and God alone knew how many more millions around the world.

Two minutes.

The Finns finished.

Guards off, out into the arena, into position, all smiles and outward confidence. Inside, the fear was still there, right up until the music started, even into the first two steps.

Then the old magic took us over, the magic of music that we loved and a warm and welcoming audience. To Jayne, it was as if a voice told her, 'Don't be stupid – you *like* doing this. Forget the rest, just skate.' Chris, too, suddenly knew it would be OK.

And we swept away into the dance, sure of ourselves at last, freed from care, hardly aware of our own movements, but aware of the audience clapping in time to the music and gasping and applauding, meshing with us, lifting us, until we felt the pure pleasure of the dance.

For those four minutes, we *were* the dance, and the dance was our universe.

Then, the final over-the-shoulder somersault, the quick sideways turn and it was over, with Jayne lying back on Chris's left arm, knowing we had given everything possible to the dance and to the audience. It was, for us, a golden performance, the best we could have done. At that shining moment, with the audience exploding into foot-stamping, whistling applause, with the burden of doubt and tension gone, we were happiness itself.

The crowd were going crazy, making the stands boom with stamping feet, throwing flowers, feeding our relief and joy. It was all worth it. We never thought we would feel like that again.

For a minute we circled the ice, with Jayne gathering flowers, until a new and different reality intruded. We heard the marks, glanced up, registered a few of them, randomly.

Technical merit: 5.8, 5.7, 5.8, 5.7, 5.7, 5.7, 5.6— 5.6!

We knew then we hadn't done it. It was as we had feared, and the audience didn't like the result. The booing and the whistles started, and went on and on as we skated off, our smiles no longer real, but frozen.

For artistic impression, the marks were better — mostly 5.9s and one six from Britain's Mary Parry — but not enough.

We made our way to the corridor, while Gritschuk and Platov took the ice. We waited, with leaden spirits, knowing the gold was lost, waiting only to know how *badly* we had lost, hating the intrusive, cold eye of Eddie's camera. Chris stood eating a banana, while Jayne drank water from a plastic mug, hardly exchanging a word, before going into her dressingroom. Bobby and Betty stood nearby. A rival passed, touched Chris on the arm. He managed a wan smile.

The marks were announced, echoing along the corridor.

Jayne came out again. 'Where did we come?'

'Third,' said Chris, quietly.

'Did we come third?'

'Yes.'

'Who came first?'

'Gritschuk and Platov.'

'Did they?' On film, her expression is dead. She felt dead inside. 'That's what they wanted.' She meant the judges, of course. Then, to escape: 'Let's get away from the camera.'

She took Chris's hand, and turned, feeling empty, drained.

Chris pushed his hand at the camera lens. 'Can we switch it off for a bit now?' But it kept running anyway, and we walked off to find a quiet corner, downcast, resigned.

Then came the presentations. First to step forward were Gritschuk and Platov, second Usova and Zhulin. There was a sort of gasp amid the applause from some of the crowd, as if they thought we might at least get silver. Then it was our turn. And again, an eruption of clapping and foot-stamping approval for us, but mixed with catcalls at our position. It was wonderful to know we had their support, though also embarrassing that we received more applause than the winners.

Back in the dressingroom with the British team leader, Kay Robinson, Jayne looked up in response to a knock on the door, and saw to her surprise that it was Natalia Linachuk, an old rival and now the winners' trainer. 'Congratulations,' she said. She shook Jayne's hand, and left. The two women exchanged astonished glances.

'I can't believe she said that,' muttered Jayne.

'Nor can I.'

There had been no congratulations from Natalia Linachuk when we won after beating her couple in the Europeans, yet here she was, congratulating us for coming third, for being _beaten_ by her couple. If this was not rubbing salt into the wound, it certainly felt like it.

Afterwards, the press conference. By now, we were beginning to see what had happened in perspective. No point complaining about anything, because in the end we were responsible for our comeback — for setting ourselves up, for choosing a style of routine, for asking advice, for taking advice. In the end, we felt that the truest balance we could find between the way we were received by the audience and by the judges was to say, 'We skated as well as we knew how, we were happy with the programme, and we felt the audience was our judge.'

Whatever we felt — and we certainly did _feel_ we had been victimised — there was nothing much more to be said, because there was no evidence. To repeat rumour and surmise would serve no purpose and simply sound like sour grapes.

Pressed later, in an interview in the empty stadium, Chris went about as far as we wanted to in commenting on the judges' decision: 'There's a lot happens out there' — waving a hand vaguely at the ice rink behind him — 'and sometimes there's a lot happens _not_ out there!'

Besides, in the end, everyone else was far more critical on our behalf than we were, or ever would be, on our own. The press were in an uproar, and demanded explanations. At another hastily called press conference that we heard about later, the referee, Hans Kutschera, and Lawrence Demmy in his capacity as vice-president of the ISU, were grilled as

335

to why the judges marked us the way they did. Lawrence, who after all had been deeply involved in our return, made no excuses, simply saying he would have come to different conclusions.

It was Kutschera who attempted to justify the marks. Deductions were made for infringements, he said, and perhaps we deserved a deduction for our final over-the-shoulder somersault. What was wrong with it? Over-the-shoulder lifts were illegal . . . but it wasn't a lift, and anyway no one had said it was illegal before, otherwise we wouldn't have done it.

Well, then, he argued, we were apart too long. Ah, journalists pointed out, but Gritschuk and Platov had been apart for longer. Where were their deductions?

Kutschera parried that the judges hadn't timed the separations. Well, why not? He was left without an answer, never offering an explanation, leaving journalists free to write scathingly about the subjectivity and prejudice of the judges.

The media in Britain, and to some extent in America, had a field day. The live TV coverage was seen by almost half the British population, 23 million people, one of the largest audiences for any sports programme ever. The papers reflected the passions our defeat aroused: 'WAS IT RIGGED?' (*Today*); 'PEOPLE'S COURT VOTES FOR T. AND D.' (*Observer*); 'AS GOOD AS GOLD'; 'GOLDEN WONDER'; 'ROBBED OF GOLD'; 'YOU'RE PURE GOLD: Daily Star speaks its mind'; 'ROBBED: Fans' fury as Torvill and Dean get bronze,' said *The Sun*, and it provided a phone number for complaints.

There were thousands. And not all the complaints and

congratulations were from anonymous fans, either. There were telegrams from Gene Kelly, Kirk Douglas, and Julie Andrews, among others.

After the interviews — there were dozens of them — we had bags to pack, decisions to make, a tour to prepare for. We had been planning to rest a few days, train some more, then fly to Japan to compete in the World championships. But we couldn't face it, not now, couldn't contemplate yet another round of post mortems, last-minute changes and political gamesmanship.

What would it all be for? The judges' panel would be similar, probably. What were they going to do? Say they had been wrong and give us the gold? No. Better to withdraw — which we did once we were back in England — and get on with the next chapter in our lives.

11

A show of
our own

Jayne and Chris

Meanwhile, throughout the time we were training for the Olympics, preparations were underway for the World Tour. Having made the decision to do it, and to delay the start for the Olympics, there were some things that could not be delayed. The concept, for instance.

We were faced with a unique opportunity – we had complete control of the content and the cast, for the first and probably only time, at least on this scale. We knew that in Phil, Debbie, Andris and Graham we had a team who would happily back us, throwing themselves into something that would tour many countries for at least a year, maybe more.

As Phil said, to start things rolling, we didn't even need to say what was going to be in the show. All he needed was one word: Go.

He was half right. We knew what *we* would bring to the show. Obviously, it had to be popular, to assure ourselves of the ticket-sales to support this multi-million-pound enter-prise. That meant using some of the elements that had made us popular in the first place, dancing a few well-established numbers, including inevitably the two Olympic routines, *Face the Music* and *Bolero*. Once upon a time, when we thought the public were about to become bored with *Bolero*, we assumed we would drop it. Previous tours had shown us they wouldn't be bored with it, and we couldn't drop it. It had become synonymous with us.

But we couldn't be the whole show. We wanted this to be the best, with more variety, talent, emotion and humour than any of the previous shows we had been in, a flow of large-scale group routines alternating with solos, or 'cold spots,' as they are known.

With these elements guaranteeing appeal, the audience would — we hoped — also accept a few new ideas, using new and surprising music. Ice-shows have to have mass appeal, but we knew from *Akhnaton* that the audience would also take quite challenging material.

When we started to devise the content, we worked without formalising all this. It was a feeling, a climate, an underlying philosophy that evolved between us and with Andris, emerging ever more strongly as we planned, contacted skaters and rehearsed.

Most ice-shows were like variety shows on stage, a collection of star turns backed by a less talented 'chorus.'

340

That was definitely not what we wanted. We knew how hard it was to struggle with starry egos, whose happiness lay in being featured all the time. That might work for a few weeks, but the concept of a world tour demanded that we plan for a show that could be on as long as two years. It would work only as a company show, with people who would be equally happy as soloists and as members of the group. We wanted a team of people, all top skaters, who would also work together, to form the greatest ice-dancing company there had ever been.

That was our aim. During the preparations for the Olympics, as we drove back and forth between London and Milton Keynes, or on coffee breaks, or sitting over meals, we discussed with Andris possible routines, possible skaters, a possible structure for the show. Our first vague ideas came into focus.

It was logical to start with _Bolero_ from 1984 and end with _Face the Music_ from 1994, the two amateur high points. In between would be four big company routines, two in the first half, two in the second. But we couldn't finish simply with our 1994 Olympic duet. It had to be part of a company number. We quickly agreed _Face the Music_ could end an extended tribute to Irving Berlin.

For another company number, Chris had always wanted to do something with the Beatles. The songs, which had been so much a part of his teenage years, had a quirkiness of subject, character and theme that appealed to him. As the routine finally developed, Chris would be doing a rare solo performance as the Paperback Writer tying other songs together, finding inspiration in a sexy, dominating Lovely

341

Rita Meter Maid (Jill) and in Jayne as Lucy In the Sky With Diamonds.

The next idea that popped up in Chris's mind was *Carmina Burana*, the collection of medieval songs set to music by Carl Orff in the 1930s. It had taken off as a popular classic in the 1960s, and we both had recordings at home. With its subject matter – monks, drinking, romance, bawdiness – and its medieval images, it would make a good contrast to the Beatles, and its poetic vignettes offered lots of opportunities for group work and solos. Andris, who had seen ballet adaptations of *Carmina*, knew at once it could work on ice, and began research.

Finally, we needed something humorous. An idea came to mind, suggested by our own experiences in ice-dancing and by the success of the Australian film *Strictly Ballroom*. We would do a spoof 1950s ballroom sequence, *Strictly Skating*. Though we didn't plan it as a comment on the Olympics, because it was outlined before, that was the way it turned out, under Andris's inspired direction. This was back-to-basics ballroom with a vengeance, with fluffy sequined dresses, backbiting rivalries, judges being bribed, and a voiceover ban on 'flashy crowd-pleasing moves.'

Between these four large-scale routines there were going to be about 10 other numbers, a couple of them skated by us, but most brought in by the other skaters. We started to make lists of the people we would like to skate with.

Of course, we already had one other star, Jill, who had decided to give up her own career in America to be a part of this show so that we could be together. This was good news for the show as well as for me, because she brought her own talents to it, and her own set of skating contacts.

Debbie recalled almost better than we did whom we had worked with and where they might be now. Lists emerged, matured and changed, with certain names bubbling to the top time and again, until Debbie had a draft of possibles. While we got on with the Olympics schedule, it was her job to turn possibles into probables, with a series of phone calls through the summer and autumn.

No point hiring anyone, however, without having somewhere to rehearse. If we weren't careful, the costs of the rehearsal period would rapidly become unsustainable. We needed to fly 30 or so people into somewhere – some of them back and forth several times – put them up for two months, and hire a rink, for eight hours a day, every day. Single rinks like Alexandra Palace and Milton Keynes couldn't spare ice for that much time, and Oberstdorf would be too expensive in travel and accommodation. As our team began to come together, it became clear that we should be in the US, some place with two rinks so that we wouldn't have to compete for time with other users. Indianapolis, with its superb facilities, proved ideal. There, immediately after the Olympics, Andris started work with the first arrivals.

They were an extraordinarily talented bunch, all stars in their own right, all with their own skills and characters, yet what united them – united us all when we joined them a couple of weeks after the Olympics – was an eagerness to work together. That sense of drive and unity was vital, because for almost all of them, the offer of the tour involved lifechanging decisions.

Mark Janoschak and Jacqui Petr were Canadian champions in 1992 and had been planning to settle down. Mark was considering a post-graduate course in sports medicine, Jacqui wanted to do nursing. Now those careers would be on hold.

Marina Kulbitskaya and Sasha Esman, who had been part of the All Stars tour after a career as internationals, both had a soulful Russian beauty and a balletic brilliance. They were coaching in New York, with their seven-year-old daughter Julia, when Debbie's call came, throwing their lives up in the air again. Now Julia would go back to her grandparents in St Petersburg, and their students would have to wait.

Scott Williams, from Alaska, a professional since being World Junior Champion, and his Canadian wife, Charlene Wong, US Open champion in 1990, were soloists, very different from each other. Scott, with his shoulder-length hair, had a wild, rock-star charisma, while Charlene was compact, neat, doll-like in her restraint.

They had just been left high and dry by the collapse of a show, so Debbie's call came at just the right time. They were ready to put everything into storage in Los Angeles right away.

'March? Really? We have to wait *that* long?'

We had met our acrobats, Kostia Golomazov and Igor Okunev, on the Australian tour in 1991, when they were part of the Ukrainian Ice Ballet. Despairing of finding work in Russia's collapsing economy, they had moved to Blackpool to teach. Their back-flips and torch-juggling made them ideal as company acrobats.

Catarina Lindgren, who keeps a trace of her Swedish origins in her accent, had been Swedish National Champion before coming to the US, where she was on the Ice Capades tour with us. She and her husband, Tom Dickson – winner of the Professional Challenge Cup in the US Open, and a well-established choreographer – had decided to settle down in Colorado Springs, where Catarina became one of Jill's closest friends.

There were others still to come, all with their own concerns. Michelle McDonald and Martin Smith had been Canadian Senior Dance Champions in 1991. Michelle was married, and had a career teaching. Martin was about to go to law school. Days of frantic talking ended in 'This is a once-in-a-lifetime chance. Let's do it!' Michelle took leave of absence from her husband Kevin and Martin put his law career on hold.

Susie Wynne, twice US national champion and 1988 Olympian, was also a friend of Jill's, so Jill knew that she and her new skating partner, Russ Witherby – they were second in the US championships – were looking for firm offers. Russ was in Delaware, Susie in Chicago, setting up home with her husband, Tyler, who was definitely not a skater – he was in the family fan-making business, Illinois Blowers – but totally committed to Susie's career, her 'biggest fan,' as she said. Among the last to be contacted, they had just four days' warning, throwing her into agonies over marriage-at-a-distance for two years.

Tammy Crowson, who had been on our first world tour in 1985, had teamed up with Joe Mero. We were keen to have them both. But Tammy's new husband, Eddie, had no connection with skating. He was a restaurant-owner in Colorado. It worked out fine in the end, because Eddie became our stage-manager. Running a restaurant had for some reason given him just what we needed

345

for getting people and props to the right place at the right time.

After our arrival, we started rehearsing in earnest, mapping out the sequence of routines, building the two-and-a-half-hour show by five minutes a day. Even towards the end of the rehearsal period, we were still short of a couple of people who could act as understudies, 'swing skaters' as they are known. It is a tough assignment, demanding self-effacement, tremendous range, and the confidence to step into almost any part in the event of injury or ill health. We were lucky to find Carla Maillard, a friend of Martin and Michelle, who had been in an ice-dance company that had gone bankrupt and was completing a psychology degree in Montreal.

Our final arrival was Doug Williams, with years of classical ballet, jazz dancing and choreography behind him. After being in the US national and international teams for 12 years, he was doing film post-production when we asked him to fill in just three weeks before we opened.

At the same time, work had to start on the costumes, anything up to 150 of them. Of course, we wanted them made by Bob Murphy, who had been doing our tour costumes for the last 10 years. With his experience in ballet and musical comedy, ideas came fast. *Carmina Burana* was easy – 'a monk's a monk, isn't it?' – and girls dancing in spring-time instantly suggested Romeo-and-Juliet styles derived from Italian Renaissance painting. For the finale, he adapted designs for costumes he had done in *Kiss Me Kate*. He and his team had the 150 costumes ready in seven weeks, finishing a few final stitches on opening night itself.

346

Meanwhile, from way before the Olympics, Phil had been building the business side.

Since we were locked into rehearsals, we were hardly aware of much of this. It was astonishing later to realise the size of the pyramid that stretched away below us, from the show itself, through Phil as business manager, to our production manager Tony Harpur, whose job it would be to organise the logistics, to the promoters hiring dozens of arenas across the UK, America and Australia. By the time the tour was over, we would have given over 250 shows and been seen by about 1.5 million people.

Gradually, as we moved into rehearsal, the promoters would begin to feed back the advances that would repay us for our investment. Every arena would demand its own set of negotiations on number of shows, sales guaranteed, advances, prices of tickets, share of profits and costs — advertising, promotion, labour, catering equipment, security, front-of-house staff, management fees.

When we were on the move — there were to be some two dozen one-night stands in America — we would be something between a travelling circus and a rock show, about 50 of us, with £100,000 worth of costumes, tons of lighting, and banks of sound gear, moving by truck, bus and plane.

We couldn't be doubling back and forth all the time, so the arenas all had to be booked in the most effective chronological and geographical sequence. Any move had to flow smoothly — wake up, coach to the airport, check in, fly, coach to hotel, check in, get to the arena, warm up, skate, back to the hotel, sleep — on a treadmill that would quickly drive everyone crazy if things went wrong.

In some sections of the tour, we would need to bring

our own £250,000 ice-floor, perhaps the most surprising, demanding and crucial aspect of this whole business. It's obvious when you think about it – the ice-floor is the foundation for the whole magic of skating – but the audience should hardly be aware of it, any more than you are aware of the foundations of a beautiful building. Normally skaters don't have to think about it either. But now we had to, and found ourselves responsible for an operation that should be enough to humble any skater.

To get a sense of it, imagine an empty arena, not an ice-rink, just the bare space, an oval of sand surrounded by 8,000 seats spanned by girders 30 or 40 feet up. In four days, we're putting on a show. The transformation that has to occur is a minor industrial miracle, cooked up from some extremely impressive ingredients – a truck-sized freezer unit, a truck-sized pump, seven tons of freezer liquid, 4,500 cubic feet of water, eight *miles* of pipes, 40 tons of sand, some 100 manual workers, and assorted wire, tape, barrows, and spades all under the control of Tony Harpur, Ian Day, and Keith Browse.

Since a mistake in any of the operations would be disastrous, Tony, Ian and Keith take it all very personally, like generals supervising a campaign. They hardly sleep for three days, relaxing only when they have ice.

Overnight, up go the lights, spread over 800 feet of steel trussing, seven tons in all. Then, before dawn, the first battalion of labour comes in, to lay polystyrene sheets, which act as a mattress for plastic strips all stuck together with tape to make it waterproof. Then the heart of the freezing operation – rubber piping, eight miles of it, which will carry glycol, the sub-zero liquid that will create the ice.

348

The pipes have to be a regular four inches apart to ensure they supply an even temperature, so they are fixed with wire ties. Inevitably, many ties have come adrift. There may be 5,000 ties to be replaced, all by hand. Then there are leaks to be repaired, perhaps hundreds of them; the pipes to be connected running back out of the arena to the industrial refrigeration unit in a truck outside; strips of wood to be added around the whole floor to form sides deep enough to hold three inches of water.

Now, with dump-trucks and barrows and spades, add the 40 tons of fine, river-washed, salt-free sand, evenly spread to act as a bedding for the pipes and a sponge for the first layer of water. Carefully smooth the sand up against the wooden edges. Fill the pipes with the seven tons of glycol. Switch on the refrigerator. Start the pumps. Freeze the sand. Spray on water, creating a winter garden of pipes, sand, and little plastic ties sticking up all over the place.

But there are devils lurking in every detail of this operation. You can't soak all the sand right through, because in a few days you are going to have to get it all out, and no one wants to tackle a hardcore of sand and ice. So you need only enough water to seal the top few millimetres. Moreover the sand must remain smooth, so it's no good squirting the water on. It has to be sprayed on delicately. And the water has to be pure – any minerals rise to the top and contaminate the surface of the ice. Ian won't trust just anyone to do this, so he does most of it himself. It takes all night.

As the whole mass cools, it contracts, and the big supply pipes spring leaks at the joints. People keep watch, cranking bolts tighter. By next morning, with the roar of the pump and refrigeration unit coming through dully from outside, the foundations are ready, the sand crusted with ice, the pipes white with frost.

And ice is still two days in the future. Now comes the white paint. That's a surprise to some people, who think that rinks are naturally white, like snow. But since ice is transparent, without paint the rink would be an unsightly mass of sand, pipes and plastic ties. So on goes the whitewash, again by hand-spray.

Then, believe it or not, a few strategically placed coins, which provide a solution to a technical problem. Once the ice is made, it has to be three inches thick. How do you measure the thickness of the ice? By drilling through it. How do you stop the drill going straight through a pipe? By drilling down on to the coins (Ian's coins − he has a running battle with Tony about whether these should come from petty cash).

Then, finally, another thin layer of water to seal in the paint, delicately sprayed in order not to wash the paint off. Then, at last the final flooding, which can be done using the Zamboni, the ice-cleaning machine.

On the fourth day, with Tony and Ian asleep, the floor is ready, the pipes covered, the entrance passageway curtained, the lights on, the stage ready for magic. The skaters swoop on to warm up, or to iron out a problematic step, or to do a press call.

And after the final show, when the audience is gone, comes the get-out, with a whole new set of problems. Lights down, pumps off, glycol to be pumped into containers. In come the first 40-strong contingent of hired labourers, wielding sledge-hammers. They lay into the rink, turning a world of lights, music and gliding figures into a battleground of thumping metal and shattered ice.

It's rough work. The men tape polystyrene pads to their shins, making them look like caricature batsmen, to protect themselves from flying ice-chips. Dump-trucks cart out the ice, leaving it piled outside in a huge heap, ready to be carried away to a place where it can melt.

Next day, the arena is clear, and the floor on its way in convoy to the next venue.

Opening night in Sheffield, with its 8,000 seats sold out for that night and for most of the three-week run, was the beginning of the best of times for us. There was tension in the air, as there should be, but good tension: 1,350 additional seats to be added to accommodate demand; plastic hard hats to be bought and fitted to stop the monks' hoods from dropping over their faces; a little guide-light to be added over the exit corridor. Nothing major.

The lights dimmed. We skated on to take our positions for the start of _Bolero_, hoping we had got the balance of the show right. How would the audience take to the relative obscurity of Janacek's _Sinfonietta_? Would the cross-dressing gag in _Strictly Skating_ get a laugh?

Two and a half hours later, we relaxed. The warmth of the reception told us all we needed to know. The applause, the foot-stamping, the whistles, the lines of home-made notices held aloft by the audience proclaiming '6.0!' — we knew that everything we'd been through over the last year had been worthwhile.

Over the next year and a half, through the crises brought on by injury, stress of travel, and the hothouse pressures

351

on this isolated little society, right through to the final show in August 1995, the disappointment of the Olympics slowly became a distant memory. Whatever the pain of the experience, there were benefits – the suffering had tempered us, strengthened us, forced us to see our sporting lives in a wider context.

Along the way, the sorrows merged with the joys, and dimmed. It had been a moment, two weeks of headlines, high emotions, and then past. Now, looking back, we see the Olympics less as an ordeal, more as simply part of a spectacle of sport and entertainment, a part of the life we had chosen. Compared with real suffering – think of what's happened to Sarajevo since 1984 – any pain we went through is nothing.

Besides, we had been so lucky. We were lifted from our little disappointment by such an astonishing upwelling of support that we could not have remained disappointed for long. And that endured.

Many of the people at every show had been among the TV watching millions who had seen us in Lillehammer. Their response then was matched by their response to the show. It seemed that our failure to win had created a great wave of affection for us, touching and releasing something deeper than a win could possibly have done.

It felt as if we had won gold after all.

And now, after it's all over?

We have no idea. Only one thing is certain: we each have our own lives, our own families, and our own interests to follow, but there are still new frontiers of ice-dancing to be explored, together and apart.

We'll skate on.

Index

T&D = Torvill and Dean